T0013671

The Healing Church

Praise for *The Healing Church*

I just completed my first reading of *The Healing Church*, and I want to:

1. read it again,
2. share it with friends,
3. thank Sam Black for his hard work,
4. and thank God for this desperately needed tool.

If you are looking for a book that heaps shame upon the porn-struggler, look elsewhere. If, on the other hand, you are looking for a book that soberly assesses the porn pandemic and then offers practical help, you've got the right volume. Porn is contaminating our generation. Yet, empowered by the grace of God and the careful counsel of people like Sam, there is hope. I urgently recommend *The Healing Church*.

Max Lucado, best-selling author, speaker,
and pastor at Oak Hills Church in San Antonio, TX

In *The Healing Church,* Sam Black challenges churches to take vital steps in growing their understanding of the effects of pornography addiction, its impact on the pews, and a roadmap to help people find tangible hope and true healing. He and the team at Covenant Eyes are leading the way.

Tim Clinton, Ed.D., president of American Association
of Christian Counselors, co-host at Dr. James Dobson's Family Talk,
and executive director, Liberty University Global Center
for Mental Health, Addiction and Recovery

Thank God for this ultra-practical book by Sam Black—fresh, honest, relevant—a "how to" book packed with wisdom to help us help others.

June Hunt, chief servant leader, Hope for the Heart

Pastors and church leaders have the God-given and unique privilege to speak into the intimate and painful areas of sexual sin and shame in congregants' lives. This sacred touchpoint must not only be handled with genuine care, but with a sensitivity and competency that avoids causing further harm. *The Healing Church* helps us be a *healing* rather than *harming* church.

Geremy F. Keeton, M.MFT, LMFT,
senior director of Counseling Services at Focus on the Family

There is a lot of hand-wringing these days when the subject of pornography comes up, and understandably so. Social mores are crumbling all around us. Sexual exploitation is rampant, and families are buckling and breaking under the corrosive influence of porn. The situation is dire, to be sure, but it is also pregnant with possibilities. For many years I have been waiting and praying for someone—someone with more credibility than I—to awaken the Church to the phenomenal opportunities presented by the porn pandemic. Sam Black's newest book, *The Healing Church*, is the one we've been waiting for. More than an exercise in biblical theology or abstract theory, *The Healing Church* is personal and practical, wide-ranging yet focused, reverent but fearless. Sam does not mince words in describing the nature and scope of the challenge, but he is not discouraged. With example after real-life example, he shows how a new generation of Christian leaders and porn survivors is bringing the healing power of the gospel to a lonely, desperate world.

Nate Larkin, founder of the Samson Society

Every church is in a war with porn; the problem is many aren't aware to what degree, who the casualties are, and how to go on the offensive. To that end, Sam Black wrote *The Healing Church* on winning the war against porn. Pastors, leaders, and strugglers alike will find this eye-opening with new statistics, heart-gripping with stories of change, and potent with a curated arsenal of practical next steps and resources for victory over this epidemic enemy. This should be standard issue for every pastor and para-church leader.

John Elmore, teaching pastor of Watermark Community Church
in Dallas, TX, author of *Freedom Starts Today: Overcoming Struggles
and Addictions One Day at a Time*

The Healing Church breaks up powerful myths that have kept churches from ministering effectively to men and women trapped in an addictive cycle. Sam has done his research and presents a bio-psycho-social and spiritual viewpoint on how to minister to those suffering with unwanted sexual behaviors around pornography. *The Healing Church* understands that healing and growth are a process not separate from discipleship. Sam Black has proved something fresh for those looking for answers to a critical discipleship issue.

Jack West, pastor of Care & Recovery at Mariners Church

Sam's honest and thorough assessment of the plague of pornography in the Church spotlights how porn is deeply affecting the lives of men, women, children, *and church leaders*. He doesn't settle for superficial solutions but provides a treasury of helpful resources as he lays out the biblical steps necessary to heal an addicted Body of Christ.

Nathan Graybill, national director of *re:generation*,
Watermark Community Church

As a former pornography addict and a person, who helps men and women defeated by pornography, *The Healing Church* is a Godsend! For those being defeated by pornography *The Healing Church* is a compassionate and healing tool to get you unstuck so you can experience freedom from porn. It's an incredible, biblical, comprehensive, sensitive resource that pastors MUST read and implement in their churches. Sam courageously includes that women also battle with pornography. The more I read *The Healing Church*, the more I knew that we have got to get *The Healing Church* in the hands of nearly everyone because of epidemic of pornography.

Dr. Clarence Shuler, President/CEO of BLR:
Building Lasting Relationships and author
of *Finding Hope in a Dark Place*

In *The Healing Church,* Sam Black addresses the issue head-on, offering great insight as to why porn is so very addictive, without heaping condemnation on the struggle. Instead, he offers grace, solutions, and resources to confront the problem. I highly recommend *The Healing Church.* Sam has years of experience working with this population and it shows clearly in his writing.

Ron Cook, president, Care for Pastors

Many pastors and church leaders who truly want to see the gospel of Christ transform people's lives are living under a fog of ignorance and fear when it comes to the issue of porn and other forms of sexual sin. *The Healing Church* is a well-researched, yet accessible resource that lifts the fog and provides wise guidance and practical ideas to empower leaders to effectively minister to anyone who wants freedom from porn and its toxic influence. I recommend that every church make *The Healing Church* available in their library.

Jonathan Daugherty, founder of Be Broken Ministries

Sam Black is a trusted expert and a man who understands the complex issues involved with sexual struggles and sin. *The Healing Church* provides the background and blueprint—with solid research and proven strategies—for you and your church to bring men to healing and restoration. If you are engaged in discipleship, you will run into this issue. And *The Healing Church* will help you provide a biblical and practical response.

Brett Clemmer, president & CEO of Man in the Mirror, co-author of *No Man Left Behind*

The Healing Church is a powerful "field guide" for churches to address the issue of pornography extensively and with grace. From the beginning pages, it is clear Sam's heart is for true healing to take place not on platforms and stages but in the day-to-day life of the local church community. He speaks from years of experience in this field to discuss the draw of pornography, the deadliness of shame, and how these things can sicken Christian marriages and ministry. This is a powerful toolkit for churches to minister to and care for people. It is filled with stories of life change and practical tools for how we, as a church, can disinfect from shame and become a place where true healing and growth can occur.

Jessica Harris, author of *Beggar's Daughter*, blogger, and speaker

This invaluable resource for pastors and church leaders cuts to the heart of the matter, offering compassionate insight and practical direction for those shepherding God's people toward freedom and growth.

Troy Haas, CEO HopeQuest Ministry Group, Christian counselor

For far too long the Church has been largely ineffectual about the plague of pornography infecting the men and women in their congregations. People are being injured by pornography and are in need of the kind of hope the Church is uniquely positioned to provide. Whether it is a combination of fear, apathy, or lack of understanding about addiction, the passivity cannot continue. With his book *The Healing Church*, Sam Black has provided a grace-filled and research-rich resource to equip, educate, and empower the Church to not just talk about porn but to provide hope and healing to those who struggle. Having known Sam personally and professionally for over a decade, I have seen his heart for those who struggle with porn *and* his heart for the Church. *The Healing Church* is the beautiful culmination of his years of advocacy that all Church leaders should read.

Crystal Renaud Day, Christian counselor, author, and founder of SheRecovery.com

As someone who served for over a decade in full-time pastoral leadership and now in recovery ministry, I have felt first-hand the divide that can exist between the church and recovery. In this excellent resource, Sam Black lays the foundation for a connecting bridge between the two. The church can be a safe place with a successful process to lead men and women to hope, healing and freedom in their sexuality. With the skill of a seasoned journalist, Black pulls expertise from the very best of ministries, resources, and research in this area. The data he reports will open your eyes to the true challenge we face over this issue, but the strategies he outlines can lead you and your church to true and lasting change. I highly recommend *The Healing Church* for any leader who is ready to stop simply talking about the problem and wants to move toward a culture of transformation in their church. Through the Gospel of Christ, we have all the answers we need to end the porn pandemic in the church. Sam Black shows us how to apply these answers in effective, life-changing ways.

Nick Stumbo, executive director of Pure Desire Ministries

Sam Black is not rehashing the same old "Don't do it . . . God hates that . . . Jesus is watching you" type of message. In this refreshing book, Sam provides a comprehensive look at *why* people return to porn and their unwanted sexual behavior again and again (even though they *want* to stop). Thankfully, God has provided the Holy Spirit and the Church to guide us along the path to freedom. Rather than another "Sermon on Purity," *The Healing Church* will help you understand the nature of porn and how to overcome the power of this complex problem.

Joe Kelty, former men's pastor at McLean Bible Church, chaplain at Good News Jail Ministry

I thank God for Sam and Covenant Eyes. I wholeheartedly agree with his passion to bring men through "a grace-filled process to the foot of the Cross, where strongholds are crushed and where stronger servants arise." *The Healing Church* is a terrific resource for you toward that end.

Brian Doyle, founder and president, Iron Sharpens Iron

THE
HEALING CHURCH

**What
Churches
Get Wrong
About
Pornography
And
How To
Fix It**

Sam Black
A Covenant Eyes Resource

NASHVILLE

NEW YORK • LONDON • MELBOURNE • VANCOUVER

The Healing Church

What Churches Get Wrong About Pornograpy and How to Fix It

© 2023 Covenant Eyes

All rights reserved. No portion of this book may be reproduced, stored in a retrieval system, or transmitted in any form or by any means—electronic, mechanical, photocopy, recording, scanning, or other—except for brief quotations in critical reviews or articles, without the prior written permission of the publisher.

Published in New York, New York, by Morgan James Publishing. Morgan James is a trademark of Morgan James, LLC. www.MorganJamesPublishing.com

Proudly distributed by Ingram Publisher Services.

Scriptures taken from THE HOLY BIBLE, ENGLISH STANDARD VERSION (ESV)® Copyright© 2001 by Crossway, a publishing ministry of Good News Publishers. Used by permission.

Scriptures marked NKJV are taken from the NEW KING JAMES VERSION®. Copyright© 1982 by Thomas Nelson, Inc. Used by permission. All rights reserved

Morgan James BOGO™

A **FREE** ebook edition is available for you or a friend with the purchase of this print book.

_____

CLEARLY SIGN YOUR NAME ABOVE

Instructions to claim your free ebook edition:
1. Visit MorganJamesBOGO.com
2. Sign your name CLEARLY in the space above
3. Complete the form and submit a photo of this entire page
4. You or your friend can download the ebook to your preferred device

ISBN 9781636980256 paperback
ISBN 9781636980263 ebook
Library of Congress Control Number: 2022943481

Cover Design by:
Creative Director: Jason Walker
Design: Grace Bolzman, Trent Reese

Interior Design by:
Christopher Kirk
www.GFSstudio.com

Morgan James is a proud partner of Habitat for Humanity Peninsula and Greater Williamsburg. Partners in building since 2006.

Get involved today! Visit: www.morgan-james-publishing.com/giving-back

To the saints who helped make it possible.

Without the support of my wife and the executive leadership team at Covenant Eyes, the hours devoted to writing this book wouldn't have been possible. I'm grateful to the church leaders, Christian counselors, and the men and women who shared their time and stories with me and gave heart-felt warmth to a topic that often receives a cold shoulder.

I also thank the men who have walked with me as allies and who continue to encourage my growth.

Table of Contents

Foreword

I n 2007, when Sam Black became part of the Covenant Eyes family, I was struck by his propensity to correlate the importance of relational accountability to the struggle for victory over pornography. What I wasn't aware of was Sam's preternatural capability to take a deep dive into the pool of despair, in which two-thirds of Christian men and one-third of Christian women find themselves drowning, and then re-surface with tools of redemption and healing. I call it God's gift to Mr. Black.

But spiritual leaders are trained, not born. Sam's proving ground during his years at Covenant Eyes has been spent in conventions and seminars, collaborating with Covenant Eyes members, pastors, counselors, and ministry leaders, and writing and teaching about the dangers of pornography and the virtues of accountable living. He is no stranger to praying with broken porn addicts. And during his time in the trenches, he has held fast to biblical principles present in Christ's healing love for the worst of sinners.

"I find then the principle that evil is present in me . . . Wretched man that I am, who will set me free from this body of death?" Paul wrote that near the end of Romans, Chapter 7. As he dwelt on his own sin, there was this voice whispering in his ear, "*Talaiporos* [wretched] you are." Like you and me, Paul struggled with sin.

Talaiporos was the whisper . . .

But Paul didn't stop there. His very next thought was "Thanks be to God through Jesus Christ our Lord! . . . There is therefore now no condemnation for those who are in Christ Jesus" (Romans 7:25–8:1). Paul knew what the church was capable of—that the church can and will transform the world, that the church is "a healing church."

This was Paul, the Apostle. As you read these words, it is highly likely that either you or someone close to you hears that whisper, "*Talaiporos . . .*"

But don't stop there! In this book, author Sam Black leads us from that voice of despair (Chapter 1) through a proper perspective on what porn is, how it works on us, and its effect on the ministry of the Church (Chapters 2–11). He then addresses why we have failed to overcome porn's temptation (Chapter 12) and shows a clear path to victory, and even a proactive zeal against the sin—even to the next generation (Chapters 13–16).

And specifically, Black addresses the need for churches to join in the battle and provides a roadmap for you to become a leader in that battle (Chapters 17–18).

Black's engaging, storytelling style gives more than hope; it gives instruction. The Church is a body of many parts, and it will take a full-bodied Church to overcome this evil that has penetrated our society.

You can't do it alone, but nobody is asking you to. But you *are* expected to be a part of the work. Paul in no way claimed he was to go it alone. Over and over, he lists his allies, his accountability partners, and his co-laborers (e.g., "I urge you, brethren . . . that you also be in subjection to such men and to everyone who helps in the work and labors. . . . they have supplied what was lacking on your part. For they have refreshed my spirit and yours" (1 Corinthians 16:15–18).

Oh, *talaiporos*, this evil whisper that comes from Satan himself, using the perfect sin, destroying families, jobs, the ministry of the Church, even encouraging suicide, and at the very time in history when the internet sets the sin before us in a cornucopia of temptation.

But who better than the Church to overcome? Who better than Christ to say there is, therefore, now no condemnation? Who better than you to take the first step toward *A Healing Church?*

Ron DeHaas,
"Pioneer of Internet Accountability,"
co-founder and CEO of Covenant Eyes

Why I Wrote This Book

God's timing is perfect, and I was in its vice.

I was hard-pressed between three voices: those of ordinary Christians who struggle with pornography, Christian counselors and support organizations that help people find healing, and pastors who want to shepherd God's people. Throughout my years at Covenant Eyes, since 2007, I've listened to people in all three groups intently, learning and growing from their stories and instruction and discovering these three segments in the Church are often distant from each other.

As I processed the challenge, I could feel the Holy Spirit's urging. For such a time as this, when pornography is a screen tap away, I felt prodded to connect ministry leaders to a better understanding of how people get hooked, why they stay stuck, and why it's so hard for them to break free.

Though I'd felt this tension for years, I felt the pressure grow during a year-long tour of Christian homeschool conferences and men's ministry events. The homeschool conferences drew 3,500 to 16,000 people, and at twenty-seven events, my teams and I listened to families impacted by pornography. I felt empathy for struggling marriages torn by porn, sorrow for young children exposed at such a tender and influential age, and sympathy for men and women who felt trapped and yearned for freedom. At these family-friendly events, I spoke about pornography in large conference center ballrooms where parents sometimes stood along the walls because all the seats were taken. These parents and grandparents understood we would talk about porn, and they often brought their kids because so many of their children had been exposed already, within environments that were much more protected than the local public or even Christian school.

It stood in stark contrast to the timidity, surface teaching, and even silence in the greater Church.

At men's ministry events, I listened to celebrity speakers provide the same warnings about the dangers of porn and directives I've heard for decades. It equates to "Stop it. Don't do that; God hates that. When you sit down to your computer, take Jesus with you."

These exultations aren't wrong. They're just incomplete.

The tension inside me peaked as I wrapped up the year with two back-to-back gatherings of ministry leaders, many of whom I've known for a decade or more. The first conclave was a workshop of pastors, Christian counselors, coaches, and influencers, many of whom had been impacted by strongholds themselves and who took a Christ-focused journey to freedom. Hosted by Dr. Doug Weiss at Heart to Heart Counseling Center in Colorado Springs, this diverse group met to debate and imagine how they might help pastors and leaders address pornography in the greater Church. The second event in Dallas was a company of pastors and men's ministry leaders who gathered under the umbrella of the National Coalition of Ministries to Men. The focus of these ministry leaders is to disciple and guide men to a stronger relationship with Jesus.

Members of both groups see the devastation caused by porn. Both are focused on restoring lives. As I listened to these leaders, I concluded each group needs the other, but there is an unintentional chasm between them. This same divide is often found in the greater Church. By and large, these barriers are not theological differences; rather, these spheres are divided by knowledge, perceptions, and activities.

At the latter event, I was honored to lead a forty-minute workshop on how men become trapped in compulsive porn use and how men's ministry leaders can help. When I first walked into the large classroom I was provided, I thought it more than adequate. After all, there were only about 120 leaders in attendance, and there would be several sessions happening at the same time. It turned out that the room was too small, and leaders stood along the walls to listen.

Afterward, I was stopped in a hallway by the event director. He said, "You must have knocked it out of the park in your session. Guys came out of there blown away by what you said."

I was both encouraged and dismayed. The truth is, I just covered elementary principles within that short timeframe. The men's ministry leaders in that room needed and deserved more than one short session. And they were eager for more.

The men and women of those two small enclaves cemented my focus. On the flight home, I scribbled the outline of this book with the hope of equipping the shepherds who serve so many struggling souls. Over the years, thousands of pastors and church leaders have sought the guidance of the Covenant Eyes team, and I hope this book serves as an ongoing reference and guide for those who serve on the frontlines.

I pray this book is a blessing to you and those under your care.

Introduction

Where Agreement Comes Easy

L et's start where we all agree.

Porn is sin.

Sin grieves the Holy Spirit. Sin divides hearts. Sin teaches people to hide and cover themselves with fig leaves. Sin rises out of the lust of the eyes, the lust of the flesh, and the pride of life (1 John 2:16). Sin causes wandering souls to eat slop with pigs (Luke 15:15–16).

As Christian leaders, we know the only power that frees, washes, and restores us from sin is the blood of Jesus Christ, who gave Himself up for us while we were still sinners (Romans 5:8). His grace, forgiveness, and restoration are gifts that cannot be earned. As pastors, you no doubt teach that once we accept His gifts, we are to turn aside from every sin that so easily entangles and fix our eyes on Jesus, the founder and perfecter of faith (Hebrews 12:1–3).

When it comes to porn, we must not only know that *right* theology, but we must also help people grasp and apply it. As a pastor or church leader, you know these simple truths. But I leave these short sentences without various denominational vocabularies here as Exhibit A, the overarching theme that we can all agree on as Christians.

Grant Me Grace

This book and the work of Covenant Eyes is an ecumenical effort. At Covenant Eyes, a coalition of hundreds of team members reflect our Christian heritage: Lutherans,

Reformed, Baptists, Methodists, Nazarenes, Assemblies of God, Pentecostals, Catholics, Charismatics, small denominations, and independents. Though our theologies differ, we all agree that porn is sin. However, we never leave our individual theologies at the door. Personally, I enjoy both the tension and revelation this ecumenical community offers.

In reading this book, you might feel a tension between how I describe pornography use among Christians and how you have perceived pornography use among Christians. For example, some Christian leaders view porn use as a simple matter of pride and self-focus. Other leaders understand porn strongholds as a sinful behavior deeply engrained over time. Most leaders agree that porn use, like all sin, can sear the spiritual conscience of men and women.

At times, my choice of words might scrape against your vernacular. Please stay with me.

I invite you to embrace the tension with an open mind. Open your heart to hear from Christian leaders and counselors who represent a swath of denominations, even those who do not share all your views of the Bible. For instance, I will use the English Standard Version for Bible quotes, but if you believe the King James Version is the only reputable translation, then please read the verses in the King James. There are ways we can work together if we remain focused on the problem: porn in our midst.

I include information about life-changing programs some churches employ. Some of these programs may cause you to have a visceral reaction, but I suspect other programs I describe will meet your church's needs. The variations included here may even inspire you to create a program just for your denomination. Several pastors have told me how hard it is to employ a program, book, or study that is not represented by a denomination's publishing house. So create one!

In researching this book, I visited churches where grace abounds, and I found its members truly alive and on fire for Christ. Not with bravado and prideful proclamations—instead, they joyfully lead with a limp because everything about their lives depends on their walk with Jesus. And God is using that humility to lead the lost to salvation. I spoke to one church member who spent the last twenty years mentoring addicts one-on-one, and God used him as a layman to bring one hundred people to repent of their sins and accept Jesus Christ as their Lord and Savior. I know there are many more churches like the ones I describe, and it is not my intent to focus on a denomination or theology. I hope you let me know about your church and how God is using your congregation to set the captives free.

You will find portions of this book hammering both myths and conventional thinking, and I ask that you keep an open mind. Porn and sexual sin may make your stomach churn or even raise feelings of anger or disappointment. You may never have struggled in the way that men and women in your church struggle with sexual sin, but in these chapters, I hope to show you why people return to porn and unwanted sexual behavior again and again, even when they promise God, themselves, and anyone else that they are done with sexual sin for good. Most importantly, the Church holds the answers and the path to freedom.

For You

Finally, this book isn't a sermon. I have attended multiple trainings for pastors and men's ministry leaders where the agendas provided sessions on the topic of porn. But instead of equipping leaders, they hear from a celebrity men's speaker who dusts off a purity sermon he delivered at the last men's conference. That's bogus. You are biblically literate, and you don't need a purity sermon from a layman like me.

While this book is biblically focused, I aim to equip you to understand the pernicious nature of pornography. While anyone may encounter lust, pornography strongholds are something more formidable. The foundation is often built in youth and the stones and bars are set in place over time. God has provided us all the tools needed to deconstruct Satan's traps, but I say tools with plural intentionality. If we only hold a hammer, then every situation looks like a nail. God has equipped us to better navigate this complicated subject.

I also understand that pornography is just one issue that impacts people in your congregation, but by the end of this book, I hope to help you see that churches that can address sex and pornography well can address other sin struggles well too.

Chapter 1

Opportunity from Brokenness

Godly men are trained, not born.
Brian Doyle, Iron Sharpens Iron

"**E**very pastor wants a layman like Dan Wobschall," Pastor Chris Johnson contends.

A leader with a servant's heart, other men are drawn to Dan and seek his guidance. He's earned a reputation as a patient and empathetic listener who assures safety and confidence. Men who struggle deeply with sin, especially sexual sin, spew their stories and confessions to Dan with raw honesty. They spend hours under his compassionate teaching and guidance and follow his enthusiastic counsel. When Pastor Chris refers a man to Dan's discipleship, he knows that if that man pays attention, his spiritual and personal life will grow, he will work to repair his marriage, and he will pursue fatherhood with greater intention.

But guys like Dan don't come free. Dan wasn't born a spiritual leader; he was discipled.

When Dan first darkened the entrance to Christ Community Church in Waseca, Minnesota, he brought a cloud of despair and brokenness with him. Though Dan had attended church services since childhood, he had watched porn habitually since early adolescence, had betrayed his marriage with a year-long online affair, and before quitting his last job, his co-workers felt he gripped a ticking temper waiting to explode. Dan's life was a cyclone of pain, sinful choices, and growing consequences, but Pastor Chris and other mature men in the church accepted Dan within his storm. They walked him to the shelter of the cross where grace rained down and washed his heart clean—not all at once but over years of patient discipleship.

Many churches would have cast Dan out or kept him at arm's length. I, and likely you, have heard examples of such wariness or condemnation. Take the student studying for ministry in Calgary, Alberta, who was ousted from his church when he confessed porn use to his pastor or the volunteer in Houston who asked for help for his porn struggle and was stripped of his duties as a greeter and told he could only attend church when his wife accompanied him.

Even at more empathetic churches, porn strugglers are left wanting for help. Often, they describe receiving prayer and religious advice but very little tangible support. A common refrain I have heard from people who gain freedom from compulsive porn habits is: "My church didn't help me very much." Instead, they found life and heart-changing guidance through supporting ministries outside of their local congregations.

About two-thirds of Christian men and a third of Christian women say they have an ongoing struggle with porn, and 69 percent of pastors say porn has adversely impacted their church. But only about 7 percent of churches offer any kind of support resources to their congregations.[1] If your church is among the 7 percent, keep up the good work! Press onward, there is more to be done! If your church isn't providing support, an opportunity awaits with valuable dividends.

With God, every challenge comes with an opportunity. Every Goliath meets not David, but the Spirit within him. Porn in the pews isn't a giant to shrink from or shake our heads about; it's a juncture to show how God's power turns the miserable into mentors. God rescues people, even Christians, and helps them turn their maladies into ministry. And when the local church sets its heart on this work, that church becomes stronger, producing servants who give greater care to others and make their pastors' workloads easier.

In researching this book, I conducted dozens of interviews, not only with pastors, counselors, and ministry leaders but also with everyday people who've recovered from a secret life of sin and are helping others who feel trapped by porn and unwanted behaviors. It affirmed in me a deeply held belief that those who experience true brokenness and who surrender to discipleship and life change become strong servants to the Body of Christ and healthier as people overall. When the selfish become selfless, when the idolators learn to worship Christ, when the prideful become meek, they become more fulfilled as servants and filled with purpose.

Today, the local church has choices. It can largely ignore the problems of porn because they are too unseemly. It can chastise, rebuke, and cast out, which will send more people into hiding. Or it can lead people through a grace-filled process to the foot of the Cross, where strongholds are crushed and where stronger servants arise.

The Risk of Doing Nothing

While the twenty-first-century Church faces many threats to its spiritual strength and purity, one of the most damaging dangers is the proliferation of pornography, the magnitude of the reach never before recorded in human history. Since 1953, with the founding of Playboy, pornography has made a steady march to become ever-more accessible and hardcore through magazines, then film, then VHS, then the internet, and now with mobile devices (see Appendix A). I hope you are ignorant of what pornography is like today. Suffice to say that when today's children see porn online, they don't see the common nudity of yesteryear. Instead, they witness hardcore, demeaning, humiliating, and often violent videos that create a lasting impact (see Chapter 16).

Repetitive and ongoing porn use among boys and girls and men and women is common in local congregations, and over time, it poisons individuals emotionally and spiritually. It changes how they think and what they think about others, God, and their place in creation.

Multiple studies show that prolonged pornography exposure leads to:

- An exaggerated perception of sexual activity in society
- Diminished trust between intimate couples
- The abandonment of the hope of sexual monogamy
- Belief that promiscuity is the natural state
- Belief that abstinence and sexual inactivity are unhealthy
- Cynicism about love or the need for affection between sexual partners
- Belief that marriage is sexually confining
- Lack of attraction to family and child-raising[2]

As you might expect, when Christians use porn, it often weakens their faith. A study at a Christian university found that among Christian students who use pornography, 43 percent of men and 20 percent of women say their pornography use worsened their relationship with Christ. Further, 20 percent of men and 9 percent of women reported their pornography use caused them to lose interest in spiritual things.[3] In reviewing several studies, researchers found that an increase in pornography use is significantly related to reduced church attendance, diminished faith, lessened prayer frequency, and diminished feelings of closeness to God. At the same time, porn use increased religious doubts.

The horizon looks troubling for Christian leadership. In 2019, The Freedom Fight surveyed Christian college students who said their faith was *very important* to them. Of this group, 89 percent of college men involved in collegiate ministries said they watched porn; 63 percent said they watched porn weekly, and 51 percent of these future Christian leaders said they believed they were addicted to pornography.[4]

It might seem elementary that pornography use is stripping the local church of possible teachers, volunteers, and leaders. University of Oklahoma sociologist Dr. Samuel Perry put this reasoning to the test and found the more frequently someone viewed pornography in 2006, the less likely they held a leadership position or served on a committee in their church over the next six years. But please don't assume your leaders are safe. As you will discover in Chapter 3, some people who struggle with porn and sex spend more time serving in the church to feel better about their sin.

As porn has become more accepted throughout Western society, fewer Christians today find porn sinful. More men and women who self-identify as religious are saying porn is okay and they are doing so at an accelerated rate. In 2017, 16 percent of Americans who claimed religion is *very important* also said that porn is morally acceptable. In just one year, that number rose six percentage points, and by the end of 2018, 22 percent said it is morally acceptable. Among Republicans, 16 percent said porn was morally acceptable in 2011, and in 2018, 27 percent said it was moral to watch porn. Among Democrats, 32 percent said porn was moral in 2011, and 53 percent said the same in 2018. Of all Americans, 43 percent say watching porn is morally acceptable, up 7 percent from the prior year.[5]

Though cultural attitudes toward porn are changing, church leaders often tell me they feel inhibitions about confronting pornography with their congregations.

Many reasons exist for why many churches address porn poorly. Pastors often describe kickback from parishioners for addressing a tawdry topic or talking about an issue that will just make people curious. And you or someone on your church team might be asking the following questions.

1. Isn't this a parent's job to guard and teach their children and teens?
2. Isn't preaching about purity enough?
3. If people just read scripture and pray, this won't be a problem in their life, correct?

Within these pages, these questions will be addressed. However, the statistics above show a clear problem for the Church. Porn isn't just an embarrassing discussion; it's an imperative one and needs ongoing attention. Pornography isn't just unbecoming. It's weakening individuals and families in your church.

Patterns

At an elemental level, using porn is a sinful choice. While that is true, the church often limits its discussion to this simplistic principle. Love God, don't sin, even though porn is tempting. That scenario creates a picture in my mind. I see an adult man or woman suddenly confronted by porn, and they simply need to make a choice. *Just say no.*

Indeed, while porn is tempting to some, it's repulsive to others. Many men and women recall seeing porn, but it just didn't have much of an impact on them. Other Christians may use porn once in a blue moon when they are feeling especially sexual or out of curiosity, but after repenting, they may have no real draw to return to it.

The audiences in the above two paragraphs will benefit from the common sermon delivered from pulpits around the world that warn people not to entertain sexualized media in their lives. These people can be tempted, but the bait doesn't command their ongoing attention. Their minds are neither barraged with incessant thoughts, nor do they fight regularly to push images and scenarios from their hearts.

Since 93 percent of boys and 70 percent of girls have accessed pornography online,[6] I take for granted that most pastors have seen porn at some point in their lives. Still, it might seem unfathomable to you that a Christian could become entrenched by its seduction. Are strugglers just stupid? Do they put their hands on stove tops just to see how much they will be scarred?

I joined the Covenant Eyes team in February 2007 and made a startling discovery along the way. My struggle with porn wasn't unique. Instead, there is a common theme among men and women who feel caged in pornography strongholds as adults.

First, like Dan in the opening paragraphs, compulsive porn users were typically exposed early. Early exposure should be especially concerning to you as a shepherd leading the next generation of Christ followers because the ages of early exposure are drifting lower due to the proliferation of mobile devices. While Dan first found porn at age twelve, more recent statistics show the average age of first exposure is between ages eight and eleven. Because of its neurological impact, the vast majority of adults can tell you when and where they were the first time they saw porn.

Second, people who struggle commonly have been impacted by trauma early in life. Divorce, feelings of abandonment, violence in the home, and sexual abuse are serious threats, but there are many more that might seem less invasive. For instance, Dan was an unexpected pregnancy for his parents, and he felt resented by his father who never told his son he loved him. "Why do you have to be so stupid?" was the rhetorical question Dan's father repeated too often.

The third common issue is repetitive use. It's one thing for a person to see porn and masturbate, but continued access and engagement create a habit that becomes engrained physically and mentally within the brain.

Often by accident, pornography use turns into escapism. At first, pornography and masturbation arose out of natural curiosity for Dan, and most others who struggle, but over time, its distraction and euphoria become coping mechanisms for adolescent feelings of fear, anxiety, stress, anger, sadness, frustration, depression, and more. With time and repetition, the list of reasons to pacify with porn might include the mundane, such as feeling bored or seeking to relax, and as an aid for sleeplessness.

Of course, this sinful and unhealthy self-soothing is self-focused. The porn user views people in porn as things to be used rather than souls created in the image of God. Porn feeds "the lust of the flesh, and the lust of the eyes, and the pride of life . . ." (1 John 2:16). People often use porn to create a fantasy of being desired, wanted, and in control. But selfishness always wants more, and threads of abuse and humiliation are commonplace in mainstream porn. All genres of pornography are devoted to dehumanization.

When sexualized media becomes a mainstay in adolescence, by adulthood, men and women face a five-hundred-pound gorilla when they try to quit.

Eric Gardener knows first-hand how the porn trap is laid—but also how to break free. He shares his story often as the California director of Marked Men for Christ and a recovery support group leader at High Desert Church in southern California. Eric finds that, though the details of his story are unique, other men who struggle with porn readily identify with the arresting pattern of early exposure, wounds, and ongoing use.

Though Eric's physicality resembles that of a bear, his stature wasn't always so imposing. At age six, young Eric sat on his front porch step with a neighborhood friend and bartered a couple of knockoff Matchbox cars for a few of his friend's toys. Pleased with his exchange, Eric showed his swapped bounty to his dad as his dad walked past the boys. In a flash, Eric's alcoholic father was enraged that his son would trade his toys. He grabbed Eric by the wrist, stood him to his feet, and slapped his bottom so hard his feet swung out like a pendulum. On his return swing toward the ground, his father's hand connected again with a force that reverberated through Eric's small body. The shock of the blow caused his bladder to evacuate. Seeing his son's wet pants, Eric's dad grabbed Eric by his neck and threw him into the house where he tumbled across the floor.

In that atmosphere, at age eight, Eric found his father's porn magazines. By adolescence, porn use had become a repetitive escape from the turmoil inside Eric's home. Pornography taught him a false sense of masculinity; sexual prowess and conquests as an adult were equated to strength and manliness.

Eric's porn addiction, pride, and self-centered behaviors followed him through three failed marriages and nearly destroyed his fourth. At a Christian men's retreat, he discovered a sex addiction support group backed by High Desert Church, and Eric began taking the first steps on his healing journey. Now, he keeps his freedom by giving it to others.

In the coming chapters, I will offer a deeper insider's view of how men and women become hooked on pornography through the stories of real people. Some counselors create prose based on a variety of clients to protect their identities. I am under no such obligation, and as a former journalist, I do my best to relay the stories told to me well while protecting individual anonymity as requested. Some of these people are mothers and fathers who don't want to embarrass or surprise their children, grandchildren, or even their mothers and fathers.

Restoring Disciples

It's not enough to say the local church has a hidden porn problem. Church leaders deserve a primer on how people become trapped, why they often stay stuck alone, and how the church can help people come out of hiding and find lasting healing and freedom. All three parts hold value. Knowledge precedes understanding and understanding precedes change. For leaders, I believe understanding creates greater empathy for those ensnared, and knowing how to help is like having a guide's map.

For the struggler, having advisors and direction is imperative because they are truly lost. They don't know how they got to their current location, where to step next, or how to get to the next post on a much longer journey. The struggler wants a quick fix, but porn recovery is a trek taken one step at a time . . . over time.

Those who are trapped want to climb out of the pits that hold them captive. They want to please God; they want to be faithful. But they construct ladders from the twigs and threads of self-sufficiency and willpower, which fall apart every time they attempt their assent.

For some leaders and strugglers, the idea of needing guided healing is a hard pill to swallow. From a theoretical perspective, quitting porn should be as simple as "turn or burn." Do people need any other assistance than prayer, Scripture, and repentance? I think it's interesting that this same question isn't applied to many other aspects of Christian living. For instance, a husband should love his wife and lay down his life for his bride as Christ loved the church (Ephesians 5:25–33). It's right there in Scripture, so just do it! If a man loves God, then he should love his wife with patience, kindness, hopefulness, and perseverance. He shouldn't be easily angered or keep a record of wrongs (1 Corinthians 13:4–7). Though churches rightfully teach these things, many also host seminars, ongoing small groups, or create opportunities to attend "A Weekend to Remember" to arm men and women with tools and guidance to fulfill God's design for marriage.

There are many amazing reasons for providing marriage counseling, hosting marriage retreats, and instructing couples through marriage books and small groups, especially for troubled marriages. Among those reasons is husbands and wives have trauma and struggles from their families of origin that encourage specific ways of thinking and reacting, especially under stress. There is a reason spouses say, "You act just like your mother (father)." They brought unhealthy and unhelpful habits into marriage, and they practiced those habits so often, they became part of their fallen natures. They react and act within marriage in ways that are impatient, unloving, demeaning, hurtful, and cruel. People often have deep regrets about the way they treat their spouses. They are ashamed of the things they say, how they shout, and the ways they storm and stew. Wisely, churches provide help, counseling, and support. Leaders provide couples with handles to hold onto that help them change behavior, turn from sin, and seek a Christ-like heart.

Conversely, churches don't tend to offer the same resources for porn use, even when it's deemed an addiction or compulsive.

It's not too hard to poke holes in my comparison, but I think it provides helpful context when we think of how people need help for specific issues inside their marriages or life in general. For example, people who rage have a lot in common with people who struggle with porn (and cross-compulsive behaviors are common). Counselors will tell you that people who rage exchange emotions associated with weakness and vulnerability for feelings of power and control. When another driver cuts a man off in traffic, his first reaction isn't anger; it's fear of being harmed and an inability to control what has already happened. His anger may feel instantaneous, but it is a secondary reaction to compensate for his lack of control and helplessness. When men and women watch porn, they often have feelings of control, which is a soothing salve for the fragility, vulnerability, and pressures they feel in life.

Throughout this book, I will point you to other books, groups, and programs that may help people in your church seek a better footing on a biblical foundation. This is not a recovery manual. Rather, it is a primer for a deeper understanding and insight into people's struggles with pornography and unwanted sexual behaviors and a guide to some of the supportive steps you can take in your church.

I have met many men and women who escaped pornography's grip through steady spiritual disciplines, close accountability relationships, and a supportive church. Nearly all of them tell me their journey to healing and freedom could have come quicker with a few more tools to help them understand their brokenness and lean more closely toward their heavenly Father.

Dan, from our opening paragraphs, took steady steps to recovery with nothing more than a Bible, prayerful companions and family, and a supportive church.

It took him seven years to live in steadfast sobriety from porn. He said if he had known that Faithful and True (which provides Christian intensives and support in Eden Prairie, Minnesota, for porn and sex addiction) was just sixty miles from his hometown, he would have made the trip. He and his church family were unaware of the support available to them.

"Structured recovery allows you to be held in place for God to do His work," said Care and Recovery Pastor Jack West, who serves at Mariners Church in Irvine, California.

"We have to recognize that we are imprisoned by our own desires," Pastor West said. "We've crafted a life in a cage of our own making, closed the door on ourselves, reached through the bars, and turned the key from the outside. That's our life until we can engage the truth. Redemption and freedom will only come from someone unlocking the door from the outside. We cannot do it ourselves because we threw away the key. No one keeps the key."

People seeking escape without help run around inside their prison cells chasing their tails. They are inconsistent in their surrender to Christ and lean on their own understanding. Guides and safe processes assist a rebellious heart from wandering to the private corners of depravity. Even though strugglers hate their prisons, their cells are well-known. And the routine is more comfortable than change.

However, to live freely in Christ, we must die daily to our desires and ourselves and be resurrected by the work of the Holy Spirit. Within a safe process accompanied by others, the wayward have an example to follow, just as the Apostle Paul said, "Follow my example, as I follow the example of Christ" (1 Corinthians 11:1).

Throughout this book, the phrase "a safe place and a safe process" receives a fair amount of attention, and in Chapter 15, I will describe several examples of biblically-based safe processes. A safe place and safe processes allow people to dig deep into their hearts to better understand what they do when they do it without the weighty barriers of toxic shame. Here are two simple examples of what people discover in a safe process to overcome porn.

First, every process suggested in this book helps people have a greater understanding of their deep need for a daily relationship with Jesus. Rather than an attitude of performance and personal justification, people need to learn to surrender . . . and not just momentary surrender when they feel shame. Luther described our lives as one of *daily* repentance, and the poor in spirit recognize their desperate need for the cleansing blood of Christ.

Second, a safe process teaches self-awareness. Here is a simple example: Many men and women explain that they often fail to fight off porn temptations at night, even when they have escaped temptations throughout the day. I hear many pastors say they create a safe boundary by going to bed with their spouses rather than staying up late and watching TV. Why should the time of day matter concerning temptation?

The recovery community calls it *decision fatigue*. Our capacity to make good decisions often wanes the longer we are awake or the more our minds are taxed throughout the day. For instance, many people mindlessly eat sweet and salty foods at night, ignoring what it's doing to their bodies. Greater awareness provides opportunities to employ tactics and strategies for healthy living. A person can think, "I'm feeling tempted, and it's because I am tired and stressed." The person can employ tactics, such as turning off media at certain times, devoting time for prayer and Scripture-reading before bed, and trying to keep a regular sleep schedule. In taking basic preventative steps, they "make no provision for the flesh, to gratify its desires" (Romans 13:14).

Through a safe process, a person seeking to overcome porn learns to think, "I'm feeling tempted. Why?" This curiosity helps them learn to step out of their emotional state and look critically at themselves. Experiencing anger, loneliness, anxiety, stress, rejection, and fear are among many emotional states, also called emotional triggers, that can cause people trapped in strongholds to run toward their long-accepted and unhealthy coping strategies rather than godly choices. Through a safe process, people learn how to run from porn, call on supportive people, and focus on their daily surrender to Christ (2 Timothy 2:22).

The Discipled Give Back

When Dan arrived at Christ Community Church, sin had wrecked his marriage, his work life, and his life as a father. In a small town where a congregation of 250 is considered large, Dan could have been considered a public relations risk to the church's image. But Pastor Chris was more focused on the local church representing Christ well. Telling the sick to become healthy before they go to a hospital is absurd; and Jesus said, "Those who are well have no need of a physician, but those who are sick. I came not to call the righteous, but sinners" (Mark 2:17).

"The church is like Noah's ark. It stinks but it's the only thing afloat," Pastor Chris said. "The Church is all we have to represent Christ to one another and to the world. God's plan is the Church. There is not a Plan B."

When God does restorative work on a person's heart, it doesn't end with the presenting problem that was so concerning. The rooms and closets of life are opened, their contents reexamined, and light fills the darkest corners. The psalmist cried out, "Search me, O God, and know my heart! Try me and know my thoughts! And see if there be any grievous way in me, and lead me in the way everlasting!" (Psalm 139:23–24).

"Addressing pornography in someone's life is an opportunity for deep discipleship," said Ted Shimer, the founder of The Freedom Fight. "When someone finds freedom, they have addressed core issues, they are walking in their core identity in Christ, and they're much more committed to holiness in their life."

Through intentional steps, those who follow paths of recovery discover their neediness and weakness and release their shame and their failed efforts to a path made straight (Proverbs 3:6). They are more self-aware, more reflective, and more able to dig into their personal stories, memories, thoughts, and emotions. They pursue ongoing change through the power of the Holy Spirit. They are sinners who get up when they fall (Proverbs 24:16) and cling to the hope and knowledge of Christ's sanctifying work in their lives. They are dangerous to the status quo. Having awakened, they pursue others. They give away the hope and life they received. Knowing what prison feels like, they are patient and kind, but also skilled in helping others find the keys to unlock shackles.

Within a local body of believers, Dan submitted his life to the patient guidance of other men in the church. But that's not the end of the story. As Dan found healing and freedom, his testimony inspired other men, women, and teens in the church to come out of the shadows about their struggles. Other churches in Waseca and surrounding communities asked Dan to speak at their services. Dan was not only mentoring men in his church but men in several other churches too. At this writing, commissioned by the small church in Waseca, Dan serves full-time with the team at Be Broken Ministries in San Antonio, Texas, where he leads weekend workshops for men in Texas and Florida and serves as a recovery coach.

This scenario isn't unique. Throughout this book, you will hear the stories of many men and women who not only found healing, they also tend to the wounds of others. Men and women who experience recovery often serve and disciple others toward a more intimate connection with Christ.

Grace overflows and can't be contained.

While some might consider Dan and Eric good examples of restoration, I see them among a battalion of saints who have become equipped to serve the church far better than most men and women who warm our pews on Sunday mornings. Having had a spiritual awakening, they share the freedom they have received because they keep what they give away.

Chapter 2
Do We Really Know What Porn Is?

I shall not today attempt further to define the kinds of material (considered obscenity, regarding hard-core pornography), but I know it when I see it.
Potter Stewart, *Jacobellis vs. Ohio*, 1964

A young man stood in the crowded lecture hall and accepted the microphone he was offered.

"Yes, my question is, what is considered porn?"

The two-day event drew lay leaders from several countries, and they sat studiously behind rows of tables. They dutifully jotted notes, some on laptops, some in old-fashioned binders. Each speaker made their points and challenged the crowd to take action. Heads nodded and more notes were taken. Was this a confab on church growth? How about evangelism? How about biblical marriage? No, this was a conference on pornography.

The event rocketed through presentations. Michael Leahy, who founded a recovery ministry called BraveHearts, told his personal story of redemption from porn and sex addiction. Clay Olsen of Fight the New Drug, a non-religious anti-porn organization, revealed scientific studies and a movement of young people who call themselves fighters that denounce and flee porn. There were counselors, pastors, and leaders diving into multiple concerns. From the audience, young people took the stage and talked about their intense struggles with pornography and what they were doing to fight back.

Midway through the conference, the lineup of sessions paused for a period of Q&A. Perched on uncomfortable high-top chairs on the stage, I was among a group of speakers ready with answers. Surely, this would be a time for the toughest questions.

The young man's question was apropos, and the audience looked intently at the stage for an answer. Leahy, who wrote the book *Porn Nation*, looked my way and grinned, "You want to take this one?"

Obviously, the guy from Covenant Eyes, a decades-old company that provides accountability software for popular devices, would know how to define porn. Hold tight, I'll get to my answer in just a bit.

When people use the word *pornography*, it seems everyone knows what everyone is talking about right up until the moment they don't. It's both simple and confusing. A person's culture, faith, politics, social views, and exposure to pornography can play a significant role. Historians, legislators, judges, pastors, and even the team at Covenant Eyes have spent mammoth amounts of effort creating definitions for pornography and related terms. While a social scientist might define porn in a dispassionate paragraph with commas and periods, a person struggling to break free from its grip or a spouse scarred by a partner's porn use might use recurring exclamation points in their narratives.

Dive deep and the emotions both pro and con become visceral. Here are some takes on porn I have heard:

One friend described pornography as a means of sexual expression, exploration, and a valued First Amendment right with the passion that gave the late pornographer Larry Flynt the same heroic status as Patrick Henry. Give me porn or give me death! I've heard several church attenders describe how their local church is too prudish on sexualized media, even though they might not say so within earshot of their pastors.

Another friend described porn as a demon that invaded his thoughts. He recalls gripping the steering wheel on his drive home from work and screaming in an attempt to force porn fantasies from his mind. He would have short periods of abstinence from porn only for its siren call to summon him in the middle of the night, when he fought with his wife, and during many other stressful scenarios.

When porn tortures a marriage, it may be defined much differently. Amy, whose marriage imploded from her husband's porn and sex addiction, described porn as the most offensive four-letter word. It's vile, evil, and composed of lies, she said.

"Porn is the nasty voice in wives' heads that tells them they will never be enough, or that they are too much, or both," Amy said. "Porn is the ultimate in sinister magicians, turning a spouse's most trusted and intimately known person into a stranger they no longer recognize. Porn is the tornado that costs spouses their safety, security, sexuality, confidence, sense of belonging, faith, future plans, dreams, and, on some days, their sanity."

Emotions run deep.

Depending on your view, what makes something porn has an obvious answer. And therein lies the dilemma. Our views on porn are shaped by our beliefs and experiences. The views of many Christians have been shaped more by culture than biblical truth.

What We Call Porn

The pornography industry and even a broad spectrum of people say that porn has been with people since they were drawing sexual depictions on cave walls and argue that today's porn is nothing new. Indeed, people have expressed adoration for the human body and sex for millennia, but I doubt any porn website would try to excite their customers with ancient pottery or papyrus drawings.

In the 1950s, '60s, and '70s, the US Supreme Court outlawed specific types of porn as *obscenity*, which is a legal term. The court accepted pornography in a limited way and gave local juries guidelines to enforce the obscenity laws based on their community standards. But with so much porn coming through VHS in the 1980s and then the internet beginning in the 1990s, community standards changed and prosecutors stopped hauling porn distributors to court (see Appendix A).

Today, most Americans governed by those Supreme Court rulings have seen what the court would have called obscenity. But people don't think to call it obscenity in a legal sense; they just call it porn, or hardcore porn, or whatever genre has become identifiable.

Most people don't simply determine whether something is or isn't porn. Rather, there's a spectrum. People describe something as either more pornographic or less pornographic. People often use words like immodest, risqué, provocative, and overtly sexual to describe what they consider the lighter fare of sexual media. Our culture invented odd words, such as *softcore* simply to say something isn't as bad as *hardcore* porn, and the softcore has become harder with time. On the other side of the spectrum are words like defecation, torture, humiliation, and genre-specific words that aren't worth mentioning. The more people watch porn, the less shocking it becomes, a 2017 study showed.[7]

The spectrum has shifted for individuals, society, and even in church culture. That shift is so individual that pastors must be more direct about defining pornography for their audience from a biblical perspective. At university student presentations, Clay Olsen is often told that Playboy nudity isn't pornography. In many students' minds, porn is only the hardcore stuff, and nudity isn't porn even if intended for sexual arousal.

Many Americans agree with these college students. Forty-three percent of American adults said a sexually arousing nude image isn't porn, according to a 2016 Barna Study. Meanwhile, 37 percent of adults said that an image of a sexual act wasn't porn as long as it didn't show intercourse, and if it did show intercourse, 21 percent said the image still wasn't pornography. But video is the mainstay of the internet, and 16 percent of adults said that a film isn't porn even when the whole video is sex scenes with little or no story.[8]

This distance between a cultural view and a biblical view is no less present in church congregations on Sunday mornings, said Nick Stumbo, executive director of Pure Desire, which provides courses and support groups to help people escape porn. "We hardly talk about sex or pornography at all in the Church, and when we do, we just assume everyone understands what we're saying," Stumbo said. "We have to be mindful, especially when speaking to multiple generations at once. People aren't even on the same page with us."

50 Shades of Questions

This cultural shift within the Church happened by osmosis. Many Christians became desensitized one ad, one episode, one magazine, one video, and one click at a time over decades. For example, conservative Protestants and biblical literalists in the United States are statistically identical to the rest of America when it comes to the use of social media, accessing the internet from our phones, and the hours spent watching

Colossians 3:1–10

"If then you have been raised with Christ, seek the things that are above, where Christ is, seated at the right hand of God. Set your minds on things that are above, not on things that are on earth. For you have died, and your life is hidden with Christ in God. When Christ who is your life appears, then

TV.[9] Many Christians aim to engage our culture, to be light in the darkness, but this interaction seems to have shifted ideals and boundaries in the greater Church.

When *50 Shades of Grey* debuted in 2012, pastors were surprised that members of their congregations were scooping up copies of a novel that detailed a BDSM (bondage, discipline, sadism, and masochism) and unmarried relationship. Author Rebecca Reilly was too embarrassed to buy the book from her local bookstore or even from the local Target, so she drove eighty miles to the outskirts of San Francisco to claim her copy. Deeply in love with her Sunday-School-teaching husband, George, she looked to *50 Shades* as a manual to spice up their sex life.

you also will appear with him in glory. Put to death therefore what is earthly in you: sexual immorality, impurity, passion, evil desire, and covetousness, which is idolatry. On account of these the wrath of God is coming. In these you too once walked, when you were living in them. But now you must put them all away: anger, wrath, malice, slander, and obscene talk from your mouth. Do not lie to one another, seeing that you have put off the old self with its practices and have put on the new self, which is being renewed in knowledge after the image of its creator."

"Even after reading it five or six times, I still get uncomfortable seeing the words describing how Mr. Grey does this or that," Reilly writes in her ebook *Diary of a Christian Woman*.[10] "Uncomfortable or not, I feel quite justified in my study of this piece of erotic literature. My goals are lofty, even spiritual. It is my responsibility to use the gift of my sexuality to bless George. And no one has ever taught me how. I remind myself of that lofty goal every time I reach for a glass of ice water to cool off."

Comparing all Americans to Christian Americans, The Barna Group found that 9 percent of both groups read the fantasy novel. The book was more popular with women. About 16 percent of American women read the book, of which 19 percent were practicing Christians.[11] In response, pastors preached sermons, Focus on the Family, Covenant Eyes, and other organizations wrote articles encouraging women to put the novel aside and skip theater lines when the book debuted as a film in 2015.

Soon after, Americans tuned in weekly and bought the eight seasons of HBO's *Game of Thrones*, which was lauded for its in-depth characters and story based on the books by George R. R. Martin. It was also condemned and praised for its ". . . oodles of nudity. Graphic scenes of incest and rape."[12] It became the most watched series in HBO's history with 17.4 million viewers tuning in on a Sunday night to watch the Season 8 finale, according to Nielson data.[13]

"The weirdest part [of directing *Game of Thrones*] was when you have one of the exec producers leaning over your shoulder, going, 'You can go full frontal, you know. This is television, you can do whatever you want! And do it! I urge you to do it!' So I was like, 'Okay, well, you're the boss.'" (*Game of Thrones* Director Neil Marshall)[14]

"This particular exec took me to one side and said, 'Look, I represent the pervert side of the audience, okay? Everybody else is the serious, drama side, [but] I represent the perv side of the audience, and I'm saying I want full frontal nudity in this scene. So you go ahead and do it.'"

While Nielson data showed Christians overall didn't watch the series as much as other mainstream shows, plenty did, especially younger men. A plethora of Christian authors debated whether Christians should watch the show, even as Christian leaders John Piper and Kevin DeYoung guided people to flee the show's temptations.

The National Center on Sexual Exploitation in Washington, DC, was definitive too: "By the excessiveness to which sexual violence is an element of the GOT plot—the graphic depictions of incestuous sex, rape, prostitution, child sexual abuse, and sexual torture, and dialogue which portrays abuses like incest as simply a matter of love or taste—GOT normalizes heinous sexual abuses and exploitation."[15]

But articles in *Christianity Today* and *Lightworkers* and others written by Christian writers gave a more nuanced view. They argued that Christians seemed overly focused on the sexual content without denouncing the violence, that the show offers theological lessons and artistic beauty, and that Christians could simply use the fast-forward button for scenes that disturbed them.

"*Game of Thrones* isn't bad because it's popular or has sex in it. Maybe it's not for you. Maybe it is. Perhaps the better question to ask, about any piece of art, is this: 'Is it beautiful?' Because, according to St. Augustine, the more good, true and beautiful something is, the closer we are to the heart of God," Hayden Royster wrote for Lightworkers.com.[16]

With this artistic gauge, it's less surprising that Americans, in general, believe that "watching sexually explicit scenes on TV or in a movie" was dead last on a list of immoral activities (including overeating and lying), presented in a 2016 Barna Study called The Porn Phenomenon. A majority of teens and young adults agreed that not recycling is more immoral than viewing what they would define as pornography. They also said that thinking negatively of someone with a different point of view is also more immoral than viewing porn.

Biblical Measurements

As you read this book, scan the results of the studies and surveys, and as you lead the conversation about pornography in your church, you must be aware there are multiple definitions of pornography to balance. In older studies conducted in the '90s, '80s, and before, you will find respondents are more strict in how they define porn, and survey respondents in the broadband internet age are less so.

When I ask you to balance these definitions, it's not a request to compromise biblical perspective. Rather, you might have to take the results of newer studies, such as The Porn Phenomenon (which Covenant Eyes and Josh McDowell Ministry financed), with a pinch of salt when so many respondents say images and videos of sexual acts aren't porn. As you preach to your congregation and counsel individuals and couples, you will need to define pornography from a biblical perspective because their personal definitions are likely compromised.

Though definitions of porn in human eyes vary, they are consistent biblically. God's measure hasn't changed since Job proclaimed, "I have made a covenant with my eyes . . ." or when Jesus said, "I say to you that everyone who looks at a woman with lustful intent has already committed adultery with her in his heart" (Job 31:1a and Matthew 5:28). Jesus provided no caveats about what a person was or was not wearing or what act was or was not being performed. God doesn't bother grading porn on a spectrum; He cares about the intent of our hearts.

Jesus taught that we are defiled by what comes out of our hearts. "For out of the heart come evil thoughts, murder, adultery, sexual immorality, theft, false witness, slander. These are what defile a person" (Matthew 15:18–20). The images of lust need not be nude, but they are made so by our hearts.

Let's return to the question that opened this chapter: "What is considered porn?"

During that conference, men and women spoke of their unique lusts. Though most people didn't label the type of porn they used, some did. One young man described how he would review websites and catalogs that showed models for men's underwear. Many men and women, whose homes were protected from modern porn, perused Victoria's Secret or J.C. Penney catalogs to masturbate to men and women in lingerie, undergarments, and swimwear. I received Covenant Eyes reports for a man whose porn was women's feet. Though some professionals might call these fetishes, no study would call these preoccupations pornography . . . and yet, they are objects of what Jesus called adultery and sexual immorality. These are what defile a person.

My answer to the audience that day was aimed at the heart: my heart, your heart, and the heart of every living soul.

"What causes you to look with lustful intent? What causes your heart to treat another as a sexual object? What do you store in your memory for masturbation fantasies? Not just the object, or image, or video itself, but also consider the lust that comes from seeking to use these things for sexual gratification. Do you not know that you are defiled by what comes out of your heart?

"That is porn.

"That is porn to you."

Chapter 3
People You Don't Suspect

People fall in private long before they fall in public.
J.C. Ryle, English evangelical Anglican bishop

Though separated by 1,400 miles, Brandon and Darlene have at least one thing in common: Their pastors never suspected them of struggling with sexual sin.

"I thought I would be the guy who went to the grave with all these secrets," Brandon says. "I wasn't gonna tell anyone."

Brandon's secret seemed secure. To an onlooker, he was in an enviable position—a successful businessman, a good father, happily married, and living in a beautiful home in southern California. But when it came to porn, he felt out of control. His wife knew he watched porn occasionally, but she ignored it as long as it was out of her sight and that of their kids. What she didn't know was how pervasive and varied it had become, how it had stolen hours of time, attention, and intimacy from the family, and how it impacted Brandon's personal and professional life.

But Brandon's life and his façade fell apart. He lost his job, and his marriage faced its most difficult period. Looking back, Brandon points to how his lies and hidden pornography use since childhood gradually stole integrity from other parts of his life. Pornography had become an escape not only from pain in his life, but also from how he felt about himself. Pornography created a fantasy space where he was loved, admired, respected, and in control. In real life, he didn't feel he measured up, and lying became part of his performance to look good and be accepted. He fudged numbers as a business manager to look better. He skipped opportunities as a father and husband to make time for porn.

"What do we have left when we don't have our integrity?" Brandon asks.

When Brandon's secrets were uncovered, nearly everyone in his life was caught off-guard, including Brandon's pastor.

Men are not the only ones struggling with sexual sin in the church. Many women and girls are struggling too. And if someone like Brandon doesn't appear to need help, that seems to be even truer for Darlene. To everyone around her, she is a model Christian.

Like Brandon, Darlene was good at keeping her sex addiction secret. She wasn't just held in high esteem at her Southern Baptist Church, she ministered as a Sunday School teacher and a church school board member, and she served on the board that oversaw the church's mission in Mexico.

Darlene wore a mask of smiles and contentment, but inside, she screamed and buried her head each Sunday and prayed for control. She was sure that if she volunteered enough, stayed busy with work that mattered, read her Bible, prayed enough, and attended Bible studies, her sexual compulsions would vanish. But her prayerful trips to the church altar and her private strategies never worked. At times, she carried on three extra-marital affairs at the same time, while balancing her work as a banker and her volunteerism in the church.

Brandon and Darlene are not anomalies. There are too many Brandons and Darlenes in churches across the nation. Based on multiple surveys, about 70 percent of men and about a third of women in the Church say they struggle with pornography specifically. Some people are occasional viewers of porn, while others have full-blown addictions. Still others lie somewhere in between.

- Of Christian men eighteen to thirty, 77 percent said they watch porn at least monthly. Within this group, 36 percent said they watch it daily.

- Overall (men of all ages) two-thirds of Christian men watch porn at least monthly, and 37 percent say they seek porn several times a week.

- Among women eighteen to thirty in the same age group, 34 percent said they watch porn at least monthly.[17]

That more than a third of men attending church have a continuous struggle with porn should cause us deep concern in the Church. But who is struggling can be elusive.

Salacious Clickers

Many secular commentators say Christians are so rigid and sexually inhibited that it's no wonder they struggle with the things that are most taboo.

The pornography industry offers a great one-liner: *If you don't like porn, don't watch it.* It's thrust as a double-edged sword to tell social and religious conservatives to mind their own business and that porn-viewing Christians must like what they're watching. The secret appetite among Christians receives the greatest smirk. Obviously, Christians who watch porn are hypocrites because they like porn while their church tells everyone it's wrong.

The American South is often called the Bible Belt because of broad church attendance. So does this concentration of Christians show that religiosity and conservative Christian beliefs make people more prone to feel addicted to porn and sex?

A multitude of authors jumped to the conclusion that Bible-belt Christians are the most likely to visit porn sites after studies in 2014[18] and 2017[19] showed searches about sex and porn are strong in states with higher populations who claim religious ties.

The results were short of a bullseye but, nonetheless, should give Christian leaders pause. For instance, even the studies' authors question if non-religious people are more likely to rely on private internet searches rather than have their conservative neighbors look down their noses when picking up porn in a more public venue. Does the lesser availability of porn in conservative communities require covert internet use? Were many of the searches about sex aimed at conversations about traditional sexual values? The studies' authors weren't sure. As well, although Texas and Georgia topped the list in the 2014 study, Michigan, Illinois, and California came right after and those states lack the Bible-belt label.

Still, the liberal Northeast, as well as Hawaii, Colorado, and New Mexico, spent a lot fewer searches per capita looking specifically for porn than did states in the American South. And the 2017 study found that if a state had higher percentages of Evangelical Protestants, theists, and biblical literalists, and if the inhabitants attended church more often, they also searched more for porn too.

Sigh.

Well, it's not all bad news.

By and large, studies show that Christians don't watch porn more than non-Christians; they watch *less overall*. But that's nothing to brag about as the statistics above reveal. A likely surprise to pastors, 10 percent of Christian women fifty to sixty-eight say they watch porn at least monthly, and these may not be the women you expect.

Under the bright lights of an expo hall a few years ago, I stood at the Covenant Eyes booth at a Southern Baptist Convention annual meeting. A fluctuating stream of teens, moms, pastors, and wives stopped at our booth to snatch up brochures and sign up for educational resources. A woman of about fifty-five, who was an SBC Messenger (or a voting delegate to the annual meeting) stopped at our booth. Though neat and modest, she was dressed comfortably for a long day of walking from hall to hall and sitting in uncomfortable chairs to hear reports and vote on the business of the SBC. She wore a warm smile, and we struck up a friendly conversation that deepened with each sentence. She explained how pornography remains hidden in the Church because it's too forbidden to discuss.

"This is so needed," she said waving her hand over the display at our table. "I have two adult boys . . ." she started and then paused. Her brow furrowed. "No. Not my boys. Me. I need this for me. I've struggled with pornography for years."

Pastors know they preach to people with secrets. But the masks are intricate; the smiles look authentic, and the charade is unchallenged. I've had the same conversation with at least one hundred pastors, and it goes something like the following paragraphs. (You'll recognize it from having had the same conversation with pastors in your ministerial association.)

"I know what you're talking about," a pastor will tell me. "I had one guy in my church who had a serious issue with porn."

Intuitively, we know that "one guy" is the one person who is asking for help for his struggle with porn. They have mustered every ounce of courage to confront a part of their life that seems unmanageable and incongruent with their faith. Often, this comes out when the marriage is in trouble and a spouse is demanding change.

Another frequent conversation sounds like one I had with a PhD pastor with forty years of experience. "Based on the statistics I've read, I know that when I preach and look at the faces in the congregation, there are men and women in my church who are struggling with pornography, but they don't talk to me about it," he said.

Another pastor with similar credentials shook his head in disbelief as he told me how one of his board members, a major financial contributor and picturesque father and husband, had unexpected secrets.

Pastor Billy Howell of Normandy, Tennessee believes there is a dead giveaway for people who use porn. "When you think someone is faithfully following Christ, you don't have as much worry," Pastor Howell said. "If a man is not following Christ faithfully, then he is susceptible to it. The faithful follower is what you see less of today."

I believe most people in Thomas's church would have described him as a faithful follower of Christ. Thomas served as a Pentecostal worship leader who led a congregation in exuberant praise. But he stepped down from his post due to the guilt and despair he felt for his ongoing porn use. No one suspected Thomas; he knew the right words to say, and he wore a flawless Sunday worship facade. More so, like so many, Thomas loves God and wants to do right, but what he wants to do he doesn't, and what he doesn't want to do is what he does (Romans 7:19–25).

People often ask me: "Why do some people who seem to love God and who faithfully serve in the Church struggle with porn and sex?" It seems understandable for a fledgling Christian, but not for a board member, a lay worker, or a steady attendee of the church. How is it we never saw this coming from the person we least expected?

And that's the crux of the problem. People you never anticipate are those who are struggling—fighting with sin and losing the battle. As a pastor, you inherit a congregation. You also inherit the hidden stories of dysfunctional families and unhealed wounds. You stand before men and women raised in church, who have had authentic and meaningful experiences with Christ, but who also feel trapped in a vise of secret sin. They don't feel safe in asking for help and continue to try harder on their own, thinking the next day—or the day after that—will be different. They are afraid of rejection and have become comfortable with plastic smiles and rehearsed religious words. They've worn masks for so long that they no longer realize they are pretending to be fine. Often, they work harder for the church to pay penance for their secret sins and to feel better about themselves; and they enjoy periods of freedom only to fall back into their long-term habits.

Most of all, they are deeply afraid. If you or others knew their true stories and their deepest struggles, not only would they lose status and respect, but they would also be rejected, unloved, and disgraced. Though we preach grace in our churches, most of our church members have not seen grace in action—especially for sexual sin.

This leads us to a very hard question: Do most churches really create an atmosphere where we can confess our sins to one another and pray for one another so that we may be healed as the Book of James directs us (James 5:16)?

Pastor Howell shepherds a Southern Baptist congregation of about sixty-five people, and he worries that even his most faithful fail to follow James's directive. "I would guess that in a small church, it's too small to deal with the shame," Pastor Howell said. "In the small church, it's too shameful to confess sins."

But is being in a small church the real hurdle?

A few hours after chatting with Pastor Howell at a National Religious Broadcasters Conference in Nashville, I spoke to a Christian couple asking for help when they heard I worked for Covenant Eyes. They attend a church that averages about 3,500 on a Sunday morning, and the husband said the church was just too big to find someone to be his *ally*, an accountability partner who would receive his Covenant Eyes reports of how he uses his devices. In other words, he didn't know a safe person with whom he could confide among a congregation of thousands.

Large and small churches alike are failing to create a culture that practices a basic tenant of the Bible: confessing our sins to one another. Individually, as sons and daughters of God, and corporately, as individual churches, it is imperative to ask: "What part of James 5:16 do we not believe?" Christians are typically well-versed in that James tells us not only to be hearers of God's Word, but also to do what it says. When we confront what we say we believe about God's truth and what we practice, we always find new growth through obedience.

Churches that create a safe place discover that the people who are thought to have it all together need help too. People, especially those who grow up in the Church, are often performers because they want to be liked, respected, and welcomed. They want to be accepted within their community. Many Christians have a deep desire to live an abundant and holy Christian life but aren't open and honest about their sin for fear of rejection.

But a safe place is only part of the remedy. People also need a safe process to confront their sin. They need help to uproot the false beliefs, lies, and patterns of behavior that keep them trapped in their stronghold(s). A safe process provides guardrails that help people focus on God's truths rather than their emotions, feelings, and even the habits engraved on their neurology. A guided path is purposeful discipleship rather than the quick prayer and the aimless wanderings of our wayward hearts. It provides incremental steps for exponential change through God's grace and the work of the Holy Spirit.

Churches that provide a safe place and a safe process open doors of unexpected healing for people that nobody anticipated needed the Master's healing touch. These churches draw people not only from their own pews but also from other churches. These churches are magnetic for people in troubled marriages, those who are struggling in life, and those hearing the Spirit's hounding call because pain often brings greater awareness of our deep need for God's grace and our repentance.

At Mariners Church in Irvine, California, a spectrum of healing groups leads men and women on a path of healing and discipleship. Depression, food addiction, anxiety, pride, pornography, drugs, alcohol, and other issues are addressed in groups that fall under the guidance of Care and Recovery Pastor Jack West. While many of the people who are present at these groups attend Mariners Church, many come from churches in the surrounding area. Why? I asked that question to several who attended. In all cases, they didn't believe their church was a safe place to address the strongholds in their lives nor did they feel they would receive meaningful guidance.

Thomas is one of those people. He attends a Pentecostal church while participating in a pack called "Guys Like Us" at Mariners Church. He has no intention of switching churches but values the atmosphere of authenticity and common purpose the men of his group share. They don't just have a list of rules to follow and teachings to study; rather, the group gives each man opportunities to talk about their journeys. The shared experience of this body of believers brings greater strength to them individually.

Brandon wasn't attending church regularly when his struggles with pornography and other issues came to light. The groups at Mariners not only gave him new hope, but the church also became a welcoming spiritual home for his family.

Similarly, Darlene found her recovery in groups at a Southern Baptist Church in Fort Worth, Texas, under the leadership of Dr. James Reeves, who likes to describe his congregation as a "hospital church where the Great Physician can do his work." Yes, she left her old church to attend City on a Hill because she had heard it was a place where you could lay all of your junk on the table without rejection. It was a church where you could learn to be broken, but that this Body of Christ would love you too much to let you remain the same.

Humility Leads to Freedom

Sometimes, God heals people of their addictions instantly. They put down booze, drugs, cigarettes, porn, and other bonds. God can do anything. But the vast majority of the time, Pastor West says, Jesus invites men and women on a journey that forces them to humble themselves and call on His name with childlike helplessness within a fellowship of believers.

That's how it was for Brandon, Thomas, Darlene, and others, whose stories are told in the coming pages. There are no quick fixes for them and their company of sojourners. No inspiring sermon, moving prayer, or Bible study creates the change they need and desperately want. They walk through the muck and up steep and unexpected terrain. Porn and unwanted sexual behaviors have men and women in a sinister grip.

As a pastor or leader, you are blessed with a Great Commission that sets captives free, even the ones who struggle secretly. That you are reading this book illustrates your desire to see bonds crushed. In the next two chapters, let's use Brandon's story and others' stories to explain how they got here in the first place. Afterward, we'll dig deeper into Darlene's story to glean why many women struggle with porn and unwanted sexual behaviors.

You will find portions of this book hammering both myths and conventional thinking, and I ask that you keep an open mind. Porn and sexual sin may make your stomach churn or even raise feelings of anger or disappointment. You may never have struggled in the way that men and women in your church struggle with sexual sin, but in these chapters, I hope to show you why people return to porn and unwanted sexual behavior again and again, even when they promise God, themselves, and anyone else that they are done with sexual sin for good. Most importantly, I hope to highlight that the Church holds the answers and the path to freedom.

Chapter 4
How Guys Get Stuck (Part 1)

It starts with a single thread . . . and before long a spider weaves an intricately designed web with only one intention—to capture prey.

June Hunt, Founder Hope for the Heart[20]

When Brandon was nine, he and his friends marched through his backyard on a lazy spring afternoon under a bright California sun. Between his family's subdivision and the next one over, a long grassy slope capped with a maze of large bushes provided a favorite play zone for kids in his neighborhood. Their adventures turned sticks into swords and the scrub became cover from enemy machinegun fire.

As the three boys climbed the slope, they noticed a magazine propped against the spindly trunk of a bush. It wasn't just any magazine. This one showed a woman on the cover, and she was large-breasted and barely covered. Though the magazine showed a bit of weathering and its cover was wrinkled from rain, the images inside remained clear and hypnotic for the boys. This was the first time any of the boys had seen an image of a naked woman. Their knowledge of sex was scant, missing even the basic mechanics, but Brandon felt strange sensations in his mind and body. He immediately claimed rights to the magazine and took it home.

To this day, Brandon can't remember who the two boys were, but he remembers how the woman posed, the color of her hair, and the feelings it awakened in him.

Finding porn at nine was a pivotal moment for Brandon. His story—though unique in details—illustrates common truths for men who become ensnared by pornography.

The foundational commonalities provide a deeper understanding of how guys get stuck and why this journey in healing takes time, grace, and a safe and directed process. Let's first discover the impact of two foundational elements common to pornography becoming a stronghold in a man's life: having seen it at a formative age and continuing to use it with masturbation in adolescence.

Much Too Young

Early exposure, like Brandon stumbling on a porn magazine, is one of the hallmarks of compulsive porn use for men as well as women. The late sex addiction counselor Dr. Mark Laaser called it one of the "building blocks" of sexual addiction. These building blocks are often collected while the human brain is still developing and more vulnerable. Because these issues and behaviors develop early, they become deeply rooted in how we think, what we find sexually exciting, and how we react to any number of scenarios and stressors.

"By 'building block behaviors,' I mean behaviors that form a foundation upon which other sexual behaviors are built," Laaser wrote in *Healing the Wounds of Sexual Addiction*. "These behaviors may start very early in the life of the sex addict, even before the child has developed enough physically to experience orgasm. Because these behaviors develop so early and are so basic, they are the hardest forms of sexual addiction to recover from."[21]

A 2014 Barna Research survey showed that many men were exposed to porn before the age of nine, especially today's younger men. Among men who were eighteen to thirty years old in 2014, nearly 20 percent of them were exposed to porn before age nine. And 88 percent had been exposed by age fifteen.[22] Millennials and generations since haven't known a world without the internet, and they have been exposed to more porn than any generations before them.

I commonly hear anecdotal stories from today's parents that their children first saw porn at six, seven, and eight years old because mobile devices are so prevalent in our homes, schools, sports fields, and our larger social circles.

Though people forget tons of things about their childhood, ask any man when he was first exposed to pornography, and he can likely tell you a complete story. In an instant, they fall through time to innocence lost and recall where they were, what happened, what they saw, and the awakening of unexpected feelings.

"Exposure to pornography for me came as a complete surprise," Nate Larkin, the founder of Samson Society, recalls. "I was ten years old; it was a few months after my mother died. I rounded the corner at the local grocery store to see a *Playboy* magazine in a magazine rack. That image just arrested me."

Speaking from personal experience, I was ten when I first saw porn. I bounced out of our house on a warm Florida afternoon and saw my nineteen-year-old brother and his friend leaning against his car. They were looking at a magazine but holding it sideways. That seemed so peculiar. How could they read sideways? When I asked what they were looking at, he flipped it around and grinned. I was mesmerized by the woman's breasts in the photo and stepped forward for a closer look. I didn't bother to open the centerfold. Then my brother's friend said, "You don't want to miss the good part," and he unfolded the full image. I knew what "boobs" were; I just hadn't seen them unclothed, and I had no idea why this lower portion of the human body was "the good part."

There are several reasons people remember their early porn exposure and why it's so *arresting* or *mesmerizing* for kids.

First, children are naturally curious about what the opposite sex looks like naked. This is normal, and it's common for children, boys and girls, to check each other out. Curiosity is typically where it ends when children see other children's undeveloped bodies. But when children see modern pornography, they see not only adult bodies, they often see explicit imagery and video of sexual acts. A child may know nothing or very little about sex, but imagery can naturally turn on neurobiological responses before they even understand what they are feeling.

In his research, sex addiction counselor Jay Stringer found that the average age for boys to first see porn is nine. It's age eleven for girls. About half of kids are exposed to porn by a peer and 32 percent were exposed by someone older.[23]

What I saw and what Nate saw was softcore nudity, and it was enticing and traumatic enough for it to be burned into our memories. But for many boys over recent decades, their first exposure is to hardcore online porn. Nothing overtly sexual is left out and too much shocking content is included. In an instant, they move from knowing nothing or very little about sex to seeing rough and abusive acts.

The event itself is traumatic, causing feelings of shock, fear, confusion, shame, embarrassment, and excitement. Natural curiosity is overwhelmed and traumatized by modern pornography, which is explicit, violent, and debasing. Children are startled and shocked by what they see, but they may also be naturally curious and want to see more.

In response, the brain releases neurochemicals like dopamine that increase awareness and focus, and dopamine loves novelty, something not seen before, Dr. Norman Doidge explains in *The Brain that Changes Itself*.[24] Dopamine makes us feel good and alert, and it can focus a person's attention to the point of tunnel vision. This neurochemical response is one reason it's so hard for a child to simply look away.

Dopamine also helps with memory and is joined by norepinephrine, which is often associated with stress and fight or flight response. Norepinephrine also helps us be more alert. And it acts as a hormone for sexual arousal and sexual memory to burn emotional experiences into our memories, Doidge writes.

A young brain is constantly learning, and to assist in this effort, a child's brain has more mirror neurons than adults. It's one reason kids learn faster. Simply explained, mirror neurons allow you to see something, and it feels as if you are experiencing it. It's why you recoil when you see a batter get hit with a baseball, or your heart races when you see runners cross a finish line. And mirror neurons are at work when watching porn, helping ignite the arousal and rewards centers of the brain. This helps explain why a kindergarten teacher told me she discovered a girl leaning over a desk while a boy pretended to thrust behind her. They were mimicking porn they had seen.

"The introduction to pornography is the left jab that sets up the right hook of a lifetime of unwanted sexual behavior," Stringer writes in *Unwanted*.[25]

There is a silver lining, if you can call it that. Early accidental or peer exposure isn't automatically detrimental. Many parents worry their children seeing porn might be their undoing, but the damage can be circumvented with open, non-shaming, and helpful parental communication.

While seeing porn at an early age is never good, greater damage is often caused by repeated and ongoing use of pornography.

Repetition

Compulsive porn use doesn't happen overnight; it comes with practice.

At a conference hosted by Man in the Mirror (a men's ministry founded by Patrick Morley who authored a book by the same name), I spoke to a man in his forties who told me about his porn recovery and his first ninety days of being porn-free: "When I got to Day Three, I realized that was the first time I had gone three days without viewing porn since I was a teenager."

With time, experience, and practice, the desire for pornography can feel like a physical and emotional need. Repetitive use of pornography physically changes the neurocircuitry of our brains. The brain learns to be triggered by pornography and pornographic thoughts and creates neural pathways that crave the neurochemical rewards of sexual excitement and orgasm. Neural pathways process information we receive and create new ways of thinking and habits.

"There are two kinds of addictions: substance and behavioral. Substance addiction involves ingesting or taking a substance such as drugs or alcohol into the body. Behavior addiction involves repetitively performing behaviors such as sexual activity," Laaser wrote in *Healing the Wounds of Sexual Addiction*.

After Brandon found the magazine on the hillside, it awakened in him a desire to see more. He discovered that if he turned the TV cable box on its side, it unscrambled channels that provided X-rated videos. At night, while his parents slept, he snuck out of his bedroom to watch porn, and he used his unscrambling trick while his parents worked in the yard or relaxed outdoors. From fourth grade to adulthood, Brandon found multiple ways to get porn, hide porn, or use porn openly. During those decades, he was angry at himself, ashamed, and fearful, and he threw away all of his porn multiple times only to gather a new stash or stream.

These stories are commonplace among men in general, but especially for men who have unknowingly wired their brains for ongoing porn use.

The lifelong ability of the brain to wire and rewire its neurocircuitry is referred to as brain plasticity or neuroplasticity. For instance, the brain can increase or decrease the strength and number of synapses that communicate an emotion or feeling. This allows information or memories to flow more or less quickly, Doidge explains.[26] And the brains of children and adolescents have more synapses (where the brain's cells talk to one another), making them wired to learn faster.

This brain neuroplasticity also operates under a dynamic of "use it or lose it." Do an activity more often, and the brain will create neural pathways that make an activity easier to think about and complete.

When it comes to creating a habit for porn in men, testosterone invigorates the process. Testosterone is a hormone that is released in men throughout the day, but when sexual cues are picked up by the brain, the testes increase production. Pornography (and the mental fantasizing that it enables) crafts a brain that generates testosterone constantly and heightens sexual desire. With this ever-present sexual desire, the brain is ready to interpret any signal (external or internal) and ramp up the perceived need for sexual activity, Mark Kastleman writes in *The Drug of the New Millennium: The Brain Science Behind Internet Porn Use*.[27] Because testosterone is slow to dissipate, men who habitually view pornography cause a chemical imbalance. This high testosterone level increases their sexual awareness far above normal. Sexual fantasies are sparked by everyday objects, and even modestly dressed women are seen as provocative.

Continued use of pornography and sexual fantasizing carves neural pathways in the brain that create greater cravings, according to Dr. William Struthers, a Wheaton College professor and the author of *Wired for Intimacy*. Just as a creek bed doesn't gouge out its course in a day, the same is true in creating neural pathways of porn use. Repetition matters. But because sexual activity launches such an amazing fireworks show in our brains, it takes less repetition to build these porn pathways than it would for us to engrain cravings for other activities. Recognize the damage early, and deep neural pathways can be prevented. However, if the stream of pornography continues, a neural pathway will develop, and it will take significant work and determination to alter.

Often these neural pathways for pornography become engrained in the formative years of adolescence, and this is especially true in today's internet culture.

"Like a path is created in the woods with each successive hiker, so do the neural paths set the course for the next time an erotic image is viewed. Over time these neural paths become wider as they are repeatedly traveled with each exposure to pornography. They become the automatic pathway through which interactions with women are routed. The neural circuitry anchors this process solidly in the brain. [...] All women become potential porn stars in the minds of these men. They have unknowingly created a neurological circuit that imprisons their ability to see women rightly [...]

Repeated exposure to pornography creates a one-way neurological superhighway where a man's mental life is over-sexualized and narrowed. It is hemmed in on either side by high containment walls making escape nearly impossible."

—Dr. William Struthers, *Wired for Intimacy*[142]

A 2021 survey of US teens fourteen to eighteen showed that 84.4 percent of males and 57 percent of females have watched pornography[28]. Many believe these statistics are underestimated because nudity and some sexual acts aren't considered porn by many people. Remember, the definition of porn in the wider community has changed over the years.

Neurologists know the brain is the last organ in the body to mature, and the pre-frontal cortex, which is responsible for impulse control, judgment, decision-making, and empathy, is also the last to develop and connect well with the other lobes of the brain. The pre-frontal cortex isn't fully developed until the mid- to late-twenties. It's part of why teens are more impulsive and take greater risks and why parents pay high rates for their teens' car insurance. Teen brains are also more impressionable to both good and bad influences, said Dr. Frances Jensen, chair of the Department of Neurology at the University of Pennsylvania.[29] She calls it a double-edged sword in which teens can develop positive habits or negative ones superbly. Addictive behaviors created in adolescence are much more difficult to overcome in adulthood, she said.

"Behavioral addictions are just as insidious as chemical addictions because they make use of the same brain circuits," Dr. Jensen writes in *The Teenage Brain, A Neuroscientist's Survival Guide to Raising Adolescents and Young Adults*. "This is why, whether it's gambling, interacting on social media, or snorting coke, teenagers are particularly susceptible to the rush of good feelings that comes with stimulating the brain's reward centers."[30]

Compulsive Behavior and the Purity Sermon

A formidable warning regarding sexual sin is found in Proverbs, Chapter 7, where "a young man lacking sense" walks toward the home of a seductive woman. She plays him like a fiddle, and he falls to sexual sin "as an ox goes to the slaughter."

The toughest thing about warnings is when they come after the fact or when they are ignored. Then what?

Ministry leaders preach this admonition from Proverbs to three groups of men at a men's night or weekend retreat: (1) wise men who are safely in green pastures but tempted to wander, (2) guys, or oxen, that might occasionally graze in the field of pornography, or (3) guys, or oxen, who have a ring in their nose and are trapped in the stockyards of the slaughterhouse.

The first two groups don't struggle with a stronghold, but as fallen humans, they can be tempted, sinful, and disobedient. They *need* to be reminded of sin's consequences, and the reminders are an important duty of the Church.

For the third group, the warning is heard and escape might be desired, but the cattle chute is cinched, said addiction counselor Troy Haas, who helped found The HopeQuest Ministry Group at First Baptist Church Woodstock (Georgia). These men want to leave the home of their seductress and they know the truth of the Proverb, but they feel chained. Purity seems unachievable. "Messages on purity generally don't help these men very much because they know they should be pure," Haas explained.

While churchgoing men have heard the biblical definition of purity, many struggle to live this out. Proven Men commissioned a Barna Study in 2014 that showed 21 percent of people who identified as a Christian worried they might be addicted to pornography. About 27 percent of born-again Christian men wonder if they are addicted to porn, with 18 percent being sure they are addicted to porn and 9 percent being unsure if they are or not. For born-again Christian men, of all ages, 14 percent say they watch porn daily and 54 percent watch porn at least monthly.[31]

Among younger Christian men, ages eighteen to thirty, many worry about their addicted state with 32 percent believing they are addicted and 12 percent believing they might be addicted. Of these men, 36 percent say they view porn daily.[32]

Over the years, I have spoken with thousands of men's ministry leaders and pastors who are concerned deeply about pornography's impact on the spiritual, marital, and familial lives of men. You have likely had similar conversations at annual conventions and ministerial association meetings.

Often, these conversations paint pornography as a simple problem of sexual temptation—a downfall of our fallen nature. At other times, the discussions draw from pep sermons about being strong men with right hearts. These views aren't wrong; they are just incomplete for the men imprisoned by compulsive porn use.

Rarely do leaders weigh how men and women have practiced corrupting their sexual neurology over years and even decades, beginning in adolescence. Proverbs 6:27 sums this truth up well: "Can a man carry fire next to his chest and his clothes and not be burned?" Scooping up burning coal leaves a mark, but a person who carries burning logs for decades can find himself or herself consumed.

Brandon didn't find himself in his situation overnight, he didn't make an "oops" and find himself in a little episode of lust. Brandon found himself in a position where his decisions were not thoughtful choices so much as impulses and obsessions.

At a roundtable interview in Colorado Springs, Christian counselors Rob Jackson, Dr. John Thorington, and Dr. Russ Rainey told me that pastors should ask probing questions in a safe environment. "How old were you when you first saw pornography? Tell me that story. At what age did it become more repetitive? How did you gain access to porn? How did that change over the years? When was the last time? How often?"

These, and other questions, begin to uncover a "stronghold," in spiritual terms, and addictive or compulsive behavior in clinical terms, said Jackson, who serves on the Focus on the Family counseling team. Uncovering the long-term nature of pornography use and unwanted sexual behaviors is the first step toward freedom. God designed our brains, our minds, and our spirit for renewal, but that change comes through deep exploration, a safe community, and a hunger to follow Christ.

Not Simple Math

Being exposed to porn as a child doesn't produce porn addicts. This is not a mathematical equation.

For some kids, the early exposure is uneventful, and the repetition is a rarity rather than a regular excursion. This is most true of kids in families that communicate well and bond well. Parents also can train their kids to be resilient to porn.

As well, not all men begin their compulsive behaviors in adolescence; instead, they start in adulthood. Andrew was raised in a Southern Baptist home where sexual discussions were limited to save sex for marriage. While attending a Christian college, he reasoned that to maintain his virginity, porn would provide an unharmful release of sexual tension. While he met his technical definition of virginity on his wedding night, compulsive porn use followed him into marriage.

Andrew had ignored the warnings and scooped up burning coals that burned neural pathways that craved porn. But porn did more than excite Andrew; it also became an escape. Looking back, he sees how he used porn to medicate and soothe his emotions and self-doubt.

Men and boys are in greater danger of repetition and compulsive behavior when they use porn to medicate negative feelings. This is especially true when they aren't provided meaningful ways in childhood to express and console fear, anxiety, neglect, and feelings of abandonment, among other emotions. Porn provides an escape, a means to soothe, a salve that numbs. In the next chapter, we'll explore childhood injuries that are common for compulsive porn users.

Chapter 5
How Guys Get Stuck (Part 2)

We can ignore even pleasure. But pain insists upon being attended to.
C.S. Lewis, *The Problem of Pain*

A s an adult, Brandon is a social guy. He strikes up conversations easily, wears an infectious smile, and people enjoy his relaxed company. Tall, with a strong build, and even handsome, Brandon's exterior proclaims easy confidence. But inside, he bears personal scars.

Brandon shares some of the hurts that are common for men who use porn compulsively. Early exposure and repetitive use of porn can create changes in the brain that cause a person to crave porn. However, just because porn excites and masturbation feels good, that doesn't mean someone will become driven into compulsive behavior. Porn grabs a stronger foothold when boys and men use porn routinely to anesthetize negative emotions and regulate their moods.

Childhood scars come on a broad spectrum in our fallen world. Physical, emotional, and sexual abuse might immediately come to mind, and they are indeed common in the histories of men who medicate with porn and sex. But sometimes, the wounds are more subtle and are ignored as too trivial compared to being beaten or sexually abused. These seemingly subtle wounds are real and impactful, nonetheless.

Let's examine the complexity of these often-trivialized wounds before also considering the sexual abuse we all recognize as deeply harmful.

Careless Cuts

American Jewish author Elie Wiesel wrote, "The opposite of love is not hate, it's indifference." Though I take Wiesel's quote out of its context, it applies in homes where parents withdraw for periods from their children's lives. They provide clothing but not regular warmth, give housing but not a reliable sense of shelter, serve food but not steady emotional nourishment, and deliver rules but not consistent safety. These families recall many beautiful memories but also intervals of distance and isolation where the damage is done.

Christian counselor Jay Stringer found parent-child relationships particularly impactful to porn and sex addiction. "In my research, 63 percent of the respondents wanted more of their father's involvement, and 39 percent wanted more of their mother's involvement," Stringer wrote in *Unwanted*. "Examples of disengagement are parents' workaholism, choosing to avoid necessary conversations related to themes every child needs to learn about (self-care, nutrition, sex), or choosing to ignore attunement (being aware and receptive) with children when they are experiencing anxiety, sorrow, or anger."[33]

Brandon's early years felt unstable. His family moved often. His dad rode the economic ups and downs of selling commercial real estate. He worked odd hours, and their family's finances fluctuated. This required frequent moves from one community to another, new schools, and new acquaintances. Surface relationships were Brandon's familiar companions.

Something else was going on too. A strange undertow of tension rippled through his family's interactions, creating a cool distance that he didn't understand until he was an adult. He learned in his twenties that his maternal grandfather had molested Brandon's older sister. Initially, his mom hid her discovery from Brandon's dad. When she finally told him, Brandon's dad desired blood. His dad wanted to kill his father-in-law and not in some figurative way. Brandon's dad pictured a dagger to the heart, a bullet to the brain. He was furious his wife had been slow to tell him of his daughter's abuse. In a compromise to bloodletting, the grandfather was banished. The police and courts were never called to exact justice. Instead, Brandon's parents simmered in their shame, anger, and secrecy. Divided emotionally, Brandon's parents held together long enough to raise their kids and then divorced. However, throughout his childhood, Brandon sensed their distance from each other, and it spilled into their muted interactions as a family.

"I wanted to be seen by Dad. I wanted to spend time with my mom. But I felt a sense of abandonment in my house," Brandon recalled.

Dr. Laaser found these kinds of strains leave children feeling unsure and unstable. "Children in these families feel as if they are held at arm's length. Starved for affection and attention, they begin to wonder, 'What's wrong with me? I must be a bad person. Mom and Dad don't love me.' To whom can these lonely children talk? They have learned that no one will listen. They feel abandoned. Later in life, they will seek to fill their loneliness with inappropriate and sinful behaviors," Laaser wrote.[34]

Rigid Rules

Being raised in strict and rigid home environments is also a hallmark for men who struggle with porn and sex. Dr. Patrick Carnes found in his research that 77 percent of men who struggled with sexual compulsivity came from rigid family systems.[35] Sometimes, the rigidity in these homes is backed by misguided or abusive religiosity.

In his book *Unwanted,* Stringer described my upbringing with precision in his chapter titled "Dysfunctional Family Systems."[36] My father ruled supreme in the childhood home I shared with my mom and three older brothers. "Don't question my authority! This is my house!" he would proclaim. "Even when I'm wrong, I'm right!!!" The use of so many exclamation points seems extreme, but you have to picture a looming red face, my father's bulging eyes, his teeth bared, and a finger thrust forward.

Unlike some rigid environments, mine was also backed with violence: emotional, spiritual, and physical. My father's "rights" were declared within biblical authority, although speaking of this within the variety of churches we attended was forbidden, never to be discussed with anyone outside the family. Our home was one of secrets and hypocrisy. Though we might be crying in the back seat from smacks to our heads, when we arrived at the church parking lot, we were told, "Dry up those tears and I'd better see a smile, or I'll give you something to cry about when we get home."

My dad was a part-time evangelist, independent Pentecostal, or Charismatic, depending on the audience, and this allowed him the recognition and pulpit he desired without the oversight of a denomination hierarchy, a church board, or even a senior pastor. We would attend small churches for months, he would preach, and then we would move on. Sometimes, these church visits came in a random rotation until the honeymoon period wore off. These small churches "needed his help," he said, but I came to recognize it also helped him escape scrutiny as a father and husband. He was granted an assistant pastor's position at one church, but when the senior pastor began to coach him in his family life, my father dropped the post and the church.

The spiritual abuse came with rigid requirements and dogmas about dating, television shows, clothes, money, movies, and dancing. These rules were not provided with informative discussions. They were simply lines in the sand, and breaking these rules was met with scarlet letters of shame and even violent punishment. My brothers weren't allowed to play sports because they couldn't always be under my father's watchful eye to monitor untoward influences.

One summer, my father declared the family would fast all food for a week for the spiritual benefit of my then-fifteen-year-old brother, Jacob (not his real name). My mother won my exemption as a kindergartener, but my ten-year-old brother, David, was required to commit. A few days into the family fast, my mom made a peanut butter and jelly sandwich for me and placed the butter knife she used in the sink. David walked by the sink, saw the knife, and licked the remaining paste from its sides. About that time, my dad walked in. He ordered to smell David's breath and then began smacking his face and head for being so pathetic and irreverent.

But all this happened behind the scenes. People at church, at school, and in our communities (there were multiple moves) saw a well-crafted veil. Even though some people knew better, they didn't intervene, and we pretended they didn't know.

People loved to hear "Brother Black's" sons sing, and it was part of the performance routine for my father's preaching. Often, our singing came with recognition, hugs, and candy from people in the church, and, like most kids, we enjoyed the opportunity to perform. One night at about midnight, my father decided it was time for us to practice. He got my brother David and me out of bed for direction, but we couldn't seem to get it right. Each mistake was met with slaps and yelling, and our tearful rehearsal made him angrier still. I can still hear my father screaming at my brother, "Sing, David, sing!"

Stringer explains that rigid family systems, such as ours, produce children who are often split as either bad or good, the golden child or the rebel.

My brothers, Jacob and David, were considered the troubled rebels and defiant out of earshot of my father until they could escape as young men. Sadly, Stringer says, the rebels often squander much of their lives in defiant protest long after they leave home. Jacob left home before graduating high school and bounced between work, two failed marriages, and at the time of this writing, chooses to live homeless in his pickup truck. David never created meaningful relationships, bounced between short-lived jobs and educational stints, and died from complications stemming from AIDS at the age of thirty-three.

"The consequences of his actions will certainly need to be engaged, but the recovery process of the [rebel] is far easier than the golden child's journey out of a life of self-righteousness and hiding," Stringer writes.[37]

I was a golden child.

As the golden child, I compromised, soothed, complied, and performed.

"He (the golden child) learns that compliance and competence allow him to maneuver as a saint within the rigid borders of the family," Stringer writes. "Although he may be struggling with depression or pornography, he correctly discerns that revealing these struggles would be far too costly. He defaults to presenting a perfect public self and elects to keep the painful troubled dimensions of who he is beyond detection."[38]

The golden children in our churches are well-rehearsed at keeping their secret sins hidden, especially porn and other sexual sin. They likely desire to change but fight an ongoing battle with shame, secrecy, and fear that if anyone knew their struggles, they would be rejected rather than helped. Men often compartmentalize pornography as one aspect of their lives—one sin area they believe requires ongoing repentance. These men, raised as golden children, might be among a church's best volunteers and Bible study attendees. Typically, they feel deep shame about their sin. They believe if they work harder and perform for others, then maybe their secret deeds aren't so damning and their hearts aren't so corrupt, after all.

Known but Unknown

There is a long list of abuses most of us would agree burn and disfigure the hearts and minds of men; physical, emotional, verbal, spiritual, and sexual abuse stand out on this painful roster. There are volumes written on these, and I encourage you to read more about their impact. However, our focus within these short paragraphs is to recognize the impact of sexual abuse.

Therapists agree that men who have endured childhood sexual abuse often struggle deeply with unwanted sexual behavior and addictions. The statistics of boys experiencing childhood sexual abuse vary widely and, in general, are under-reported to authorities.[39] A 2014 study found that 5.1 percent of boys had experienced sexual abuse by the age of seventeen.[40] Meanwhile, a 2005 study conducted by the US Centers for Disease Control on members of a San Diego HMO found 16 percent of males were sexually abused by the age of eighteen.[41] While the statistics vary by study, the deep feelings of shame and secrecy are common.

Gender and age are the two factors that stand out most in defining whether a man or woman becomes sexually inhibited on one side of the spectrum or sexually compulsive on the other side, according to a review of multiple studies.[42] Boys, much more than girls, are at greater risk of becoming hypersexual when they experience childhood sexual abuse at any age. However, when boys experience sexual abuse before the age of twelve, they are even more likely to develop compulsive and aggressive sexual behaviors. The study explained that boys tend to be molested at younger ages since they are better able to defend themselves in adolescence.

Understanding

Acknowledging childhood wounds is not about shifting responsibility. Blaming family, friends, and abusers doesn't release the compulsive porn user or the sex addict from self-examination, changing their behavior, and rebuilding their heart and mind. However, uncovering the harm that was done and conceding that these individuals didn't deserve the wounds is paramount to understanding, acceptance, and healing.

Children are exceptional at deflecting hurts and escaping pain with strategies that are born out of desperation and immature reasoning, Dr. Gregory Jantz writes in *Healing the Scars of Childhood Abuse*.[43] Their strategies of evasion and comfort often and over time damage their growth into maturity and adulthood.

Watching porn might sound disgusting to many Christians. But porn provides a gateway to

Fear is a four-letter word; addiction is not.

Many Christian leaders fear words like porn addiction, sex addiction, or compulsive behavior. A big reason is these words are seen as excuses and releases from responsibility. Others see them as labels, robbing a Christian of their identity in Christ.

The opposite is true.

We should be more fearful of religiosity than addiction.

In our modern culture, it's easy to see how celebrities and their attorneys have used the word *addiction* to escape responsibility. However, Christians have used religious phrases, such as a fantasy for both men and boys where they think they are safe, admired, desired, wanted, masculine, and in control, which may be the opposite of how they feel in real life. As a boy escaping to porn, I wasn't just lustful toward the women in the magazine photos. In the fantasies I created around the images, I was accepted, received and gave affection, and felt connected. With so many sermons describing prurient sin, I was surprised in a Samson Society meeting that all four of the men in the session described the same thoughts and emotions. They sought intimacy and acceptance in their fantasies. Certainly, continued porn use typically escalates to other fantasies and actions, but for a boy seeking escape, these emotions of acceptance and affirmation are common.

"Children who are abused may adapt by looking to outside sources for relief and comfort," Dr. Gregory Jantz wrote in *Healing the Scars of Childhood Abuse*. "If people are unreliable and unpredictable, children who are abused may find certain behaviors and substances appealing because they appear more constant and certain. Children turn to a variety of outside sources to feel better: food, cigarettes, drugs, alcohol, sexual activity, video games—just about anything that produces a pleasure response."[44]

Whether porn use becomes habitual in youth or adulthood, one theme persists. Pornography becomes a salve of escape that is used to tend to wounds, whether those wounds are emotional, physical, sexual, or spiritual. Having a bad day? Medicate it with porn and masturbation, and the brain will get a spritz of neurochemicals that will

"our fallen and sinful nature," in the same fashion. Worse, religiosity has made private confessions to God (and public confessions, if found out) a simple prescription. The slate is clean. There is no more work to be done. Move on.

True repentance requires more of us. It requires we turn away from sin, take responsibility for our sin, and set a different course with action and purpose.

Every recovery model in this book requires a person to conduct a searching and fearless moral inventory of oneself. It requires making a list of the people harmed by our actions and becoming willing to make amends. In other words, I am responsible for my sin, for the pain I have caused others, and for my sin against God. These models require total submission to God because we admit that we have made a mess of our lives and that we are absolutely nothing without the Great I Am. Not only must we recognize our sin, but we must also confess that sin to another and ask them to pray for us so that God may bring healing (James 5:16). In addition, these recovery processes require us to make amends to those harmed without causing more harm.

provide a temporary respite. Feeling the pains of youth or the past? Run to the refuge of porn. Soon, porn and masturbation are just a part of life, or even what many therapists characterize as an addiction. The relief it brings is fleeting, however, and the porn binge is less and less satisfying, leading to cravings for more.

"What works in the moment to numb or alleviate the pain can cause collateral damage in the long term. These costs can be extensive and can complicate a person's emotional, intellectual, physical, relational, and spiritual health. These costs eventually become unavoidable, no matter how fast or far you try to outrun them," Jantz writes[45]

Accepting words like *addiction* also reminds us we are susceptible and to be on guard. Too often in the Church, we have swept addiction under the rug and then acted surprised, disappointed, or disgusted when a person's life falls apart. When we take our sins seriously, we're not afraid of a process that digs to its roots to pluck them out. We seek regular support from fellow Christians and confess our weaknesses. We create boundaries to guard the gates of our hearts (Proverbs 4:23). We recognize our ongoing neediness for the body of Christ and the transforming power of the Holy Spirit.

Ignoring Wounds

If your Christian and adult experience is anything like mine, woundedness and compulsive behaviors might seem irrelevant and inconsequential to your faithfulness today. Athletic coaches, religious and secular teachers, and Bible studies urge people to think about the positive and ignore the negative. Good Christians are overcomers that are not weighed down by the past—at least that is the message I received.

Growing up in the Church, my Christian experience taught me to ignore the underlying wounds. Not only would other people in the Church look down on me and my family, I thought, none of it mattered anyway. All of these unaddressed and unexamined issues were to be washed away. Good Christians forgive and forget. Bury it. Hide it. It's too embarrassing, and it's definitely not part of the Wednesday night Bible study.

I bought that philosophy wholeheartedly. Years ago, as part of a church Bible study, I remember reading *Wild at Heart* by John Eldredge and thinking, *This talk about woundedness is silly. I don't have any wounds. This is a bunch of whining.*

These false beliefs cheat the body of Christ often and keep men and women from experiencing God's complete healing. Dr. Laaser wrote that it is difficult for a man to accept the message of God's grace fully when the words of the Bible are filtered through childhood wounds. A man can hear the words that he is "fearfully and wonderfully made" (Psalm 139:14) and because God loved us he sent his son to die for us . . . but did our families help or hinder us from understanding these truths?

"It is like a coffee filter," Laaser wrote. "You put coffee grounds in the filter and when you pour water through it you get coffee. Our human spirits and our minds have filters. When you put various forms of abuse into them, you can pour the living water (John 4) of Christ's love into them but what comes out is still tainted with core beliefs that we are bad and worthless people." [46]

That's how it felt for Brandon.

He came to Christ as a high school student. After another move to a new town, Brandon fell in with a clique of high school skateboarders who were the outsiders at his new school. He didn't even skate. He was an outsider even among his collection of outsiders.

Two of his new skater friends attended a church youth group, and he tagged along one Wednesday night and liked the sense of community and a larger group that welcomed him. Brandon's family seldom attended church, usually twice a year at Easter and Christmas. In this youth group, he began to understand the traditions behind holiday services, and he sprouted a growing and deepening faith. His teacher was a dynamic youth pastor who inspired him.

Heartened by the teachings of his youth pastor to live a pure life, Brandon tried repeatedly to stop using porn, but his efforts were short-lived. It didn't feel safe to tell anyone, so he fought solo, certain that only he struggled this much. Praying, reading Scripture, and trying harder failed him each time, but he kept doing all three, continuing a pattern of white-knuckle days of sobriety only to fall over and over.

This revolving cycle of acting out and private confessions to God continued until his dynamic youth pastor announced he was leaving for another church . . . in Hawaii, no less. If he was pastoring at another church in town, Brandon could have switched churches, or at least occasionally visited for a spiritual shot in the arm. Brandon felt like he'd lost his second father. Then, his parents divorced. To Brandon, it seemed like his authority and spiritual figures abandoned him, like so many people he had left behind in repeated moves from one community to another.

Brandon left the Church, continued his porn use, and mixed in a party lifestyle that lasted into his young adult years. While the gospel was poured into Brandon's heart, his filter was soiled. Change for Brandon wouldn't come until the pain of his sinful behaviors forced him to focus on cleaning the silt that tainted his heart. This time, rather than covering and hiding, a new group of Christian brothers at Mariners Church would show him how to come clean.

Dealing with Wounds

Whether porn use becomes habitual in youth or adulthood, one theme persists. Pornography becomes a dirty bandage that is used to tend to past wounds, whether emotional, physical, sexual, or spiritual. People trapped in pornography strongholds are often unaware they use porn to regulate their emotions and calm self-incriminating feelings about their worth.

Recovery groups and programs at Mariners Church and other churches in this book create safe environments to deal with underlying pain because the Great Physician "heals the brokenhearted and bandages their wounds" (Psalm 147:3). Dealing with our woundedness is paramount to this journey because the ultimate goal is wholeness through Christ. In a safe environment, people confess their sin, get honest about their sin in detail, and dig below the surface to find why sin has such a hold on their hearts and minds.

Left without a safe process, some people put enough boundaries and restrictions in place to loosen the grip of pornography, only to slip back into its grasp months later. Some people become hypervigilant against porn, but their self-soothing merely changes from one sinful habit to another.

When we examine our wounds, study their impact on us, and do so with a competent counselor, coach, or safe friends, we become more conscious of our thoughts and emotions and the hidden pain points that drive them. This healing assists us in honoring God with our minds, bodies, and spirits. We mature by confronting our hurts and the sinful ways we use to calm our minds. In doing so, we submit ourselves to the Holy Spirit to redeem and renew our hearts.

An example from my own life might help illustrate this point.

When I was about twelve years old, I was working with my dad in our shed. There was an old and tangled hemp rope that had endured Florida's daily cycles of pouring rain and baking sun in the back of a pickup. It had been thrown some weeks before onto the plank floor of the shed, and it was a gnarled mess. My dad directed me to coil the rope. When I began to wind the rope around my hand and elbow, he told me to stop. He wanted me to loop the rope hand over hand. I had never done that before, and the weather-beaten rope twisted defiantly. Each time a twist showed in the coil, my dad would hit me on my head, back, or face. As though waiting for the next mistake, he pounced repeatedly as if hitting would help me wind the rope perfectly. I panicked and returned to winding the rope around my hand and elbow. More hits. He told me I was a "dummy," and an "idiot," and that I "can't do anything right."

As an adult, every time I coiled a rope, an extension cord, or a similar item, my mind would recall that memory unbidden. I didn't simply remember it, I relived it. Sometimes, I tried to shove the memory aside; other times, I fantasized about coming to that boy's rescue.

Winding a cord was a physical and emotional trigger for me that would interrupt my day with feelings of anger and resentment. I also felt shame. I felt shame because *wouldn't people think less of me if they knew our family secrets?* Typically, I would try to stuff or block the memory, but my mood and emotions were tainted and bitter. *Forgive and forget*, I would repeat to myself. Despite my best intentions and most sincere prayers, I couldn't get there on my own. I would say to myself, *I can forgive all that was done to me, but I can't forgive what happened to my mother and brothers.*

With safe people in a safe process, I learned how to stop stuffing pain and confront it head-on with Jesus. Christ endured more pain, more anguish, more rejection, and more temptation than any one of us will ever know. Through the Body of Christ, fellow believers listened to my stories, confirmed I didn't deserve those wounds, and guided me in coping with my trauma in healthy ways. I had never connected the dots, that the act of coiling a rope was just one among many prompts in my teen and adult life that would lead me to seek pornography.

As an adult, I couldn't stop coiling my ropes and extension cords, but I could allow Jesus to be there with me. So, as I did that work, I would sing hymns about my loving heavenly Father. A favorite for me was Stuart Townsend's 1995 song "How Deep the Father's Love for Us." The beat worked well in coiling a rope, regardless of how I decided to do it. And I could finish feeling accomplished, refreshed, and at peace.

Little by little, I became more aware of other social, emotional, and environmental triggers—what I call SEE Triggers. When I felt tempted to view porn, I learned to ask *Why am I being tempted?* And that greater consciousness was exceedingly helpful. With practice, just deciphering the trigger was often enough for me to think clearly and take thoughts captive. Of course, I could also interrupt temptation by calling a friend or taking other actions.

Woundedness is not an excuse for sin, but understanding it helps us exchange self-defeating escapism for healthy ways to live, grow, and cope. We gain greater freedom to follow our true hearts' desires.

"But I say, walk by the Spirit, and you will not gratify the desires of the flesh. For the desires of the flesh are against the Spirit, and the desires of the Spirit are against the flesh, for these are opposed to each other, to keep you from doing the things you want to do" (Galatians 5:16–17).

Read that last phrase again, but in a positive light: ". . . doing the things you want to do." That is what a journey to healing is about. When we nurture the mind, body, and spirit, we enjoy living in the fullness and peace God wants for His children.

Missed Opportunities

Most adults look at childhood wounds in unconstructive ways, and in doing so, they miss opportunities for healing. Here are just four examples.

First, they may **downplay them** as not being as hurtful as other people's wounds. "Compared to being beaten, my feelings of being ignored in my childhood just isn't a big enough deal." However, this is looking at past pain points through the rational eyes of an adult, which is far different from the emotional thinking of the child who endured the trauma or neglect. And it is the child's pain that remains deeply rooted in the soul, only to be triggered by current negative events. In denying or minimizing our wounds, we miss opportunities for healing.

Second, teens and adults may **create a before and after wall**. What happened before a specific period is in the past, and we ignore it by keeping it there. A person might say, "I'm a grown adult now, and it's time to move on." But we can never "move on" if we have not identified the hidden triggers that lead us to act out.

Third, some people **bottle up past injuries** because they seem too painful. When they are triggered by a negative event or someone's words, they may stew over them, play the memories in their minds, and fantasize about different outcomes. Often, they just stuff them because of shame and self-doubt. They think no one else would understand.

Fourth, some people feel anger about past wounds but **haven't found a safe place** to voice their stories. They may bring up past hurts at family gatherings while playing a game or eating a meal. It might be a quip, a dig, or a confrontation. But instead of being heard, they face denial and more pain.

For comfort and healing, men and women need to tell their stories through a safe process with safe people. Here are two reasons why this is imperative:

First, it allows a man or woman to get out of their head. When we tell our stories to an ally or a group, we are expected to take time to tell our story. They listen without interruptions, denial, and defensiveness. We provide context and related dynamics. In doing these things, we discover details and feelings we might otherwise ignore. This is part of our healing.

Second, when we tell our stories we often help others open up about their lives. By hearing their stories, we learn from them and gain new perceptions and perspectives. We also empathize with them, and in doing so, we more readily accept their empathy for us. We discover we are not alone. The stories may not be similar, but receiving compassion creates a greater bridge for healing for everyone involved. "Carry one another's burdens; in this way you will fulfill the law of Christ" (Galatians. 6:2).

Telling one's story is not only about the wounds received, but also about examining how those hurts influence behaviors. Please note: What people uncover are not excuses; they are opportunities for understanding. Each person must own their sinful conduct and the harm it caused others. But a good investigation takes a person closer to making substantial changes that lead to freedom.

Chapter 6

How Women Get Stuck

The deeper the injury, the more severe the scar tissue.
Mary Ellen Mann, *From Pain to Power*[47]

Without intention, Catherine crushes stereotypes with the feminine force of a sledgehammer.

Dressed modestly with no makeup, she appears to have stepped away from a conservative Sunday morning worship service most days of the week. Raised in a Christian home, she attends church faithfully with her husband with whom she shares a deep bond after five years of marriage. She didn't date in her teen years, and she wore white proudly on her wedding day, grateful that she'd saved sex until marriage. She's slender, cute, and sometimes shy, but she's also well-spoken, smart, and intuitive.

On some days, she asks her husband to hide their Chromebook because it's the one device in their home that isn't protected with Covenant Eyes accountability software, and her inner ache to watch porn can feel overwhelming. True to a growing trend among young women struggling with porn, she's not reading erotica as older surveys show; she watches porn videos and masturbates. Short looping videos, called gifs, that have no storyline and all action are what Catherine calls her Achilles heel. Days after watching one, the loop replays in her mind for weeks.

One stereotype that rings true for Catherine is she feels her church should be a place to find help but doubts anyone in her congregation would understand.

"What I hear more than anything else from women is, 'I thought I was the only one,'" Counselor Marnie Ferree said during an interview at Bethesda Workshops in Nashville, where she provides clinical intensives for porn and sex addiction.

Though Catherine felt like a unique sinner for many years, one study showed 73 percent of women (mainly between the ages of eighteen and thirty-five) used porn in the last six months and 26 percent in the last week.[48] In an online survey of young women eighteen to twenty-nine, 14 percent said they watched porn a few times per week, and 18 percent watched porn about once per week. Twenty percent of all of the women surveyed said they worried that they watched too much porn.[49]

While many Church leaders have watched these statistics grow in recent decades, they have difficulty connecting them to the diverse and caring girls and women under their care.

When Jessica Harris was called to the Dean's Office at her Christian college, she was certain she was in deep trouble. On the dean's desk rested Jessica's internet history report that showed twisted and even sexually violent web page addresses. After a brief lecture on the evils of porn, the dean finished by saying, "That being said, we know this wasn't you, women just don't have this problem."[50]

"I didn't have the strength to tell her she was wrong. I was a woman and that was my history report. Therefore, at least *one* woman had this 'problem.' Perhaps I was the only woman who had 'this problem.' If that was the case, what was wrong with me?" Harris wrote in *Beggar's Daughter*.[51]

As a church leader, you may have a difficult time accepting that some girls and women in your church struggle with porn, and that's understandable. First, the majority of Christian women don't struggle with porn like the majority of Christian men do. Second, growing up and in your adult life, you've likely heard women speaking negatively about our sexualized culture—and for good reason.

Third, the Church has often given women a great deal of responsibility to shoulder regarding sexuality. Women are to dress modestly to not provoke a man to lust, and this can be especially true within specific denominations or sects of Christianity. Wives are to be sexually available to prevent their husbands from lusting. Girls and women have to be careful in so many ways to guard men, Ferree said, and many leaders in the Church give shallow consideration to women as sexual beings. Stereotypes, she said, have often viewed women as either seductresses or reluctant participants.

"That women themselves could be struggling with love, sex, relationships, and pornography addiction many times never crosses the radar," Ferree said. "It does not occur to people within our church culture, and when it does there is an added stigma, disbelief, shame, and judgment associated with women who struggle."

Let's confront several popular stereotypes and changing dynamics and discover how cultural shifts are impacting girls and young women in churches like yours. Please recognize this single chapter faces the daunting task to review a complex issue. Throughout, I will reference helpful resources for deeper study.

Let's journey through the lives of a few women to find the significant commonalities that these women share. Again, the connection between the human heart and mind is not an equation. People respond in different ways to experiences, abuse, and trauma, but common denominators are often shared by women who struggle with porn and unwanted sexual behaviors.

Men and women have more in common than you might think. Early childhood exposure, repetitive and ongoing use of porn, dysfunctional homes in childhood, and trauma can contribute to compulsive and unwanted sexual behaviors, including porn addiction.

Rewind, Early Exposure

Catherine's story provides common elements for women who struggle.

When Catherine's parents brought the internet home in 2002, they would never have guessed she would intentionally seek online pornography at eleven years old. (Eleven is the average age for girls to be exposed to porn, Stringer says.[52]) Her fifth-grade friends whispered about sex, and with her new online access, she had questions and a deep curiosity. Her home computer had no filters or monitoring software, and she quickly learned how to cover the tracks of her growing online habit.

Catherine found the images and videos she saw stuck in her memory, and she could replay them at will, and sometimes, they played against her will. Like most females, Catherine naturally excels at recalling imagery, objects, and everyday events—more so than males.[53] To avoid getting caught seeking porn on the family computer, she would simply replay porn from her memory library. When she felt stress and anxiety, the videos would loop through her mind, and it served as an escape. As a teen and then an adult, she knew what she was doing didn't match her Christian convictions, but she couldn't seem to stop.

"Pornography doesn't stop; it lives in your head," said Harris.[54] "You can take alcohol away from an alcoholic; you can take drugs away from a druggie, but you cannot take pornography away from a porn addict. It stays with you until you kick it out yourself."

Dr. Carolyn Ross laments the internet is exposing girls to porn earlier today than ever before, often at ages eight or nine, and studies are showing that this early exposure often leads to earlier sex (girls exposed to explicit media were twice as likely to engage in oral sex). In one study of 932 sex addicts, Ross writes, 77 percent of women reported that pornography was a factor in their addiction.[55]

Unlike past generations, today's young women grew up with mobile access to the internet. The first iPhone was released in 2007, and the first iPad in 2010. Women younger than thirty likely would have received their first (unmonitored) mobile device before they left home, and even if a girl didn't have a device of her own, her friends did.[56]

Since joining the Covenant Eyes team in 2007, I have had many conversations about girls seeing pornography at an early age. At a Christian homeschool conference in Arkansas, a fifteen-year-old girl brought her parents to the Covenant Eyes booth. Well-spoken and fashionably dressed, she explained that at age eight, she overheard boys using words she didn't understand. Curious about those words, she used her dad's smartphone to look them up. That was her first exposure to porn. Presuming her innocence, her parents would hand over their phones when she asked. She continually sought porn for two years before her parents discovered her activity.

As a whole, women were most likely introduced to porn by people they know, be it a peer or an adult. Many of Stringer's clients reported finding family members' porn stashes in "hidden," yet obvious, locations like a bathroom or a treehouse. At ten years old, Christian counselor Crystal Renaud Day found her brother's porn in his bathroom, "which catapulted me into an eight-year addiction to porn and other sexual behaviors."

Parental Relationships

Though girls should never see porn, parents play a pivotal role in helping girls when they do encounter porn. Girls who have strong parental relationships, especially deep connections with their fathers, are less likely to struggle with porn and sex in adulthood. Counselor Jay Stringer found in his research that women are 56 percent less likely to struggle with significant pornography viewing as an adult when they have fathers who are emotionally and physically present.[57]

Another key driver associated with the introduction of pornography is when a child wants more emotional involvement from their parent. Consider the following:

- The risk tripled of being introduced to pornography by someone older for those who, to a very great extent, wanted more of their mother's involvement.
- The risk quadrupled of being asked to sexually stimulate someone during or after pornography when women wanted, to a very great extent, more of their mother's involvement in childhood.
- Women were two times more likely to be introduced to pornography by someone older when they, to a very great extent, wanted more involvement with their father.
- The risk of being introduced to pornography by someone older increased from 9 percent to 38 percent when they reported their father showed a very great deal more interest in a sibling.

Women who want more involvement from their parents are not only introduced to pornography at a greater rate, but they are also more likely to be sexually abused.[58]

For Catherine, her dad was present physically but emotionally absent. He rarely interacted with his only child and was reticent with his wife except when yelling was involved. Throughout her childhood, Catherine never saw her dad kiss her mom or even hold her hand.

"Growing up, I felt extremely distant from him, and I felt like I had to be perfect in order for him to recognize me," she said. "The few times that we would go out to eat as a family was when I got straight As. I got to spend time with my dad if I performed well in school. So I was very scholastic, always very into my schoolwork."

Two decades ago, Ferree pulled back the veil of women's unwanted sexual behaviors in her book, *No Stones, Women Redeemed from Sexual Addiction*. Since then, she has written and edited treatment guides and workbooks and led thousands of people through intensive workshops.

Ferree said there are multiple ways that a child can feel abandoned by her parents. Physical abandonment can come in the forms of a parent's death, the strained relationships that come through a divorce, or a parent's workaholism. Emotional abandonment can happen simply because a parent lacks the skills to emotionally nurture a child because the parent never learned these skills in their childhood.

Sexual Abandonment

Though common, especially in the church, parents often don't consider the impact of saying little or nothing about sex. One woman told me her dad asked her as a teen if she knew what sex was. When she replied that she did, he said, "Good. Don't do it." That was her only discussion of sex with her parents.

Sexual abandonment occurs when parents ignore their responsibility to provide their children instruction about the design of their bodies, Ferree said. Worse, our modern mobile device culture fills young people's gaps in knowledge with pornographic lessons.

Catherine married without a single conversation with her parents about sex, everything she knew came from her peers and porn. And porn wasn't sex, right? So she was doing the "Christian thing" in not dating, not having sex, and preserving her virginity until marriage. In the book *Dirty Girls Come Clean* by Crystal Renaud Day, multiple women explained how they justified porn in their formative teen years as a way to preserve their virginity.

Jessica Harris said that while the purity movement of the 1990s and early 2000s provided guidance about saving sex until marriage, it missed any meaningful understanding of sex.

"As a young woman, I wasn't supposed to ask about it, talk about it, think about it, or dress in a way that made men think about it. [She continues] Pornography was not sex. In fact, pornography seemed like a perfectly acceptable alternative to sex. I could explore and indulge while keeping my virginity intact and avoid all the nasty STDs and the whole potential pregnancy problem. It made perfect sense."[59]

"Truth was, I had learned most of what I knew about sex from pornography,"[60] Day adds.

Watching pornography and even having sex delivers poor instruction to women. "In my experience, female sex addicts are woefully ignorant," Ferree writes. "In terms of factual concrete knowledge about anatomy, how the body works and normal sexual response, they often know very little. They may have loads of sexual experiences, but they know little that's accurate about the subject." [61]

Multiple studies[62,63] show that when children grow up with good information about sex, they have less need to experiment, have a safe place to discuss their temptations, and make safer choices. When good instruction is lacking, they turn to an overly sexualized culture that makes kids more susceptible to abuse and exploitation, Ferree writes.[64]

Sexual Abuse

If sex education is difficult to discuss within families, sexual abuse is often buried or taboo.

Childhood sexual abuse (CSA) is one of the strongest drivers of unwanted sexual behavior in adulthood for both men and women. A 2014 study found that 26.6 percent of girls had experienced sexual abuse by the age of seventeen.[65]

Gender and the age of onset of CSA are the two biggest factors in whether someone becomes sexually inhibited on one side of the spectrum or sexually compulsive on the other side, the study showed. Women whose sexual abuse began after age twelve are more likely to become inhibited and fearful of sex. When girls experience sexual abuse before the age of twelve, they are more likely to develop compulsive sexual behaviors.

Remember Darlene (who we met in Chapter 3), the overperforming church volunteer and perfect mom with a secret sex addiction? Her story is neither short nor sweet, but it will likely ring familiar for women in your congregation—though, hopefully with different outcomes. Darlene's story, like other women's stories, deserves to be told. So often in our church culture, we ignore the pain of women who have endured sexual abuse, underplaying the impact it has on their minds and spirits. We ask them to move on, and we ignore how it has impacted their behaviors, their thinking, and even the sin in their adult lives. Darlene's story helps us understand that she had more than just a lustful adult heart in her sex addiction. For years, she was drowning, and the buoy of an inspirational Sunday message or a chat with the pastor's wife wouldn't be enough to help her float.

As a child attending church and from her mother, Darlene heard that girls must be modest. If girls were not modest, it would invite boys to do "dirty" things to them. Though she didn't understand modesty or dirty things at the age of five, an older boy did those dirty things to her anyway. Later, she understood what those things were and wondered how she could have invited them at such a tender age.

During the summer after her fourth-grade year, Darlene was occasionally sent by her mother to the local grocer for bread and milk. A short walk from their house, the store was a family-owned affair, and the employees presented a brightly colored sucker to a child who visited with her family. When Darlene visited by herself, the man would ring up her items personally and return her change along with an awarded sucker. Sometimes, he gave her a handful of suckers to take home, and once, he presented her with a full-sized chocolate bar!

It was a pleasant walk to and from the store. The bright sun that warmed her skin was interrupted by the intermittent shade of sycamore trees that clapped their hands in the breeze. Sometimes, Darlene saved money to buy candy or gum and looked forward to her mother's request to visit the store. Once home, the milk and bread delivered, she would run to her room and open the stitching of a stuffed bear where she hid her treats inside. Hiding in plain sight was a good tactic, and neither her mother nor her siblings ever discovered her secret.

One summer day, at her mother's direction, she bounded out the door to retrieve the family's supplies. Inside the store, she made her way to the aisle stacked with loaves of hamburger and hotdog buns and bread. The man who owned the store followed behind. He grabbed a loaf of bread from the top shelf—the brand of bread she usually selected—and handed it to her. He smiled warmly as his one hand gripped her shoulder, and his other hand grasped her hip so that his fingers awkwardly touched her buttocks. She froze. Then his hand moved up her dress, his smile never faded but somehow it hollowed into an ugly grin.

She felt dirty leaving the store and dropped the gifted chocolate bar on the sidewalk. Quietly, she walked home, and the trees and wind made no sound. At home, she placed the milk in the fridge and left the bread on the kitchen table before running to her room.

In the following weeks, Darlene would be directed to visit the store where dirty things happened in plain sight and no one knew. After another two visits to the store, Darlene's mother noticed her daughter's newfound reluctance to run the errand and asked her what was wrong. Darlene's emotions and story gushed out through tears and convulsions of panic. From her kneeling position, Darlene's mother stood and stated matter-of-factly, "Well, just don't go there anymore."

And that was that. "Just don't go there anymore."

Darlene wanted to reach out and hold onto her mother, be held, but nothing else happened. The store owner wasn't confronted. The story wasn't mentioned again. Cover it over. Ignore it. Hide it inside a stuffed bear in plain sight.

Covering up sexual abuse cuts a wound more deeply, Ferree said, especially when that person is supposed to be your protector. This classic no-talk culture asks the harmed child not to feel their pain, fear, sorrow, remorse, possibly confusing pleasure, and anger. That Darlene told her mother at all in her family's shaming culture is astounding, Ferree said, "but she learned, 'I'll only tell once because I'm not going to get any help.'" Whether it is implied or not, the child can assume the parent is blaming the child for the sexual encounter, exacerbating the feelings of guilt and shame.

Darlene would have more to hide in the years to come.

She hid the encounter she had with the man who lived down the street; she just didn't go near his house anymore. As a teen, she hid months of oral sex abuse with the married man who volunteered for her church youth group.

"I wasn't driving yet, so he would take me home after the youth meetings," Darlene recalled. "I never talked about it; it was never addressed. I shoved it under the rug."

At nineteen, Darlene married her knight in shining armor, Carl, who was twenty-two. Young and hopeful and both leaving dysfunctional homes, they were giddy about striking out on their own. They lived in a modest home and collected a mix of pots, dishes, and used furniture. Carl was starting his career as an IT professional, but as a junior in his field, he often worked the evening shifts, which the more experienced people didn't want.

One night while Carl was at work and Darlene ironed clothes, she smelled the acrid smoke of an electrical fire in her unfamiliar home. She unplugged the iron and waited, but more smoke filled the room, so she turned off the main breaker and a dark blanket covered the house. In the darkness, she called her parents. Her father owned an electrical contracting business, and he would be right over to repair the problem. The relationship she had with her father was thin—he was a workaholic in growing his business, and on weekends, he left the family behind to sing in a gospel quartet.

A knock soon sounded at her door, and she peeked through the curtains to see her father standing on the front step. In short order, he found the problem and fixed it. He gathered his tools and set them by the door.

Relieved and grateful, she hugged her father tightly and thanked him for coming to her rescue. He responded by forcing a kiss on her lips and reaching down her blouse with one hand. She shoved him off, and the glare in her eyes was fierce. "Leave! Get out of here," she demanded. He stooped, picked up his tool bag, and walked out.

The next day, she told her young husband what had happened. "We didn't know what to do with it, so we just shoved it under the rug," Darlene said. "It was never talked about. We just moved on."

But something happened on the night of her father's visit that flipped a switch in Darlene's mind, she believes. Soon after, she began to have affairs with men while her husband was at work . . . three affairs in the first six months of her marriage. One of the men was a layman at her church, a man so respected that he was appointed the interim pastor while the church sought a new pastor.

Stringer's research found that women who had high scores on his sexual abuse scale were four times more likely to want an affair compared to women who had low sexual abuse scores.[66]

"She's a classic sexual trauma survivor," Ferree said. Though Darlene feels something changed within her mind after the egregious assault by her father, Ferree suspects that the "switch was flipped" long before Darlene was aware. Her early childhood sexual trauma was conflated by the trusted church youth volunteer who brought a sense of relationship to the sexual abuse. Then the affair with the interim pastor is likely trauma repetition, where she unknowingly revisits trauma scenarios hoping to manipulate a better or a more controlled outcome for the harm inflicted years before. Darlene would continue her affairs with men for her first seventeen years of marriage—with co-workers and friends but never a one-night stand or hookup. After all, the affairs weren't really about sex; the sex was something she gave to receive relational scraps, snippets of emotional attention, and fragments of affirmation. Never satisfying, she felt an endless hunger that pulled her deeper into addiction.

If you are a sexual addiction counselor, you likely want to know more about Darlene's story, and your mind might be flowing with questions and recognition. If you are a pastor with limited sexual addiction counseling experience, you might feel a bit overwhelmed and wonder how you would help Darlene. We will return to Darlene's story to learn how Christ intervened in her life and how a church community helped Darlene not only recover but thrive. Here's a teaser: Darlene's marriage will be saved; she will learn to be true in marriage, to herself, and in her faith. Today, she serves through her church, helping other women escape unwanted porn, sexual behaviors, and addictions.

Fighting the Impulse to Hide Behind "Fine"

Dr. Ted Roberts, a former senior pastor and founder of Pure Desire Ministries, broke down different types of trauma into what he called "whacks" and "lacks." Whacks are events of extreme impact while lacks are the small wounds that occur over and over. Roberts further broke these into three categories: extreme, moderate, and mild. High-intensity whacks include physical, emotional, and sexual abuse, failure in school, and others. Medium whacks might include being bullied, and mild whacks might be name-calling and feeling unheard. An example of a high-intensity lack could be feelings of familial abandonment; a medium intensity example is frequent moves, and a low-intensity example might be receiving little validation from peers.[67]

Though Roberts admits that "whacks and lacks" are a gross simplification, it puts in layman's terms how overlooked trauma, as well as seemingly insignificant harm over time, has a cumulative impact on the heart and mind. Trauma victims often attempt to control their inner struggles through any number of means of self-soothing. Sometimes, poor but reliable sources of temporary mood management come through shopping, eating, drinking, doing drugs, masturbating to porn, or using sex.

The woman who is struggling with porn and unwanted sexual behaviors desperately wants to control her actions but continually fails under her own power, Ferree writes in a *L.I.F.E. Recovery Guide for Women*. The unresolved issues become an excuse (often subconscious) for continuing in sinful behaviors. Acting out comforts internal distress and might be fun at first, but over time, the compulsive behavior becomes burdensome, Ferree writes. In fighting back, women and men may find periods where they stop the behavior only for it to return because they haven't embarked on the more difficult road of healing and recovery.

"What you need is wholeness," Ferree proclaims. "Being whole means you are practicing real intimacy. It means you are self-aware and capable of modulating negative emotions through healthy means. It means you are present in the moment instead of being lost in your head. It means you no longer hide behind 'fine.'

"Being whole means God is having His way with you, and as a result you are being transformed inside and out."[68]

Despite the struggle, there is hope for wholeness in Christ. He came to make us new. As Christ-followers, we must lean into this hope because often, we not only tend to mask or minimize our trauma and hide behind "fine," we also tend to battle shame, trauma's sneaky offspring.

Chapter 7

The Shame of the Salacious

The devil knows your name but calls you by your sin.
God knows your sin but calls you by your name.
Matt Smethurst

Horses on merry-go-rounds never travel far, and Eric was going nowhere. Eric was trapped in a cycle that always brought him back to porn.

We first met Eric as a six-year-old boy who wet his pants because his dad hit him so hard. Further enraged by the sight, Eric's father not only threw his son across the floor, he screamed at Eric: "You piece of crap! I wish you were never born! I hate you! Go to your room; I never want to see you again!"

Decades later, Eric recites these words without the expletives.

As a grown burly man, Eric could box his way out of anywhere except his addiction to porn. He had tried to quit so many times. Instead, he knocked out three marriages. Against the ropes and about to lose his fourth marriage, Marked Men for Christ[69] came to his corner at a weekend retreat and coached him on how to fight.

"In that weekend, I came face to face with Jesus," Eric recalls. "I always felt my life was a mistake—that I was a mistake. When I came face to face with Jesus through another man, I found that my heavenly Father doesn't make mistakes. That man said, 'First, your Heavenly Father created you exactly as He wanted. Quit trying to be someone else, and be the man who your Eternal Father wants you to be so you can do the mission he has for you.' Second, he said, 'It wasn't that your earthly father didn't love you. He was just so broken and wounded that he didn't know how to show his love, so have some grace and mercy with him as well.'"

"It dropped me to my knees. That was a huge turning point for me," Eric said. "I finally understood why I lived the way I lived and why I wore a mask. I thought being me was the way I got beat, yelled at, or scolded, but that was just my father's woundedness coming through in my life."

Embarking on a healing path, Eric discovered he was in a revolving cycle driven by deeply rooted shame, and it continually looped back to sinful behavior with pornography. Dr. Patrick Carnes explained this paradigm in his Cycle of Addiction model.

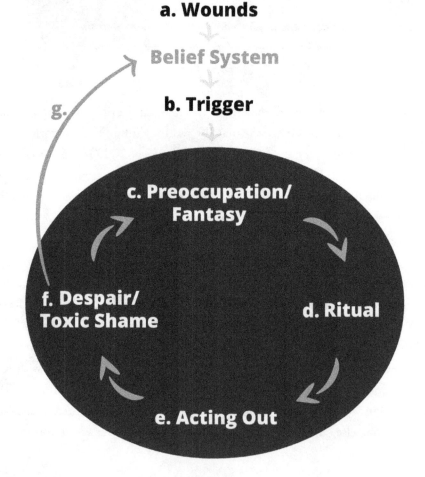

With feedback from Christian counselors, I simplified Carnes's model to make it easier to use and understand, but its elements remain. Understanding this cycle of pain, shame, and sin helped Eric step off his porn merry-go-round and walk a new path.

A. The **wounds** of drama and trauma work to create an underlying foundational belief system that creates doubts about self-worth. A voice in a person's head says, "I can't be loved as I am," "I'm just not quite good enough," "I'm a failure," and "God can't or won't meet my needs, and other people can't either."

   People might struggle with depression or anxiety but hide it well. They might work hard to perform, especially in front of co-workers, fellow church members, and others—even as a voice inside says, "When I perform well, I can be liked. When I make mistakes or perform poorly, I'm not valued."

   People often hide their woundedness behind wealth, education, or careers. Sometimes, people bury their hurts and self-doubt behind bravado, religiosity and religious practice, projected self-confidence, or boasting. But healthy, authentic human beings know they are flawed and need others.

B. This underlying current of unworthiness provides a shaky foundation that is susceptible to **triggers**, which are prompts that lead to unhealthy escapism and self-soothing. Pornography is our focus, but some people use food, sex, shopping, alcohol, or other distractions.

   I call them SEE triggers because they come in *social*, *environmental*, and *emotional* situations. These three aspects often intermingle. These triggers may bring up painful or uncomfortable memories or thoughts about past sexual or pornographic episodes. Smells, hair color, media, and body parts may act as triggers.

   Common triggers include being hungry, angry, lonely, and tired (HALT). But with repeated escapes with porn, this list greatly expands to include being bored, overwhelmed, stressed, or anxious about common problems in life.

C. Triggers lead to **preoccupation, obsession,** and **fantasy**. A person might shout at himself to stop obsessing, but the more he focuses on *not* thinking about a fantasy, the more it sticks.

D. The preoccupation with sex and fantasies drives a compulsive porn user toward **rituals** that can be long or short. A brief ritual might be as simple as taking a phone to a bathroom to act out. Before smartphones, we often heard stories from Covenant Eyes clients of how people would make excuses to stay at home alone so they would have access to their computers in privacy. Getting their family out of the house with smiles and waves became part of their ritual.

E. After the ritual of preparation, the next step is **acting out** with porn and masturbation.

F. But after using porn, the person feels **despair and toxic shame**. When a Christian falls to porn's temptation, they can feel a great sense of failure. This isn't an "Oops, that was naughty. Shame on me." It is toxic shame that eats at a person's feelings of self-worth. They may feel hopeless, isolated, and unworthy to be called a member of the Body of Christ.

"There is even greater stigma and greater shame for Christian women who struggle with porn," said Marnie Ferree (a counselor and founder of Bethesda Workshops in Nashville, Tennessee, you may recall). "It's suffocating, it's paralyzing, it's the Chinese water torture dripping on her head every moment, and church culture can make it worse."

G. This toxic shame reaffirms the person's core belief that they are a failure. "I knew I wasn't a good person, and my acting out proves it once again."

After a period of wallowing in self-hatred, the person recommits to quitting porn. They may try to escape shame by shopping, eating, or using drugs or alcohol. They may spend extra time doing good works for their church or family and hide their thoughts of failure from others and even themselves. But underneath their distraction, good deeds, and religiosity lies a shaky foundation of wounded core beliefs that are self-condemning. And Satan whispers in their ears that they are worthless, that God's sexual standards are impossible, and that they can't handle life without porn.

Of course, this underlying Addiction Cycle works in tandem with neurobiology. When a trigger is sprung, the obsession and fantasy deliver a spritz of dopamine to the brain. Feelings of self-doubt are replaced with pornographic fantasies where a person may feel desired and in control. The feeling brain overwhelms the thinking brain in regard to consequences, and sexual activity and orgasm provide a neurochemical rush. The more the cycle is repeated, the deeper the neural pathways become for future porn use.

Many times, people try on their own to block the places where they can view pornography. But that doesn't work because access is only a contributing issue. When the wounded heart is triggered, it will obsess on how to leap over any physical wall set in place. They will run to familiar soothing because the escape with porn and orgasm seems like their greatest need.

"I had to learn that I had a brain problem," Eric recalls. "I had turned my brain into a factory that craved that high. I was medicating my woundedness and brokenness.

"Sexual release is the only chemical that can bring you up when you're down and down when you're up. If I'm feeling tense and stressed out, that release can calm me. If I'm feeling down, bummed, or horrible, it can lift. It's the most addictive drug that I found, and I was addicted to it."

The Power of Shame

Sinful behavior with porn fuels shame, and shame fuels the addiction cycle.

It's often referred to as the *shame cycle*. A person may use porn to medicate bad feelings, then feel shame for using porn, which creates self-loathing. This underlying damnation combines with triggers like anxiety, anger, and boredom, and the cycle of acting out starts over again.

Sinful behaviors and shame shape an insulating bubble of isolation that separates us from God and our relationships. We make private confessions to God and promise to do better and be stronger. But the isolated confession rarely builds our capacity to grow stronger, to cope better with life, stress, and temptation. So when the triggers and temptations rise within our hearts and minds, no real transformation has occurred, and we travel a familiar sinful path, only to feel more shame.

Christian Counselor Jim Cress, the founder of Integrity Redeemed, has created the perfect acronym for **SHAME: Self-Hatred at My Expense**.

This toxic self-hatred not only shouts, "I messed up," it also says that as an individual, I *am* messed up. I am uniquely defective. A voice inside wails, "If anyone knew what you did in front of a screen, they would know how pathetic, disgusting, and warped you are. What's worse is that you claim to be a Christian, but you're nothing more than a hypocrite. God doesn't hear your prayers! He can't love you because He can only forgive so many times. And God knows how many times you have asked for forgiveness. Even if you think God might forgive and love you, you know your friends, family, and, heaven forbid, your fellow church members would never stoop to your level. You deserve to be shunned by those around you, and they would surely oblige if they knew your secrets."

Ouch. It's ugly.

Many porn struggling Christians conceal these emotions behind self-righteousness and acts of service to the church and for others. The benevolence makes them feel better about themselves if only for a short period.

Cress likens it to two sides of a coin that flips routinely. On one side of the coin is perfectionism, even grandiosity. An over-the-top example was shown in Darlene's constant volunteerism. Often, this side of the coin is focused heavily on rules and outward appearance. But this perfectionism doesn't deal with the roots of woundedness and shame, and a person can try harder only for so long. When the person fails, the coin is flipped, and he or she faces incredible self-loathing. After a period of wallowing in self-contempt, the coin is flipped again, and the Christian returns to working hard, praying, and serving but is trapped in the shame cycle.

This is Satan's perfect revolving trap: perfectionism and shame.

We need a new way to look at sin. The healthy companion amid these feelings is *godly guilt*, said Christian counselor Troy Haas. "Shame says you are bad, but guilt says what you have done is bad," Haas said.

Guilt reminds me that I have fallen short of God's standard, that I am hurting others, and that my actions are not only unhelpful to myself, but also damaging to my relationships, character, heart, and personal and spiritual wellbeing. Guilt prompts a desire to grow, to change, to renew my mind.

Guilt is an urging of the Holy Spirit that pushes me toward my need for my Savior and fellow believers. I might be the lost sheep, but Jesus wants me to join the ninety-nine, and He endlessly pursues me. My sin is not a secret to Him, and His grace is sufficient.

Guilt provides an opportunity—a door to walk through—to break the shame cycle. It leads to honesty, confession, and repentance with fellow believers. Unfortunately, people often live and cope with shame because they don't feel safe confessing to others and because the shame is so deeply rooted.

The Deep Roots of Shame

While porn use itself causes people great feelings of shame, often shame has a deeper foundation in our lives. Our feelings of self-reproach and our desire to hide are much broader than a specific sin. Shame grabs at our hearts with many tendrils.

Often, attitudes of shame were cultivated in men's and women's lives at an early age. Teachers humiliate poorly performing students, children denigrate each other for body size, hair color, and freckles, and teens deride each other for just about everything.

Some people struggle with shame because shaming was used as a weapon of control in their youth. Unfortunately, parents and adult authorities have tried to use shame to stop or change behavior in children, but typically, it inflicts scars instead.

Darlene can recall her mother saying, "Darlene is my little darling," with a tune to her voice, but Darlene felt like no one's *darling*. The moniker sounded hollow when it fell from her mother's lips. Never said privately, "My Little Darling" was just the rehearsed nursery rhyme of her mother's creation, a phrase spoken publicly that somehow reinforced an illusion to others looking in at their family. The facade was wrapped in Sunday dresses for church, brownies for the neighbors, and dishes served at church dinners.

Shame. Yes, that alias fit Darlene well, and it was what her mother surely knew was true. At five, Darlene stood with slumped shoulders at the bottom of the steps, looking up under a bowed head at her mother's disappointment. One finger wagged and pointed down at Darlene while her mother's other hand rested on her hip. "Shame on you," her mother said with more sincerity than the My Little Darling rhyme. "Yes, shame on you." Darlene couldn't remember what she had done, but the memory of "shame on you" would be reinforced many times over. Shame was her mother's way of exacting control over her children, and it bowed them quickly.

Remember, guilt says, "**That thing** that I did **was bad**." Shame says, "**I am bad** for what I did."

In a study released in 2016, 380 fifth-graders were assessed to ascertain their proneness to feelings of guilt versus feelings of shame. When the children became adults—ages eighteen to twenty-one—they were interviewed again. Children who saw their actions through the lens of guilt were much better protected as young adults than their shame-prone counterparts. The kids who harbored feelings of shame in youth reported more sexual partners and were more likely to have unprotected sex, use illegal drugs and alcohol, and have contact with the criminal justice system.[70]

"When the people you love the most, and whose opinion matters most, say bad things about you, it can be more than hurtful—it can affect your self-esteem in ways that can become ingrained and permanent," Dr. Claire McCarthy wrote for Harvard Medical Publishing.[71]

In our schools, communities, and churches, we have stuffed shame into the backpacks of children and adolescents, and they carry those weights into adulthood. We learn to carry shame about abuse, poverty, disability, neglect, trauma, health, physical appearance, our bodies, socio-economic status, and even our athletic or cognitive abilities. In our worldwide and worldly culture, image often seems to matter more than substance, and people become distracted from their true worth by themselves and others.

To top it off, sexual feelings and emotions (things that God designed) have been among the most shameful topics to discuss in the Church and in the homes of Christians. The majority of men and women I meet tell me their parents never had a meaningful discussion about sex, let alone the ongoing conversations that are needed. Many Christians, especially those raised in strict religious homes, learn early that honesty is punished and struggles are met with humiliation. I tell parents often that shaming their children when they discover porn use will only teach them to hide better.

Shame Teaches Us to Hide

As adults, we are supposed to just get over it. Most people don't, however, and their shame is reflected in their emotions and reactions: self-consciousness, bravado, anger, boastfulness, regret, anxiety, remorse, insecurity, feelings of being alone, and more.

This doesn't mean people are cowering in a corner. They function well enough. They work, raise families, attend church, go on vacations, and manicure their lawns. People often find self-value and self-esteem in their work, hobbies, and roles in their homes and church. But that doesn't make them vulnerable and open within the Body of Christ. People keep friends for fun, companionship, camaraderie, and excitement but avoid revealing their secrets, weaknesses, and doubts about themselves. We often put on a good front to prove our self-worth through pleasing people, self-promotion, over-identifying with our work or profession, and even our religiosity and perfectionism.

This underlying struggle with protectionism causes us to grapple with our standings in our communities and societies. Do we come from the right side of the tracks or the right side of town? Do we have the right education, family, marriage, job, car, house, or finances to be accepted by others?

"Look behind the resume and you often find an ashamed little kid who is still trying to prove his or her worth," Christian counselor Edward Welch wrote in *Shame Interrupted.* "What about the people who are self-confident and boastful? There is more trouble there than you might think as well. Authentic human beings know they are imperfect and needy creatures, and they are not compelled to boast. Boasting and arrogance are for those who have deceived themselves into thinking that shame can be banished with a hyped press release."[72]

When Grace Church in Greenville, South Carolina, decided to host a women's event addressing shame, they prayed for a good turnout. Instead, they were overwhelmed. The auditorium that would easily hold the attendance of the average American church was packed. To meet demand for the "Shame: Finding Freedom" event, they published the video to serve more women and even other churches.[73] One of the most impactful efforts of the conference was that women in leadership at Grace Church, including the executive pastor's wife, Ruthie Delk, gave the gift of going first. They told their stories of experiencing shame to add to a church culture where it is safe to come clean and receive support. These women leaders opened up about difficult issues they had faced as children and even as adults, from abandonment to sexual abuse and abortion to having a child out of wedlock.

They also explored the seemingly small shame traps. "As a recovering addict with a criminal record and a history of sexual rebellion, the thing that trips me up the most is the fact I never went to college," Chrystie Cole, the then women's discipleship advisor for Grace Church, told the crowd. "Isn't that funny? I have this past that is littered with shame and sin, legitimately shameful things that I did, but [that is] the thing that just gets me. I am an introvert anyway, and when I'm in a social situation, I hate the question that always comes: 'Hey, where did you go to school?'

"Shame rarely shows up as shame. It's a very complicated issue. It operates best when it is undetected. It is often elusive and hard to identify," Cole said.

People can find how shame invades their hearts by asking simple questions:

What would I hate for someone to know about me?
What do I want to avoid?
What makes me avoid others?
Why do I feel unworthy in certain circles?

"What do you want to hide? That is a shortcut to identifying shame in your life," Welch writes.[74]

Some of this might seem like petty pride, but people often live in their own protective bubbles, even within the Church. Unconsciously, they say, "If you don't truly know me, you can't reject me." We are afraid of being truly seen and truly known. Because if we let down our walls, we might be ostracized, cast out, less valued, less admired, or less respected.

From this false framework, confessing sin to one another seems a formidable task. Shame must be dealt with to find the freedom and healing that God designed for the Church to provide.

"When you feel that shame, you are either going to move toward the Lord and biblical community, or you are going to sin again in some form of self-soothing to medicate that shame, which then just creates more shame and you just get stuck in the endless cycle," Cole said. "This is why shame is directly and so highly correlated with addiction, and depression, and violence, and eating disorders, and suicide, and perfectionism, and workaholism. Shame can't go unaddressed."

Chapter 8

Killing Shame

Shame knows you're powerful when you're honest.
Christian Bosse, SHE Virtual Recovery Summit 2020[75]

Every Tuesday at 1 p.m. EST sharp, I log onto my computer and talk to strangers about porn.

I often wonder, "Will this Tuesday be the day no one shows up?" But I'm never alone. Typically, a half dozen guys log on as well. They attend this online newcomer meeting to learn about the Samson Society, an international recovery community of Christian men who seek healing and freedom, mainly from porn and unwanted sexual behavior.

On this particular day, the men on the video call include a high school principal, a shop owner, a seminary student, and a delivery driver. After an opening prayer and a reading of the 23rd Psalm, I follow the script:

"Welcome to this meeting of the Samson Society. We are a company of Christian men. We are also:

- **Natural loners** who have recognized the dangers of isolation and are determined to escape them.
- **Natural wanderers** who are finding spiritual peace and prosperity at home.
- **Natural liars** who are finding freedom in the truth.

- **Natural judges** who are learning how to judge ourselves aright.
- **Natural strongmen** who are experiencing God's strength as we admit our weaknesses.

"As Christians, we meet at other times for worship, for teaching, or for corporate prayer. Today, however, we meet to talk. Our purpose is to assist one another in our common journey. We do so by sharing honestly, out of our own personal experience, the challenges and encouragements of daily Christian living in a fallen world. Our faith rests in the love of God, as it is revealed in His Word and in the life of His Son. This is the Great Fact of the Gospel, which is the foundation of our charter."

These men show up seeking a safe place where they can be honest before God and other men about their sin, struggles, and desperate need for the Body of Christ. Admittedly, these guys are discussing topics as it relates to their battle with sexual sin. But could you imagine those words being read at the start of other small group sessions at your church? Would people in your church be honest about their lives? How would that be received? What might hold them back?

Let's explore why people often hold back in being authentic with others and how Samson Society and small groups within churches overcome these hurdles.

Freedom Begins When We Stop Hiding

Sin, shame, and secrecy reinforce each other.

Sinful behavior brings shame, and shame powers the addiction cycle. Secrecy maintains the momentum of both sin and shame. We're as sick as our secrets.

Although major tenants of the Christian faith are confession, grace, and forgiveness, as practitioners, we exercise these tenants poorly, especially when it comes to sexual sin. We have misinterpreted the Apostle Paul's warning about how "the sexually immoral person sins against his own body" (Corinthians 6:18). Paul did not say that in God's eyes, this sin is worse than other sins; instead, he divinely warned us that the effects of sexual sin are more damaging to the person in mind, body, and spirit. Sexual sin detonates not only in the soul of the individual but creates a painful blast zone for all those around them. Paul is begging us to pay attention to sexual sin, please. Flee from it! Run baby, run! It's more hurtful to others and more damaging to you than you know, he implores.

Addiction provides an endless supply of grenades. To stop pulling pins, a person needs to be transparent about their shame and their sin. Unfortunately, men and women fear they will be ostracized, especially if they regularly attend church. Instead of confession, we hear silence.

In early 2020, restrictions over COVID-19 locked down many American states and entire countries. People were isolated from friends and family, and many felt the triggers of isolation, boredom, frustration, and anger. Christians who struggle with porn were in a tough spot, and porn sites were providing free premium accounts to cities and nations. In that atmosphere, the National Coalition of Ministries to Men asked me to provide an overview of how porn was impacting the Church. During that online meeting, one men's ministry leader posed a question that was on everyone's mind: "How do I get men to even start talking about porn in their lives? When the topic of porn comes up, guys get as quiet as church mice."

The simple answer is safety and grace.

Within a safe environment, people learn to shed their shame, anxiety, fear, and self-reproach. All of the pent-up angst can be overcome in a safe environment over time. Men and women won't pipe up about the sin that causes them shame unless they feel safe, and creating a sense of safety doesn't happen overnight. It requires intentional steps over time.

Fortunately, safe environments exist many times over within Christian communities and churches. There is no need to reinvent the wheel. We can borrow from their examples. Let's first look outside the walls of the Church.

~~Strong~~ Safe Like Samson

Some years ago, I crammed Danny Bledsoe, a friend, pastor, and accountability partner, into my Ford Fusion for a ten-hour drive from Michigan to Eva, Tennessee. A six-foot-two man with a beefy build, Danny had barely fallen under the maximum limit to pilot Blackhawk helicopters in the Army, which included tours during the war in Kosovo. With his knees bumping the glove compartment, he played navigator and kept a steady stream of music playing.

Our relationship was built over time. Conversations come easy. We have fished, hunted, camped, and traveled together. I'm a godfather to his daughter. Over the years of our friendship, Danny and I have shared our deepest wounds, weaknesses, secrets, and sins. Our struggles aren't the same, but we still relate and bestow empathy. He tells me that few pastors have such a trusted confidante, and I know that most men lack our brotherhood.

Reasonably, Danny suspected time-honored friendship is the rare place where raw honesty happens safely. But the men at this Samson Society retreat stunned him. Men from across the United States have learned to practice vulnerability and candor in a safe fraternity, and almost immediately and seemingly without hesitation, they bear their souls and support each other. The event includes the typical Samson Society meeting that is well-scripted. And the playbook provides a specific time for sharing where men talk about their struggles with sin. This time of sharing is preceded by what you might call Samson Society liturgy.

The meeting facilitator reads: "In sharing, we speak honestly out of our own experience. We tell the truth about ourselves, knowing that our brothers will listen to us in love and hold whatever we say in **strictest confidence**." The final two words reverberate through the room as every man says them in unison. Whether you are attending a Samson Society meeting for the first time or the hundredth time, the message rings clear in all of the men's voices. *This is a safe place.* The society makes it clear they will protect anyone in danger, and they obey the law. But when it comes to the sin that so easily entangles, this cadre of men is serious about authenticity, community, humility, and recovery.

Serious, not grave. From early morning to late at night you hear guys playing guitars, traipsing through the woods in conversation, talking around campfires and folding tables. These guys are the opposite of the quiet church mice.

Danny felt uneasy at first, watching as an honored observer. As an Army pilot, he made friends quickly, but the conversations remained surface-level because, within a short timeframe, he might have found himself deployed to a new location or even to a different unit. In ministry, conversations with other pastors ran deep about theology, preaching, and administration but were otherwise guarded.

At this retreat, men talk straight. In small groups during the weekend, one man describes recurring nightmares he has about his father's abuse. Another confronts being sexually abused as a child. Others talk about how they ripped apart their marriages with pornography use or multiple affairs. It's all on the table. No hiding. No hedging. And no judging.

Unlike the typical Bible study, where everyone is expected to give that "special sinner" advice, the men of Samson are quick to listen and slow to speak. Listening and learning are high priorities because what another man says can impact your life. Plus, you don't need advice when you just spilled your guts; you need to hear your secrets exposed, get them out into the light. Telling someone else what to do during a meeting is considered "crosstalk" and is frowned upon. Such discussions are reserved for private moments after the meeting. This doesn't mean men are devoid of instruction. The opposite is true. Most are reading and participating together in recovery and scriptural curricula, but during their regular meetings, they work to maintain a safe place for vulnerability and honesty.

"Men were vulnerable and honest first, and then they became friends, not vice versa," Pastor Danny said looking back at their camaraderie. "Trust preceded the relationship because safety was established. Everyone there had a common goal to slaughter sin and live in the freedom that only Christ gives."

Though the Samson Society is not a twelve-step program, it borrows from the process. After witnessing such authenticity, Pastor Danny was deeply moved. When he accepted a senior pastor's role at a church in Bay City, Michigan, where a Celebrate Recovery program was already in place, he didn't just endorse it, he participated.

Safety in the Church Too

More and more churches are taking the lessons learned from support groups into the Church itself.

Safe spaces are part of the DNA of City on a Hill in Fort Worth, Texas. Like many medium-sized churches, they have a variety of small groups for in-depth study of the books of the Bible, community service, fellowship, and membership. But they intentionally encourage everyone to attend Life Groups or Freedom Groups with highly engaging topics, including common struggles that just about everyone deals with in life. These topics are often reviewed in sermons with testimonies from leaders and respected church members. Pastor Emeritus James Reeves and Senior Pastor Derrick Bledsoe understand that before you can talk about something like porn, new attendees might be more willing to talk about their need for control, destructive anger, discouragement, and depression.

Like many church studies, these groups are boxed within twelve-week timeframes to fit a school semester. Pastor James wrote a group curriculum, *Life Change for Every Christian,* and most adults attending the church have been through the study. The underlying message is that everyone has wounds, hurts, and hang-ups, and the Church is a safe place to heal, grow, and draw closer to Christ by dealing with your issues in safe spaces with safe processes. This class isn't for the bums, sickos, and perverts; it's for everyone. When a person finishes *Life Change for Every Christian*, they might repeat it or move into more specialized groups that deal with specific issues from depression to anger and alcohol to porn.

Every week, small groups of men or small groups of women gather in the various rooms at the church. These groups aren't like a Sunday School class or a Bible study, per se, because everyone participates, and everyone expects a turn to talk.

And talk they do. They are a chatty bunch. They don't yak about football, raising kids, or other easy small talk. They speak honestly about sin—their sin, their weaknesses, their struggles. And using words like "we" is nearly forbidden, and words like "me," "my," and "I" are used instead.

The church also hosts ongoing support meetings where members seek to live in freedom from their strongholds. Let's step into a session of men who meet on Tuesday mornings and call their meeting The Island of Misfit Toys. It's a diverse group: young single men, married guys, grandfathers, line workers, a pastor who drives an hour, business owners, those who are unemployed, and even a millionaire. What they have in common is a desire to follow Jesus and a recognition that they need the Body of Christ to overcome their compulsive sinful behaviors, including the use of drugs or porn. About twenty guys sit in a circle facing each other. It's honest, raw, and most important, safe. When one person talks, everyone listens. This particular meeting is more like a conversation where men are not only heard but also ask questions and pursue answers together.

Safety and grace aren't about being nice but about being Christ-like.

Safety and authenticity exist on a continuum among churches today, said John Cox, the executive pastor at Watermark Community Church in Dallas. On one side of the continuum are super safe churches where people are loved just as they are, but they are not called to change—to be restored and transformed. On the other side of this continuum are churches where it's horrible to have faults. In other words, the pervasive perspective is people who love Jesus, who are even mature Christians, can't have issues. In that environment, people hide and bury their sins so no one will see them or help them.

"So the challenge in a church is this: How do you create an environment where it's safe to come as you are, but it's not okay to stay the way you are?" Cox asked.

At Watermark, safety grows out of small, close-knit groups where authenticity is taught and practiced. More important, it's modeled by its leaders. From its founding in 1998, elders fostered these community groups, said Todd Wagner, a founding elder and former pastor of the church. Pastors, elders, and leaders are not only part of a community group, most also complete the church's one-year recovery program called re:generation recovery. They also complete re|engage, Watermark's group-based marriage help program.

When members attend re:generation and other programs and tear down strongholds in their lives, from porn to pride or something else, they strengthen their community groups, which then strengthens the church.

Joining a Watermark Community Group is required for church membership. These groups are neither supper clubs nor mini-inquisitions. They are made up of imperfect, flawed, and fallen men and women who are learning to love and honor Jesus and helping others to do the same. These groups are guided by six standards, backed by Scripture, that are explained in a twenty-nine-page guide called *Together: Six Core Values of Biblical Community*:

1. Devote ourselves daily to a personal relationship with Jesus.
2. Pursue deep relationships with one another, based on love and acceptance.
3. Offer and receive biblical counsel in all areas of life.
4. Live authentically, sharing our struggles.
5. Encourage and admonish one another faithfully toward maturity.
6. Engage intentionally with our communities and the world to make disciples.

This is not a list of platitudes. Adherence and practice by community group members create a church culture of safety, authenticity, and love to which many churches should dare to aspire. Restated, Watermark doesn't have community groups; instead, community groups are the bulwark of the church.

In its early days, Watermark's philosophy was put to the test. Nate Graybill wasn't a new Christian, rather he was a lay leader. Nate struggled deeply with pornography in his teen years and as an adult, but he thought he had it whipped as a married Christian volunteering at Watermark. One day, he stumbled onto porn online, and it drew him. He didn't tell anybody; he just tried to put the failing aside. Then he watched porn again the following week, and then the week after that, and then the next day, and so on.

"A year later, I was back into a full-blown addiction," Graybill said.[76] "And I remember one night I got on the internet, and I just saw stuff that scared me, and I knew I was in trouble."

When Nate confessed to his wife about his sinful behavior, she gave him wise consequences even through her hurt and anger.

"'I think we need to tell our pastor,'" Nate recalled Teresa saying. "And I said, 'Well, I don't want to tell our pastor.' To which she said, 'I'm going to go stay with Mom until you're ready.' And I said, 'Okay, I'd rather tell our pastor than tell your mother.'"

Nate's counseling session with Todd Wagner (who was the senior pastor at that time) didn't go as planned. Nate asked for an additional counseling referral, but Wagner looked at his layman and saw a common problem that he knew was plaguing many more men and women in his church. If the Body of Christ at Watermark couldn't support one of its laypeople, then what did it say about its vision for a culture of authentic community. Wagner told him a counselor would be helpful, but first, he wanted him to connect with a small group of believers in the church that would walk with him daily.

"I discovered through the process that porn was just a symptom of a deeper struggle," Nate said. "I was a people-pleaser, a performer. I liked people to think well of me. I was a pastor's kid. I learned how to hide shameful parts of my life but display the good parts of my life. Whenever I was afraid of failure or feeling rejected, I would run to a fantasy world where I was always successful, always affirmed, always approved. I never failed or had to think about anybody but myself in the fantasy world. When I discovered that, it changed everything for me because I realized that I had an idol issue and not a porn struggle."

Nate found healing and wholeness in his church rather than being whispered about and shunned. Church leaders loved Nate too much to let him stay the same. The lessons learned helped Nate and Watermark launch *re:generation recovery*. This biblically honed program isn't for the sickos, it's for the entire church. More than 60 percent of Watermark's pastors and staff have been through the year-long, twelve-step program. After a commencement ceremony at the end of a year, members are called to serve as leaders and ambassadors of the gospel in their communities.

From a small gathering in 1998, Watermark has grown into multiple campuses and planted several independent churches. And the re:generation recovery program is provided free to other churches that want to employ it.

The Healing Power of Safety and Grace

Whether authenticity, safety, and grace happen in a group setting or one-on-one, there is a common thread. We were wounded in relationships, and we heal in relationships. God provides forgiveness, but He uses relationships to provide confession's healing power (James 5:16).

"Shame is only combatted in the context of relationship," Christian Counselor Troy Haas said. "Where I'm able to be honest, I show you intimately who I really am. And instead of rejecting me or judging me or criticizing me, you love me, you embrace me, you walk with me, you become an ally and a friend. That makes all the difference in the world. And now shame dissipates. And I'm able to just know, 'Hey, I'm loved by others and loved by God. I love others and I can love myself. And now I can make different choices. I have the power to make different choices.'"

Certainly, there is more to healing and growth than talking. Men and women need biblically sound tools and curricula to grow. Safe and directive processes like re:generation provide direction and increase a person's knowledge and capacity to heal and live in wholeness. But reading curricula or books in isolation fails to produce lasting results. That's why every program and group in this book encourages its members to recruit a mentor or an accountability partner with whom a person can talk, confess, voice temptations, request prayer, and seek support between meetings.

Newcomers to these groups or discussions are often wary. They have lived for years with shame and a veiled public persona. Being authentic is frightening. That's why Nate Larkin, the founder of Samson Society, gives the gift of going first. When Nate tells his story of brokenness to another guy first, Nate typically becomes the safest person that man knows. That man may not deal with porn, but he likely has something in his life that feels bigger than he is. Suddenly, he can unload the weight he has been carrying alone for too long.

Authenticity builds an intimate connection that is contagious. Within a safe space, people hear, *You are a person, not a problem. Your identity is found in Christ, not in your sin.* People enter feeling shame but gain a sense of value and worth. They enter hopeless and discover longing and a belief that God can renew their mind, body, and spirit.

"I spent years begging God for a private solution to my private problem. I am a colossal failure as a solo disciple for the very simple reason that Jesus doesn't have any solo disciples. That's not His program," Nate said. "Thankfully, I have a freedom today when it comes to porn. But I am well aware that it's a fragile freedom. It's something I protect with the help of boundaries, and brothers, and accountability. It's something I keep by giving it away."

Chapter 9

The Lies That Keep People Stuck

The simple believes everything, but the prudent gives thought to his steps.
Proverbs 14:15

Escaping pornography requires men and women to shake off the lies they accept as truth.

But it's not easy. If casting off these distortions was simple, there would be no point to this book or the dozens of other books aimed at helping individuals heal compulsive behavior. The most pernicious lies about compulsive porn use feel legitimate. The lies sound right. They feel true. Yet they are subterfuge to evade God's direction, to escape the consequences of broken promises, and to hide shame and brokenness. Proverbs 14:12 warns us, "There is a way that seems right to a man, but its end is the way to death."

So far, I've shown how early exposure, repetitious acting out, trauma, and wounding can combine to create a compulsive habit with pornography. We also reviewed how shame keeps people in a revolving cycle of porn use and holds them back from asking for help. Let's review the lies that secure the locks on the cage. Porn distorts how we think and how we feel. Some of these lies might seem ludicrous to the outsider, but in my brokenness, I believed many of these concoctions myself.

From earlier chapters, common lies likely already come to your mind: "I don't need help; I can quit porn on my own. I just need to try harder with

91

my self-discipline." Indeed, these self-assuring lies are among the worst because they lead to failure. And failure combined with secrecy and isolation leads to hopelessness and resignation. If you have never struggled with porn use personally, this try-harder mentality likely sounds like the right tactic. But think about areas where you are not strong. For example, one survey showed that 41 percent of pastors are obese compared with 29 percent of all Americans. What are the lies that interactions with food tell us when we feel down or stressed? We call it comfort food for a reason. In a difficult period, I recall asking my accountability partner to meet me at a Chinese buffet. "My treat," I said, and I filled my plate at least three times. The double portions of moo goo gai pan were an escape, but thankfully, they at least came with a healthy helping of godly wisdom from my friend.

"Food and sex are among the more difficult addictions because we need food and we are sexual beings," said Erik Troyer, a Christian counselor and the director of God Speed Resources, which serves Christian missionaries. "You can stop using alcohol and heroin, but sex and food are issues that must be tempered, realigned, and redeemed."

Here are common porn lies I hear from Christian men, some of which might make your skin crawl.

- "I need to watch porn and masturbate just to feel normal. There is a tension that needs release."
- "I watch pornography because evolution made me this way. I was meant to roam the savannah and mate with as many females as possible, and that's why I seek a parade of different images, videos, and online interactions."
- "My sexual needs are more than my wife can or wants to meet. It's her fault I watch porn."
- "God made me this way. God created this sexual drive within me, and it overpowers 90 percent of guys. Look at Samson, David, and Solomon."
- "We will have a lifelong battle with porn and our sexual thought life with plenty of failures because of our fallen nature." This one borrows from the prior example, and worse, many church leaders teach this lie as truth. It sounds true because there are so many current stories and so many biblical examples.

Let's not leave out women, because they have common lies to battle too. These are a few among the many that Christian counselors Marnie Ferree and Crystal Renaud Day hear.

- "Porn and masturbation are safer than sex. I don't have to worry about pregnancy or an STD/STI. I'm actually being very responsible sexually."
- "I deserve this. God hasn't brought me a husband, so using porn is my best option right now."
- "Porn and masturbation don't count. It's not really being sexual; I'm still a virgin . . ." or "I'm being faithful to my spouse by not having a physical affair." (Perhaps you thought only guys think this way.)

An important part of believing lies and misconceptions is hearing them often enough to believe them. Eating carrots improves your eyesight. Shaving thickens hair. Vikings wore horns on their helmets. None of these are true, but most people believe them because we've heard them our entire lives.

Repetitious messages are a common weapon in politics. Every election season we see repeated political ads that provide grains of truth from a strained point of view and social media fables spread far and wide. Dictators and autocrats throughout history have repeated their lies to make them seem true to the masses. After World War I, the German army trained Hitler and other soldiers as propagandists to thwart communists, and Hitler used that knowledge for his own rule. In Mein Kampf, Hitler declared that propaganda "must confine itself to a few points and repeat them over and over."

The porn industry has been repeating its messages for decades, and what once was considered despicable is now acceptable. Throughout these decades, parents didn't teach their kids healthy sexuality, and the Church remained mum. If you are an older pastor, you likely grew up around women who thought only gross men viewed porn. However, with the porn industry's consistent messaging and easy mobile access to porn, millennial and Generation Z women often view porn as sexually liberating and believe violent and degrading sex and objectification are healthy sexual expressions.

"Porn is where I learn about sex," a teen girl told Ferree at one of her Teens & Parents workshops aimed at Christian families. "My parents didn't teach me anything, and school just talked about where babies come from, and the Church won't go near the subject. I need to know what all the interest is about and see what my boyfriend wants me to do with him."

The Neurology of Sticky Lies

Our beliefs and feelings, whether they are true or false, are often integrated into our very anatomy. In our church culture, we have sometimes tried to make our bodies somehow separate from who we are. But the Apostle Paul says that though he seeks God in spirit, he is still a man of flesh and that his members wage war against his mind (Romans 7:23). Neurology and biblical principles go hand in hand because we are God's creation. Our biology and neurology are God's ideas. God designed our beautiful brains to learn, and from the Garden of Eden, we have been learning both truth and lies. Psalm 139 tells us, "For you created my inmost being; you knit me together in my mother's womb. I praise you because I am fearfully and wonderfully made; your works are wonderful, I know that full well."

A basic principle of neurology is that of *brain plasticity*. In simple terms, it means the brain is more like moldable plastic than hardened ceramic. It used to be thought this plasticity ended in one's late twenties, and then the brain's neuropathways became hardened and set. This idea lent to the phrase, "You can't teach an old dog new tricks." But in recent decades, neurologists have discovered that people can create new neural pathways throughout their lifetimes. For instance, the brain can increase or decrease the strength and number of synapses that communicate an emotion or feeling. This allows information or memories for our habits to flow more or less quickly.

This learning plasticity not only applies to learning a language, defining the foods we like, and performing tasks, but also to our sexual appetites and beliefs. In his book, *The Brain That Changes Itself*, Dr. Norman Doidge explains that our brains and our sexuality are molded by our experiences, interactions, and other means of learning, which is why people vary in what they say is attractive or what turns them on. The brain creates neural pathways that label a specific type of person or activity as arousing.[77]

This will come as sad news to many. The attraction and compulsion to porn are learned behaviors, which means people play a huge role in their own habituation—what they do out of habit without even giving it much thought.

Habitual experience is only part of the learning equation. After all, people experience a variety of activities that never stick. You probably do some things over and over in an attempt to learn something new and get incredibly frustrated at your lack of progress.

So why does porn have such an impact? In a nutshell, it has a lot to do with the therapy term "attachment." Therapists and neurologists use this term to describe how the brain neurochemically bonds and remembers how to react to a stimulus. "It's not so much the stimulation [the image, video, experience, etc.], it's what is done with the stimulation," Christian sex addiction counselor Dr. Doug Weiss told me. "The initial arousal of novelty will be there, but that is not much of a threat until it's attached to the sexual experience [through masturbation]."

Pornography attachment can be very strong because masturbation and orgasm produce intense neurochemical rewards, and repetition builds neural pathways to enable patterns of behavior. The episodes are even more enhanced with other feelings, including the fear of getting caught, secrecy, and novelty. This chemical and hormonal explosion takes learning to a whole new level. As the porn pathways deepen, people in everyday life become objects of sexualized fantasy, and inanimate objects, clothing, and situations not designed for sex become sexually charged.

Proverbs warns us: "Keep your heart with all vigilance, for from it flow springs of life" (Proverbs 4:23). Proverbs provides the imagery of flowing water from a spring. And this spring is our heart! Our hearts and brains go together. Our spiritual selves and our thinking selves are intertwined. "For as he thinks in his heart, so is he" (Proverbs 23:7, NKJV). Jesus taught us (Luke 6:45) that when you store good stuff in your heart, your mind thinks of good things. Conversely, when people look at porn, sexual fantasy will exact control over their thoughts.

The problem is that a person's spring has been poisoned over time. Maybe he was seven years old and exposed to porn (a common experience today). His brain got turned on, and little by little, over time, he returned to porn, further poisoning his well. This repetition caused his heart to crave and lust for porn, and as a man, he feels stuck, searching and seeking pornography, even while he is begging for freedom.

Carving the Porn Rut

With time and repetition, these porn behavior neural pathways become deeply rooted, and they are expressed in the way a person thinks about porn and the emotions they feel about porn. The lies about porn seem true because they are etched into what I call the Porn Rut. The four parts of the Porn Rut are common clinical terms that are part of all compulsive behaviors.

Sensitization

A person who uses a pornographic image, video, or story and masturbates for the first time begins a learning process of how to respond to porn in the future. With repetition, the brain responds not only to the initial stimulus, but also to related stimuli. After a person becomes sensitized, very little is needed to trigger a response; a superhighway is connected to the rewards circuitry. This superhighway has many entrance ramps; sexual cues are seen everywhere, and sexual fantasizing comes easy. Because porn provides a state of arousal, the brain creates pathways that make initial arousal easier.

Triggers

Cigarette smokers can name a list of activities that spark a physical and mental desire for a smoke: drinking a cup of coffee, finishing a meal, or sipping alcohol. When these cues or triggers are presented, the brain gets a shot of dopamine that motivates a person to smoke, ingest nicotine, and fire the rewards circuitry of the brain. These are examples of environmental triggers. I use SEE to remind me that triggers can be social, environmental, or emotional. Smokers also feel a strong need for a cigarette when they are stressed, sad, or angry, and those triggers are emotional.

Triggers also surface for porn and masturbation, and these sensitization cues can vary greatly from person to person, depending on their gender, marital status, environment, emotional states, memories, and the types of porn and activities they use.

In the early days of Covenant Eyes, before the advent of the smartphone, people would tell us that simply being home alone was enough to prompt them to rush to their computers in search of porn. Others would lie awake at night, taunted with thoughts of getting up to view porn online and masturbate while the family slept. Why? Because they held not only memories of using a computer for porn, but also of opportunities of secrecy, and even of getting up or staying up for a late-night fix.

These compulsive feelings are engrained from repetitive and powerful experiences. Dopamine flows easily in response to the learned pornographic triggers driving a person to act out, and the sensitized neural pathways lead easily to the rewards circuitry.

Desensitization

Though not true for everyone, most compulsive porn users find they need a greater amount of or more intense porn to activate a state of arousal. After multiple excursions with the same porn image or video, the brain reduces the amount of dopamine released for that media or even that type of media.

To escape this desensitization, people expand their pornographic tastes to more novel stimuli. In simple terms, the desensitized porn user is chasing the original high, and so they need a new or bigger dose. Dopamine likes novelty, even startling novelty. What was once considered hardcore—a heterosexual couple engaged in intercourse—is now considered mundane, Dr. Doidge says. Varied forms of sex mixed with force, violence, and humiliation are now fused into today's most common pornographic scripts. As tolerance expands, people often become disgusted with their own pornographic pursuits . . . but do it anyway, broadening the cues that lead to arousal.

"When pornographers boast that they are pushing the envelope by introducing new, harder themes, what they don't say is that they must, because their customers are building up a tolerance to the content," Doidge writes.[78]

Hypofrontality

Compulsiveness is a good descriptor of hypofrontality. Many porn users feel focused on getting to porn and masturbating even when a big part of them is saying, "Don't do this." Even when negative consequences seem imminent, impulse control is too weak to battle the cravings.

A person stuck in compulsive porn use may have excellent self-control for many other scenarios in life, from budgeting money to working hard, but they lack self-discipline with pornography.

A Poisoned Well Accepts the Lie

Once firmly stuck in the Porn Rut, all of the lying makes sense to the person struggling. People exchange the truth for a lie because with time and repetitious acting out, they *feel* the lies are true at a gut level. They have overwhelming *feelings* and desires to watch porn. Over time, they have achieved the opposite of what Romans 12:2 directs; they have conformed their minds to the *feelings* and the lies that pornography teaches.

Feelings aren't facts.

- "I *need* the escape of porn and masturbation to ease my stress and anxiety and to fill my physical and emotional needs."
- "Nobody is getting hurt."
- "This is natural and beneficial."
- "I have tried to quit so many times; I can never be free."
- "I am a shameful failure as a Christian and uniquely defective."
- "Porn provides the variety that gives more sexual satisfaction."

This wayward thinking and accompanying emotions are intertwined with the fantasies of a pornified mind. These fantasies provide fictitious interactions of being accepted, loved, and admired without the relational sacrifices of giving, loving, and caring for the needs of another. People may also feel dominant, strong, and irresistible in porn fantasies, but the feelings are fleeting. Why? The answer is obvious, right? When feelings are based on fantasy, there is nothing tangible. The feelings aren't based on facts.

For instance, every scientific study ever conducted on sexual satisfaction comes to the same conclusion: people in long-term, monogamous relationships have the greatest sexual satisfaction. God designed us for satisfaction in marriage. He made it "very good" (Genesis 1:27–31). Yet the porn industry promises greater satisfaction in a never-ending sexual parade, and people gobble up the lie, even though studies repeatedly show less sexual satisfaction among regular porn users.

From a scientific point of view, Dr. Doidge explains that porn is more exciting than satisfying because we have two separate pleasure systems in our brains: one for *exciting* pleasure and another for *satisfying* pleasure. The exciting system, fueled by dopamine and anticipation, is all about appetite, such as imagining your favorite meal or a sexual episode.[79] The *satisfying* system involves actually eating the meal or having sex, which provides a calming, fulfilling pleasure. This system releases opiate-like endorphins that provide feelings of peace and euphoria. Pornography, Doidge writes, hyperactivates the appetite system. But the satisfying system is left starving for the real thing, which includes actual touching, kissing, caressing, and a connection not only with the body, but also with the mind and soul.

The porn-saturated brain is fixated on sex, Dr. William Struthers explains in his book *Wired for Intimacy*, but real sex is intended for intimacy.[80] The pornified brain is ready for multiple partners, images, and sexual possibilities, but real sex is intended for a narrow focus of exclusive sharing. Porn's neurological superhighway is built for speed, but satisfying sex is designed for the slow and evolving discovery and appreciation of a loving partner. Porn is focused on masturbation that offers a fleeting (and usually quick) escape that hastens the need for more. Meanwhile, a committed couple can have long and satisfying encounters with many creative expressions of intimacy that are not genitally oriented.

Porn users believe the lie that porn will spice up a marriage. Yet studies repeatedly show that after prolonged porn exposure, men and women alike report less sexual satisfaction with their intimate partners, including their partners' affection, physical appearance, and sexual performance.[81,82]

Battles for Truth

The man or woman seeking freedom in Christ has a war on their hands with daily battles for His truth that requires the whole armor of God (Ephesians 6:10–20). It is not a battle to simply push down the bad but to enjoy all the good God created for us to enjoy. Through His truth, we discover and enjoy His design for relationships, exciting and satisfying habits, and a way of thinking that reflects the fruit of the Spirit.

Admittedly, it is a prolonged battle to cast off the imaginations and fantasies that a man or woman has nurtured since adolescence. Struggling men and women must deconstruct the habits forged in deception and rebuild them with all the amazing pleasures that God prepared for us. They must recognize the deception of their feelings that are often rooted in woundedness and self-soothing behaviors and open themselves up to trust godly friends who can guide them to healing.

In the war against strongholds, truth is vitally important. Here is a practical and common example. A man, especially a compulsive porn user, may seek porn when his wife says no to sex. The lie is, "I feel rejected. I'm angry. She doesn't care about my 'needs.' I should withdraw from her emotionally. I deserve to look at porn." But the Bible teaches husbands to ". . . live with your wives in an understanding way" (1 Peter 3:7). The truth teaches husbands to love their wives and even sacrifice their lives and to "love their wives as their own bodies" (Ephesians 5:25–29). God's truth instructs us to listen and be slow to anger (James 1:19) and not to look to our own interests but to those of others (Philippians 2:4), including a spouse.

The beauty of this truth is backed by biology and psychology. A woman's natural cycle of menstruation and a greater desire for sex at certain times of the month create a beautiful tension that enhances emotional and sexual bonding. In God's design, a husband is patient, listens to her physical and emotional needs, and provides support. In doing so, he learns to love and bond with her through non-sexual touch and conversation, grows in self-discipline, and when the awaited sexual encounter arrives, the couple finds deeper sexual satisfaction. His wife is not simply on tap for sex, but rather, sexual intimacy is nurtured through compassion, trust, non-sexual intimacy, and care.

The pornified mind ignores these truths for a quick release of sexual tension and loses the reward of God's design. "Stinking thinking" leads to excuses and lies that lead to ongoing deception. The small lies compound in our hearts like a snowball rolling downhill. In Ephesians 6:10–20, Paul tells us we need the whole armor of God to withstand evil, and he begins by fastening the belt of truth. Truth protects our hearts. When we remove the belt of God's truth the enemy is poised to strike.

We often think of the belt of truth as a simple two-inch strap worn by a Roman soldier (Ephesians 6:14). Instead, a soldier wore a hefty four- to six-inch-wide leather belt that supported his trunk to help him hold up the weight of his armor. The belt held his sword, allowing him to fight. It held his food and water to keep him nourished. As well, the Roman soldier's belt had weighted leather straps that hung down in front to protect his groin from low blows. When it comes to our mental, moral, and spiritual selves, Satan wants us unsupported and weak, and he strikes below the belt. It's the attack that is most painful and most shameful.

Counselor Troy Haas framed Satan's assault in more stark terms. "Think about it. Would you rather be beaten or raped?" Haas asked me. "I've never met anyone who said the latter."

To resist the assaults of our culture, "to stand against the schemes of the devil" (Ephesians 6:11), to overcome the war within oneself, the Christian must listen to James's directive to be doers of the Word and not just listeners (James 1:22). And that doing comes through obedience. If there was a key word in the Christian life, it would be *obedience*. It's not the truth we know; it's the truth we obey that will make the difference in our lives.

Obedience comes at a cost. It requires me to lay aside my feelings and emotions. Obedience requires me to acknowledge God's design and purpose for my life. Obedience requires my trust, my submission, and my surrender to His higher authority. "For my thoughts are not your thoughts, neither are your ways my ways, declares the Lord. For as the heavens are higher than the earth, so are my ways higher than your ways and my thoughts than your thoughts" (Isaiah 55:8–9).

This leap of faith is not simply a matter of making a decision, although it starts with a choice to yield to Christ. Many Christians have prayed for change, but their hearts and minds have not grown in capacity to embody the truth of Christ or the daily obedience to live out the truth. They require a safe place and a safe process to grow, climb the stairs of obedience, and yield and accept the work of the Holy Spirit.

"The loving heavenly Father wants to 'renew' our thinking into right, healthy thinking, so the result will be right, healthy behavior," Dr. James Reeves writes in *Life Change for Every Christian*.[83] "The process of growth requires patience and perseverance."

So far, we have found that most church attendees don't become unstuck overnight from these lies and the resulting strongholds. And shame and fear often keep them from seeking help. If that is true for a church attendee, how much more do ministry leaders experience despair and panic over their sexual sin. How much more do they tremble at the thought of asking for help.

Chapter 10

Porn's Impact within
Christian Ministry (Part 1)

Failure is not falling down but staying down.
Dr. Dan Erickson

After thirty-eight years of preaching, visiting the sick, and baptizing believers, Pastor Wayne Johnson's career as a pastor collapsed. No public explosions, no firestorm of publicity. Rather, it resembled air being let out of a balloon.

Wayne thought he was alone in his church when a deacon's wife walked by his office and spotted him watching porn on a church computer. When confronted by the deacons of his church, he told them, "It was just a one-time thing. A pop-up ad appeared on my screen, and I made a bad choice."

He told his wife about the confrontation with the deacons, and she immediately came to his defense. "In spite of what he did, Wayne has the purest heart of anybody I know," she told the deacon's chair. She believed every word she said, but the sheriff's detective who served on the church board didn't buy it. The board allowed Pastor Wayne to resign, or else he would be fired. Under the pretense of addressing family obligations, he preached a final salutation to his congregation the following Sunday morning.

In truth, at age sixty-two, Wayne harbored a secret war against porn and lustful fantasies that he had battled since his early teen years. He could fight off the urges for periods, but when life became stressful, as it often does for a pastor, he would return to the self-soothing he learned as a boy. He was exposed to pornography at an early age, was sexually abused by an older boy, and when Wayne's dad got drunk, he would tell his young son sexual stories about his conquests, objectifying women as he did. Like many Christians, Wayne never told anyone about this trauma and downplayed its impact on his life.

At age seventeen, Wayne gave his life to Jesus, and he felt a deep calling on his life to share the gospel with others. He understood Christ's call to purity and believed life at a Christian college would help him leave porn and sexual fantasies behind. He, indeed, found greater periods of freedom. So Wayne extended his Christian training at seminary, where he embarked on a double-major. After graduation, he entered a career as a minister of education and administration at large churches, and he spent five years at his first post and nineteen years at his second, where he also met his devoted wife. After two decades of ministry, Wayne felt led by God to serve a smaller church as its senior pastor.

"I remember telling the Lord, 'I just want a small congregation to love,'" Wayne recalled.

But with the stresses that come as a senior pastor, Wayne found a resurgence in his secret. Absent from longtime friends and family, in a new community, threatened with church conflicts, feeling unexpected anxiety, and left alone for hours in his office with high-speed internet, pornography made a subtle and progressive reentry into Wayne's life. After a few years as a senior pastor and with no one knowing of his struggle, Wayne tried the location cure in which he accepted the senior pastorship of another church where he was sure he could start over and transform. But the change was short-lived, and porn use returned with a vengeance and seared his conscience (1 Timothy 4:2).

"The enemy had convinced me that no one was being affected by my porn use as long as no one found out," Wayne told me. "That, of course, was one of his lies. Along with my marriage, my ministry was being affected more than I would ever admit to myself. My preaching and our worship lacked power because of my habitual sin of porn use, lust, and masturbation.

"Even though I told the Lord I was sorry every time I had a session with porn and I promised to never do it again, I could not stop on my own," Wayne continued. "I was addicted. This caused so much shame, and the intense shame fueled my already low self-esteem. Shame and self-loathing over the double-life I was leading caused me to crave affirmation. So when I received words of affirmation, as most pastors do, my self-centeredness intensified. My desire to please people in the churches I served took precedence over pleasing the Lord or pleasing my wife and family. My motives and reasons for doing ministry became polluted, confused, and convoluted."

A Leadership Dilemma

Over the years, you and I have heard multiple versions of this story from people serving in roles of spiritual leadership, your denomination or non-denomination included. Men's ministry leaders, worship leaders, youth pastors, and others describe seeking a deeper closeness to God (often through prayer, biblical study, service, and self-discipline) and, at the very same time, fighting a secret and ongoing battle with pornography.

A few years ago, I was invited to speak at a major conference for missionaries of multiple denominations. Throughout the conference, I engaged one counselor after another who described a common theme: pornography use is a common issue among missionary ranks. Counselors described pulling back the layers in counseling men and women about marital strife, depression, burnout, and other issues and would regularly find pornography use as part of the equation.

A 2016 Barna study reported that 57 percent of pastors and 64 percent of youth pastors said they struggle with porn currently or have in the past. About 21 percent of youth pastors and 5 percent of senior pastors believe they are addicted to porn. In 2014, pastors.com surveyed 1,351 pastors and 54 percent of respondents said they had visited a porn site in the last year, and 30 percent had visited a porn site in the last thirty days.[84]

Many people would say these men and women are simply unfit, lack true love for Jesus, and haven't experienced the power of the Holy Spirit. These faux servants are not "above reproach" and should be disqualified, and if they had basic morals, they would disqualify themselves. Further, they should be fired and never trusted again to assume a ministry role.

In some cases, I affirm these critics are spot-on with their sentiments. In more than twenty years of serving people with accountability software and educational resources, we've heard some startling stories at Covenant Eyes. For example, a youth pastor and Covenant Eyes subscriber told our team that he walked into his church to find his senior pastor watching pornography on the sanctuary's media screens. When the youth pastor confronted his senior, he was met with threats and intimidation. "No one will believe you over me, so you better keep your mouth shut if you want a future in ministry." The church's board believed the youth pastor after they discovered the senior pastor was accessing porn through his office computer too. Despite the evidence and even admitting to using porn, the pastor was indignant and unrepentant, saying the board had no right to discipline him. The board rightfully stripped the senior pastor of his post. ("You are to deliver this man to Satan for the destruction of the flesh, so that his spirit may be saved in the day of the Lord" (1 Corinthians 5:5).)

That's an unfortunate and extreme example.

In some churches and denominations, a pastor found struggling with porn might receive a forgiving path. But the route to restoration is often limited to a public (or even private) confession, a period of not serving in ministry, a span of church discipline that varies greatly, and sometimes, discipleship or mentorship in the spiritual disciplines. You might have witnessed other scenarios as well that included counseling, a weekend intensive, and other efforts. Some of these restorative efforts are strong and some are window dressing.

We should be wary of cheap grace to pastors and church leaders caught in sexual sin. From my youth, I recall a pastor being prayed over when his affair was discovered. With instant renewal, he returned to the pulpit. Those who doubted the sincerity of the exercise were ignored, splitting the church.

I'm also disheartened by immediate abandonment for porn use. We are sons and daughters of God, and He disciplines those who have a repentant heart (Hebrews 12). As the Body of Christ, leaders of the church must correct and restore those with a willing and truly repentant heart (1 Thessalonians 5:14, Revelation 3:19, Galatians 6:1). Too often, the Church ignores these Scriptures for a more expedient route. For example, a Fort Worth, Texas deacon confessed to his fellow board members that he was struggling with pornography. He wasn't caught by anyone; he simply approached them with a repentant heart. Their response was to not only remove him from the board but also oust him from the church.

Finally, I feel sad for those who struggle in a variety of ways and even more secretly after going through poorly designed efforts of restoration. In some cases, people stop using porn, but they haven't achieved wholeness and remain unhealthy emotionally and spiritually. It's common in counseling circles to find that people quit one sinful habit only to exchange it for another when they don't find true spiritual renewal and wholeness.

There is a better way forward. A truth that I have witnessed time and again is those servant leaders who go through a true process of repentance, church discipline, and holistic restoration come out on the other side better equipped to serve the Body of Christ.

That was my worst understatement of this book.

What I mean is that these restored servants catch fire for Christ. They are driven to give away the grace and freedom they have received. These restored sons and daughters express greater humility, guard their boundaries, and have a deeper understanding of themselves and others. They are magnets for others seeking hope, restoration, and a healing community. They nurture healthy relationships and support and guide meaningful change in the lives of others. Going through a strong recovery process makes them more effective to the Kingdom. This is not to say that leaders should necessarily be returned to their previous roles, but God can use a repentant, safe, and restored heart.

"For the moment all discipline seems painful rather than pleasant, but later it yields the peaceful fruit of righteousness to those who have been trained by it" (Hebrews 12:11).

Ted Shimer has mentored men since 1991 through Student Mobilization and other missionary work. He has witnessed how Christ restores the hearts of fallen leaders and uses them for His glory. "I know many former pastors who have fallen, vulnerably repented, and are now serving the Kingdom by helping others break free from sexual sin," Shimer wrote in *The Freedom Fight*. "If you love Jesus, are repentant, and free, then you have a role to play, no matter what you've done in the past."[85]

The Wounded Want to Serve

The woman who washed Jesus's feet with her tears, dried them with her hair, and anointed them with ointment had serious issues (Luke 7:36–50). She was not as put together as Simon, the Pharisee, with his stellar education, a fine house, and honor among his people. After extending a dining invitation to Jesus, Simon plopped down at his table and gave Jesus a skeptical eye, doubting that this dusty Nazarene could be the Messiah. Simon even ignored the basics of Near Eastern hospitality, such as offering his guest water to wash His feet. But this woman whose sins "are many" goes to work in an extreme approach. Can you imagine crying enough tears over your sin to wash someone's feet? Her sobbing and efforts show her immense sorrow for her sins and her desire to be made right before Jesus, who grants her His eternal grace.

Troy Haas had serious issues. His sins were many. He was exposed to porn well before puberty, and from the age of ten, when he felt overwhelmed, lonely, anxious, or afraid, he looked at porn and masturbated. He lost his virginity in middle school. Porn, sex, and drugs in his teen years were habitual means of escape. At seventeen, he received his first felony drug possession charge and his second came at nineteen. He was sure he was going to prison for up to five years.

Instead, Haas spent five months in the Harris County Jail in Houston, Texas, where he learned about Jesus. He spent hours for days on end reading a Bible and learning to pray. As soon as he was released, he sought a church to learn more about his Savior.

In a new Christian community, he felt loved and accepted and was mentored like never before. He discovered help for his drug and alcohol habits within the walls of the church but found no resources for his struggle with porn. "The church really didn't know what to do with that. The only advice was 'Don't do it. God's not for it. You just need to get married and love Jesus more,'" Haas recalled.

Within his own will and reasoning, he did his best to do just that. He registered for classes at a Christian college, where he met and later married Melissa. He then attended Southwestern Baptist Theological Seminary, and after graduation, he and Melissa became missionaries in Africa. He was sure that as a missionary, focused on his service, he would no longer struggle. However, in Western Kenya and Southeastern Sudan, Troy found himself struggling with culture shock and loneliness. They were the only Americans in an area the size of South Carolina.

Haas bared down against porn, praying, fasting, and reading Scripture, but his deliverances (yes, plural and many times over) from porn didn't last. Instead, his behavior escalated to affairs and prostitutes. When his secret struggle was discovered, he was recalled abruptly. But he was also provided a path to restoration.

Today, with more than twenty years of restoration and freedom behind him, Troy believes he better understands why many in ministry struggle with any number of issues, including pornography.

"What makes anyone vulnerable in leadership is not taking your own personal journey and understanding where you're vulnerable," Troy told me. "A lot of people who end up in professional ministry roles do so because they care—because they have their own hurts that they are overcoming. They want to give back. They don't want other people to be hurt the way they have been hurt."

It is often said that "hurt people hurt people." My dad was a Pentecostal preacher who spoke in tongues, took food to the hungry, and picked up hitchhikers just to share the gospel; he was also violent, demeaning, and domineering with his family. I believe he preached, prayed over others, and served God because he wanted others to know the salvation he had received during his service in the US Army. I can navigate Scripture well because my dad played it consistently on records in our home, but he had demons that he never excised with the support of others. My uncle said as a punishment, my grandfather once strapped my dad to a dog leash in their backyard, where he was fed from a dog bowl and slept outside. Though traumatized and wounded, these events were secreted away and ignored. "The fathers have eaten sour grapes, and the children's teeth are set on edge" (Jeremiah 31:29).

"While it is very biblical to give back the comfort we have received, if we've never really received comfort in the first place, we're going to be a sitting duck in ministry," Haas said. "If I'm going to set out to partner with God in saving the world, then I need to know where my wounds are because, I promise you, the enemy does know and was there when the wounds happened. If I underestimate my wounds, they will take me down."

Imagine that I shatter my leg in a car accident; I need a skilled person to support it with a rod and to place it in a cast. Even with that expert care, it will take time to heal. If I try to fix it myself with a splint and duct tape, my leg will likely reform but will function in a weakened and distorted way, causing me to limp through life in some fashion. I'm surviving but not thriving as I would have with help.

"So many souls are like that," Haas said. "Their hearts have been shattered by what's been done to them. But if you don't receive care, then your heart may somehow knit together in a functioning way because God created us to survive, but it won't be whole, and it won't be supported."

Prime Targets

In 1777, General David Morgan organized the 11th Virginia Regiment, and he filled its ranks with 400 of the finest marksmen he could find. The start of the American Revolutionary War was a time when officers still came from the so-called "gentlemen's class" and were not to be targeted like the poor saps they led. Morgan made his mark in the history of sniper warfare when he ordered sharpshooter Timothy Murphy to shoot British General Simon Fraser, who was rallying his troops to crush the American forces. Fraser's death turned the tide of the Battle of Bemis Heights. Though only one man, he was worth a regiment of troops in the fight.[86]

Satan has his sights set on you and every leader on your team because when he takes down a leader, he takes out a multitude of troops. Jesus said, ". . . it is written, 'I will strike the shepherd, and the sheep will be scattered'" (Mark 14:27b, Zechariah 13:7).

People have a habit of pinning their inspiration on ministry leaders rather than God. When a pastor or church leader falls, the whole church hurts, causing pain and despair that can send shockwaves through the faithful as well as those on the periphery of the Church.

Helping the staff members in your church find safety, healing, and corrective heart surgery may be among the most impactful services you can give, not only to your team but also to your entire congregation.

The Ambush Is Hidden in Plain Sight

Haas said earlier that Satan not only knows our wounds, but he was also there when they happened. You've likely heard similar statements, but it's worth repeating. You and every member of your team have been studied closely and an ambush is waiting.

When we think of Satan prowling like a lion, seeking whom he may devour (Peter 5:8), it's easy to think of a lion sitting on its haunches ready to leap at its unsuspecting prey. Certainly, that is part of Satan's plan. As a Church of the Nazarene superintendent of missions in Southeast Asia, Dr. Michael McCarty recalled how prostitutes in Bangkok would flash known Thai pastors in what seemed like a game of "trap the Christian."

But often, Satan's tactics are subtle, even mundane, aimed to push the faithful to a weakened state. We are all more susceptible to our deepest struggles when we're hungry, angry, lonely, exhausted, stressed, and anxious.

The lion chooses the adolescent antelope as easier prey, rather than chasing the alpha bull, unless the bull becomes wounded and weakened. When captured, the average World War II American POW was about five inches taller and thirty to forty pounds heavier than his Japanese counterpart, but that imbalance changed quickly with starvation, deprivation, and disease.

Though hurts, history, and hang-ups are often well-hidden, the common threats that weaken Christian leaders are often laid bare for everyone to see and thus taken for granted. These pits are so common, most people ignore their power. We underestimate what many Christian leaders navigate daily.

Here are just a few examples. Missionaries face loneliness, anonymity, changes in cultural norms, long-term stress, and unmet needs. They face sickness without modern hospitals, changes in climate, political and cultural hostility, and many more unexpected stressors. Pastors and leaders deal with many of those same issues, while also counseling people through complex and draining crises. Men and women in spiritual leadership are always on-call, with many missed opportunities to disconnect from the underlying pressures. Throw in personal family struggles (because every family has them), the strains of balancing church and personal budgets, and other conflicts, and you discover the traps for anxiety, stress, and depression.

The aforementioned Barna pastors survey found: "Almost half faced depression, while one in five pastors has struggled with an addiction—most commonly, to porn."[87] Because of the stressors pastors face, the allure of escapism and unhelpful self-soothing is a real threat that might come in the form of food, drink, porn, and even ministry.

What a Shame

Shame can be draining. Most pastors, missionaries, and leaders are acutely aware they are held to a higher standard biblically. They are also aware that others hold them to account with specific Bible verses, which must indicate that good and holy Church leaders *never* fail.

Falling short, even briefly, of these high standards for porn can bring immense shame to a Christian leader. A servant leader (or a leader in training), who carries the hefty weights of shame and fear, typically believes he is the only one struggling in his community of peers. So he repents and promises God in private that this last porn session is the final one. But if it doesn't work, he remains stuck in a cycle of shame and acting out, partly because he lacks the healing of confession to others and the support of a community.

Despite the terror of being found out, a person in Christian service may not seek help for several reasons: 1) he may lose his position, wasting years of study and feelings of purpose; 2) he will lose face, not only with the Church body, but also with his spouse, family, friends, and his greater community; 3) he may fear his spouse will divorce him; 4) his income will vanish, and 5) he may be unaware of available help. You can likely add to this list.

One of the surprising companions to shame is perfectionism, Haas said. Many leaders either grew up with or adopted a Christian performance mindset; they must achieve, and failure is not an option. It can be reinforced with fear-based religion and accountability questions with yes/no answers in hierarchal relationships. The perfectionist's self-worth and value to God and to people are based on adherence to rules and achievement. Many people view perfectionism as a positive trait, but research shows that perfectionistic tendencies are strong predictors of depression, anxiety, stress, and even suicide.[88] The perfectionist leans on their self-discipline paired with religiosity, rather than God's immense grace. A perfectionist's confession is a secret conversation with God because they fear examining failures with the support of others.

When they fail, as we all do in some way, self-loathing gains even more power. Because of the perfectionist's pride, their failures become skeletons in a secret closet, rather than a treasure chest of insight, experience, and renewal.

For those who have experienced temptations and shame regarding porn, there is a better way forward.

Consider the Ant

For some leaders reading this book, you recognize the draw of pornography. That draw might be a strong pull or something that feels like distant gravity, tugging ever so lightly on the edges of your heart and mind at the least opportune times.

In times of strength, people tell themselves, "This kind of moral failure won't happen to me." Unfortunately, there is a long list of celebrity pastors and unknown servants who simply pushed against the draws of sexual sin in private, without support, and they fell with a splat.

When our marriages are tightly bonded, when our spiritual hearts are inspired, when the sin of our past seems distant, that is the very time to prepare for an assault.

Proverbs 6:6–8 tells how the ant prepares in summer before the times become tough in winter.

Address the temptations you have felt in the past. Consider how sexual sin has impacted your heart before. Then, prepare before the next assault begins. Don't wait for the time when you and your spouse are distant or when the stress of service to others seems overwhelming. Certainly, recognize when you are under attack, but don't wait to prepare your defenses at the time of an incursion.

Billy Graham's longevity in ministry was protected because he gathered his closest friends in 1948 to formulate what would become known as the Modesto Manifesto. It yielded him to oversight and accountability to protect him from four traps in ministry—finances, immorality, an independent spirit, and exaggerated success. This accord is probably best known for the Billy Graham rule: "From that day on, I did not travel, (nor) meet or eat alone with a woman other than my wife."

Many pastors install accountability software not only to guard themselves online but also to serve as an example to others. Every office at Covenant Eyes has windows and nearly every computer at Covenant Eyes faces a direction that fellow workers can view. (A few mature and older women who view pornography to improve our software are exempt and have ready access to counselors.) Wayne Johnson, who we met at the beginning of this chapter, conducts his Bible study from the kitchen table these days, a single boundary among many more in his recovery that he wishes he had put in place before his fall.

Guard your life and ministry in community. Ecclesiastes 4:9–12 reminds us that we are most vulnerable alone. In brief, these three practices can have a major impact on anyone's life, including those in Christian service: 1) Confront your weaknesses in a safe community with godly counsel; 2) Seek healing and nurture your weakness with godly companions; 3) Keep your freedom by giving it away to others.

"The reality is this, no matter what we struggle with, the path forward is with real and authentic relationships with God, ourselves, and one another," Troy said. "I would encourage pastors to find someone that they can be real and authentic with. There is no other way than to look at my own life, my own heart, lay it on the table, and say 'I'm going to find somewhere, someplace, somehow, that I can be honest, authentic, and real.' And when that happens, I at least know I'm headed in the right direction, and God can work and God can move."

Chapter 11

Porn's Impact within Christian Ministry (Part 2)

You demonstrate biblical love when you take steps
to restore a fellow-believer overtaken in sin.
John C. Broger

D
r. Eric Geiger attended his first ministry conference at just twenty-two years old and heard a dire warning.

A conference speaker told Geiger and the audience of leaders that he started in ministry with twenty friends and wrote down each of their names, but year after year, he scratched through the leaders' names as they were disqualified from ministry because of sin. Only two were left. Geiger hoped his generation of leaders would somehow be different, but the senior pastor of Mariners Church in Irvine, California, has seen many of his contemporaries fall.

Just down the hill from the main worship center at Mariners, across a pond where fountains spritz the California wind, is a square building filled with classrooms. Nearly every day here, people meet in small groups to work through the messes their lives have become. They are guided by others who found healing through Christ. Care and Recovery Pastor Jack West, a former alcoholic and drug addict, oversees a broad sphere of support groups, where I met former church leaders and lay ministers alike who seek God's grace and wisdom to restore their lives.

No one either points a finger at the former leaders or gives them deference. Here, everyone is on an even battlefield seeking healing.

Geiger, who also authored *Simple Church* with Thom S. Rainer, wrote on his blog that local churches typically hold one of three views on the restoration of pastors and church leaders:

1. **No restoration to ministry.** An elder must be "blameless" or "above reproach" as directed by 1 Timothy. A scarlet letter lasts for a lifetime, at least regarding ministry.
2. **Immediate restoration.** Based on how Moses led his people after murdering an Egyptian and how David remained king and wrote Scripture after adultery, murder, and lying, a church leader who repents should be immediately restored to his post.
3. **Deliberate restoration.** Under this view, a plan of action is created to restore a pastor or leader, and at its conclusion, the person can and should be restored.[89]

You may have drawn yourself already into one of those three camps, and you can also point to the dangers within any of those options. While the three strategies above would include restoration to Christ, I feel they offer only a shaky hope. Option 1 often leads to abandonment; Option 2 offers a forgive-and-forget mentality that is ripe for repeat behavior influenced by pride and self-centeredness, and Option 3 is like a mathematical formula that leads to an expected result.

~~Training~~ Renewing Grounds

I ask you to consider a fourth option.

I do so only because of the relationships I enjoy and the witness I have seen among former leaders who fell to sexual sin but who repented and found healing and a closeness to Christ and a filling of the Holy Spirit that is inspiring. My friends, Troy Haas, Mark Denison, Dr. Clarence Shuler, and Nate Larkin, are just a few ministry leaders who fell and whom many Christians would have written off as depraved. Today, these men are leading in new ways and helping thousands of people live in purity and wholeness. Larkin wrote *Samson and the Pirate Monks* and founded the Samson Society, which provides in-person and online support groups for Christian men. Dr. Shuler has written more than a half-dozen books, provides marriage and men's seminars, and is a contributor to FamilyLife and other ministries. Through their ministry, There's Still Hope, Mark and Beth Denison are passionate partners in helping married couples weather the storms of sexual sin and renew their marriages rather than divorce.

In these examples, God wasn't finished with their lives and their service to the Kingdom.

Admittedly, I hesitate to include this chapter. It deserves a book of its own. The purpose of *The Healing Church* is not to provide a comprehensive plan for restoring a ministry leader, but when I think of the Church's important role in helping laypeople who struggle with porn and sexual brokenness, it would be an oversight to ignore restoring ministry leaders who wrestle with this sin as well. I will point to resources for additional guidance.

My description of Option 4 is an open concept similar to the other views mentioned above rather than a specific process. Leaving it as such provides room for the practices and standards of your denomination or theology. Instead of drawing diagrams and step-by-step directives, I will point to the commonalities and processes others have followed in their ministry restorations. Specific steps and themes indeed stand out. A loose framework and nuggets of wisdom are awaiting discovery in the experiences and stories of fallen ministry leaders who found healing, some of whom were also restored to ministry.

The Right Focus

The overriding theme among the processes in this sphere is centered on restoring the person to Christ first and foremost. No promise or focus is made on returning to ministry. This Option 4 might lead to faithful church members who spend the rest of their lives in the secular workforce, but it might lead to Kingdom-focused service.

Only God knows.

This uncertainty can be disconcerting for those removed from their posts, often because their identity has become intertwined with their ministry. As American Christians imitating our culture, we meet people for the first time and ask, "What do you do?" as though our worth in Christ is tied to our daily tasks and livelihoods. For a fallen leader, this can be exceptionally painful because of the shame of falling from the higher standard demanded of those in Christian service.

They have also earned credentials, spent years focused on ministry, and worked to maintain a reputation even under false pretenses. You will recall from the last chapter that Wayne found his self-worth in how others saw him in ministry, even if it was a façade. Wayne craved affirmation, not only because of pride but also because of self-doubt.

Restoring the heart has more value than restoring a title. "For what does it profit a man to gain the whole world and forfeit his soul" (Mark 8:36).

In the book *Restoring the Fallen: A Team Approach to Caring, Confronting & Reconciling*, a group of six authors recount their journey toward restoring a Christian leader. They hold Galatians 6:1 as their guiding verse: "Brothers, if anyone is caught in any transgression, you who are spiritual should restore him in a spirit of gentleness. Keep watch on yourself, lest you too be tempted."

From their experiences, they landed on four aspects of the restoration process.

1. The person being restored must be truthful regarding their sin. No lying, including omissions, hiding, or minimizing their sin.
2. Complete repentance.
3. Establishing or re-establishing spiritual principles and disciplines.
4. Restoring and making amends as possible without causing more damage and harm.

Pain Is Part of the Process

Christian counselor Earl Wilson's pastoral friend was shocked at Earl's confession, Earl wrote in *Restoring the Fallen*. The pastor recoiled, thinking not only of the ramifications to Earl but also about the pain it would cause Earl's wife Sandy and their children. Then the pastor considered the impact on the seminarians who attended Earl's classes and on the throngs of people who attended his speaking sessions at conferences and who read his prose. [90]

Earl's confession was prompted by the discovery of his affair with one of his counseling clients. But his full confession revealed ten years of stewing in pornography, which led to massage parlors, nude bars, and prostitutes. The pastor's knee-jerk reaction was to keep this confession private to spare others, and even Earl, agony.

But Earl's confession to his pastor friend was secondary. His original confessor, and only after discovery, was his mentor Paul Friesen, who knew the truth sets us free (John 8:32). Paul and the other members of Earl's newly formed spiritual care team knew that Earl and those in his sphere would feel a great deal of pain.

The explosion of sexual sin always creates a blast zone. The closer one is to the individual, the greater the damage of the detonation. The sinner isn't the only one blown apart. Family, friends, the local church, and others are struck by the shrapnel. But pouring dirt over wounds to hide them only creates infection and disease. Only when there is a clear understanding of the damage can healing begin and reparation made. "Restoration is a very painful process, because sin brings painful consequences," Earl wrote.

He lost the façade of his reputation, relationships were damaged, and his career and income were curtailed. He faced shame, depression, anxiety, fear, and uncertainty, and he grieved losses caused by his sin. But taking responsibility and submitting his heart and mind to the guidance of spiritual mentors, set Earl on a path where he could learn to be honest with himself, others, and God.

Lead the Willing

After a nationally known leader and author's moral failure cost him his family, his ministry, and his job, he sought the guidance of Pastor James Reeves at City on a Hill church in Fort Worth. Pastor James listened while the fallen leader blamed the church, co-workers, friends, and even God for his failings. After a moment of silence, Pastor James told the author and speaker, "I don't think there is much that can be done to help you right now because you have not come to brokenness. You are still trying to blame others for your failure. You haven't come to the end of yourself. When you do, we'll be here to help you in any way we can."

"Pride goes before destruction, and a haughty spirit before a fall" (Proverbs 16:18).

The Church has witnessed too many church leaders collapse in moral failure only to suggest that they have repented, and all is well. In their arrogance and pride, they reject church discipline and guidance. Fallen leaders must consent to surgery for the healing to be effective, and there is nothing you or Pastor James can do for those too caught up in their personal grandiosity and false identity.

When people fall, they are their own worst advisors. Even when they recognize their sin, they tend to deflect, blame, and minimize. You will recall from earlier chapters how Darlene used her good deeds to feel better about her ongoing sin. Left to their own advice, the fallen make poor choices. "A person who has chosen to pursue sin must be willing to be carefully scrutinized and guided by others," Earl wrote of his journey. "Restorees are in no position to make independent decisions regarding their restoration. They must follow, not lead."

Form a Spiritual Care Team

When failure is disclosed, the fallen often watch their friends turn away. If a person caught in sin cannot trust themselves and their friends aren't willing or equipped to help, to whom can they turn?

In *Restoring the Fallen*, the writers suggest a spiritual care team should be made up of four to six people. They should be Christians who emulate the men found in Acts 6:3—"of good repute, full of the Spirit and of wisdom . . ." Both Earl and his wife Sandy had a voice in selecting the team because of the great need for trust.[91]

I also believe a senior church leader should have a voice in the selection process because they likely know church members who are a good fit.

Earl had two married couples at the nucleus of his care team. But this makeup of men and women doesn't fit some denominations. Troy Haas's care team was made up only of men, which reflected the more conservative views of his denomination. Both of these teams worked well, but Earl benefited from the wives on his team who helped him understand the rollercoaster of emotions his wife experienced.

Before a person agrees to be part of a restoration effort, each team member needs to understand the immense commitment involved. Time spent listening, praying, guiding, and caring can take its toll. Both Troy and Earl spent more than three years meeting with their care teams. These spiritual restorers will experience strains on their emotions, and they may hear gory details that rob them of innocence.

As the authors walked through Earl's restoration process, they discovered six purposes of a spiritual care team.

1. **Spiritual Health.** Though a professional counselor may be enlisted for emotional maladies, the spiritual care team uncovers the spiritual roots of sin and helps the person become grounded in their relationship with God.
2. **Body Life.** Within the Body of Christ, we have different gifts, such as intercession, discernment, admonishment, encouragement, mercy, and serving. As a care team, each member brings something to the process of restoration that "can unleash God's love and power to the restoree."

3. **Accountability and Sensitivity.** This one is tricky because of our fallen self-centeredness. The person under care may not realize how they fool or blame others, including a spouse, for their behaviors and sin. This is more than asking a list of yes/no questions in isolation. This requires deeper conversations that might include family members, as appropriate, and the team will act as an advocate for the injured spouse and family members.

4. **Penetrating Denial and Clarifying Reality.** A fallen leader may be a powerful person and a gifted orator and debater, one who might intimidate others. A team is less intimidated and can better sort through distortions. "A spouse or family member who might otherwise be too wounded, confused, or insecure to stand alone will benefit from the strength and support of the team."

5. **Synergy.** A team benefits from the wisdom of the group. "It is an awesome responsibility to have someone voluntarily put himself or herself under your care for a period of time, so the combined wisdom and consensus of the group, led by the Spirit of God, is very important."

6. **Intercession.** No one person can pray constantly and consistently, but "praying for God's mercy, strength, and restoration is probably the most critical function of the team." As the authors point out, "Restoration ministry is divine in nature and is characterized above all by grace. It cannot be driven by anything apart from consistent intercession."[92]

Christ Restores

"Remember that Christ mended the wounds of a broken fisherman named Peter and how He restored him to feed His sheep (John 21:15–17). And don't forget the story of John Mark. After Paul rejected him, Barnabas worked with him and brought about spiritual growth. In the end, he became useful to Paul.

"When the actions of the disciplined staff person exhibit remorse and repentance, then hold him or her up as a trophy of grace to others. After all, Peter became the rock on which Christ built His church."[143]

Additional Support

The spiritual care team and the fallen leader need support from the local church, a pastor, and often a professional counselor.

For churches with a limited staff, a pastor should not be part of the care team for three reasons, the authors of *Restoring the Fallen* point out. First, few pastors' schedules can absorb the time demanded. Second, it allows more than one care team to be fielded at a time. Third, the family that is part of the crisis needs the pastor to fulfill his role with them. That might be compromised if the pastor is part of the care team.

Also, a fallen leader who has exhibited sexual compulsive behavior would benefit from a Christian counselor who is certified in sex addiction. These specialties provide the specific training needed to address compulsive porn use and sexual addiction. The person being restored might also sign a waiver, allowing the spiritual care team and the therapist to communicate as is appropriate.

A Christian sex addiction counselor can also help a church decide if a leader should step down from his post or continue working within limitations. I am not prescribing that every ministry leader who has watched pornography has to step down from their role. It's important to examine the depth of their involvement with pornography. If they are facing compulsive behavior with porn (a Christian sex addiction counselor can help you define this) or if physical adultery has taken place, the ministry leader should vacate or be removed from their ministry role to focus on their healing. But the denomination, ministry organization, and the local church have responsibilities to restore to the Body of Christ those who are willing to accept guidance and discipline.

Consequences, Not Abandonment

So much can be said on this topic, but let's follow Troy Haas's journey to see what this process looked like for him. From the last chapter, you'll remember how Troy and Melissa Haas were missionaries in Africa when his sexual sins surfaced. The International Mission Board promptly called him back to the United States. With Melissa left behind to pack their belongings while nearly nine months pregnant, Troy's missionary overseers directed him to a residential treatment facility in California.

Troy looks back amazed at the gift that the International Mission Board provided. First, in his sinful mindset, Troy agrees that he did not belong in ministry. Second, instead of casting him aside, the missionary leaders sought to restore him to a right relationship with Christ. It was *not* an effort to restore him to mission work. That was off the table. But through their support, Troy took his first steps toward being honest with himself and someone else. For the first time in his life, he found a safe place to spill every part of his story. With guidance, Troy and Melissa dug through core issues, not only for Troy's compulsive behavior, but also for the core issues that impacted their marriage, their daily living, and their relationships with Christ. It set a foundation for their healing.

The problem was that the support could last only so long. They had a basic foundation that stabilized their marriage and a path to continue the healing journey, but they didn't know what to do next. They considered staying in California, where they had developed a community of spiritual support, or returning to be near family in Texas. Both ideas lacked appeal.

Unexpectedly, the couple was invited to First Baptist Church Woodstock (Georgia) to participate in a fledgling effort that extended God's grace and love to fallen ministry leaders, who often feel lonely, abandoned, and worthless. Through this program, Troy and Melissa were provided counseling, basic financial support, and a place to live. Troy received help in finding a secular job so he had steady work and could provide for his family. They were welcomed into a weekly small group through the church. Their new Sunday School class threw Melissa a baby shower soon after their arrival and volunteered as babysitters so the couple could enjoy date nights. No finger-wagging came their way. No whispering conversations halted as they walked into church throughout the week. They were welcomed without condemnation.

A spiritual care team guided Troy's renewal. Because of Woodstock's large staff, two pastors served on Troy's team, and they suggested spiritually mature laymen from whom Troy selected three. Troy yielded his life decisions and his recovery journey to five men who met as a group every two weeks and over three years, they gradually reduced the meetings to once per month. These meetings were in addition to the counseling sessions and ongoing accountability conversations.

There was no expectation and no opportunity for Troy to return to ministry. He and Melissa had one job at the church: to work on their recovery in all its aspects so that they could enjoy a right relationship with Christ. One aspect of this quest was for Troy to apologize and make amends as possible to those that had been hurt by his sin. His care team arranged calls and in-person visits with pastors and church leaders who had released their platforms for Troy and Melissa to speak and raise funds for their mission work in years past. Troy apologized and confessed to missionary colleagues and missionary leaders with whom he had worked.

Throughout this period, the Haases lived life like most church members. Troy made a living as a clerk earning $12 an hour before finding a more lucrative sales job at a cell phone store, where he would become the general manager of the small company. He and Melissa worked on daily living, their recovery, and their marriage and dove headlong into the fellowship of the Church.

"One of the things I really appreciated about Troy was that he fought for his relationship with God, me, and the Body of Christ," Melissa said. "He didn't give up. It would have been very easy to give in to hopelessness, depression, and shame—and he would struggle with those things—but there was enough hope alive in him that it enabled a path toward recovery. If our mind is hopeless, if we feel hopeless, we're more likely to revert to our old coping strategies and fall back into our sinful ways."

Through the authenticity that Troy and Melissa learned in their recovery journey, their story became known to others in the large church. After sixteen months of recovery work, Troy found men in the church coming to him and talking about their struggles with pornography. As a layperson and with permission from his spiritual care team and the church, Troy started a small group called Walking Free. Calling on the experiences of his ongoing recovery journey as well as his seminary training, he wrote two sets of curricula for the class. (After many revisions and fine-tuning, these workbooks are called *Building for Freedom* and *Walking in Freedom*.) The men practiced honesty and accountability and supported each other to fight sin successfully, which brought even more men to their ranks.

Of course, these men had wives who were frustrated, angry, and disappointed with the impact pornography was having on their marriages. Melissa knew that pain all too well. So as a layperson, she started a small group for wives. She also wrote a curriculum called *The Journey* to help wives heal.

"God calls all of us to minister out of our stories, out of what He has done in our lives," Troy said. "But [at this time] we're not vocational ministers. We're just laypeople. It was so encouraging to realize God loves me because I'm His child. And it was so freeing to be able to just serve God and serve others out of the overflow of that relationship, not because I was paid to do it, not because I am supposed to do it, not because I went to seminary to do it, but just because it was out of the overflow of that relationship with God."

After Troy and Melissa had been at Woodstock for three years, she asked her husband if he could do anything, what would he want to do? He was making a good salary in 2002 as a general manager, but if he could do anything? Without hesitation, Troy said, he would love to use their experiences to help fallen pastors and missionaries.

Unexpectedly, the following week Woodstock's leadership asked Troy to do just that as the director of Restoration Ministries, a position—and a department—that was brand new. His job was to create spaces, opportunities, and resources for those impacted by addiction at Woodstock. Part of that effort was to serve fallen pastors, missionaries, and ministry leaders through a new ministry called City of Refuge.

Troy levitated with excitement. Though Troy wanted to say yes, he had to ask permission twice. Of course, he had to ask Melissa. But Troy had given his rights to return to ministry to his spiritual care team. They also would have to agree that the situation and the timing were right. And they had to agree unanimously.

"I just got offered my dream job, and yet I've given this group of men veto power over my dream job," Troy said. "But I trusted them, and I trusted the process."

The oversight these godly men held over Troy was important to Melissa too. These men had come to know every part of Troy's story and his recovery, including that serving as a missionary had propped up his feelings of self-worth. He had clung to his identity as a missionary while in that service, and it had given him a sense of value and recognition. It even covered his feelings of shame; because if he did enough good then maybe he could make up for his sin. Of course, these feelings were hidden to him as a missionary and were only understood with deeper reflection with his spiritual care team.

Separately, the stakes of returning to ministry were high. Melissa and Troy suspected everyone would be watching him. Every decision would be held to the greatest scrutiny. "It helped me know that Troy's desire wasn't just a fleshly pattern of going back into ministry to get a personal need met, to somehow redeem himself after moral failure," Melissa said. "Having these men say, 'He's ready; he's done the hard work, and we see true heart change,' was important to me as a wife because any time you enter ministry for Jesus, the enemy shows up big time."

Troy's mentors gave him the nod, each one.

Over the next fifteen years, Restoration Ministries served not only FBC Woodstock but also other churches with recovery programs. More than 250 men at a time attended Walking Free groups and a comparable number of women attended Journey groups at Woodstock.

Separately, more than 300 pastors, missionaries, and ministry leaders went through an eighteen-month City of Refuge program, following many of the steps that Troy took himself. In caring for pastors, the program provided for up to fifteen families at a time. They received housing, childcare, job search support, access to support groups and church small groups, as well as marital, group, and individual counseling. Of course, each former leader met with their own spiritual care team.

"Beautifully, God called some of those men back into ministry," Troy said. "And for the ones that didn't return to ministry, it was obvious they didn't belong in ministry. The goal was to see lives restored, relationships restored, and marriages restored. If a guy went back into ministry, that was bonus extra credit, but it wasn't the goal of the program."

In 2004, due to insurance reasons, the residential treatment programs became a separate entity called HopeQuest Ministry Group, where Troy is CEO and Melissa serves on the team of counselors. It has grown over the years and is a Christ-centered, accredited, residential addiction program near its founding church that also offers outpatient treatment and support groups. The City of Refuge program continues through FBC Woodstock with help from HopeQuest, but for financial reasons, serves just a few fallen Christian leaders at a time. However, about 20 percent of HopeQuest's clients in its twelve-week residential treatment plan are pastors, missionaries, and ministry leaders.

Right Relationships

In America today, pornography is more pervasive than at any time in history, and young men and women entering Christian service have been impacted by porn in some way. Church leaders should evaluate and mentor these young men and women when they come under their wings. Some will be in a current struggle, and others may believe they are immune. Both need support.

Looking back, Troy and Melissa see their younger selves as a man and woman with credentials, but they were unprepared in many ways, including in the area of spiritual formation. They were unaware of their emotional and spiritual immaturity. For example, they overidentified with, and drew significance in, how others saw them through their ministry. Much of their identity and personal security was wrapped up in being missionaries rather than finding their identities in Christ.

"All of those things, in addition to my addiction issues, really contributed to a heart that wasn't free," Troy said. "I look back and realize nobody really knew me. I was admired by my peers, but nobody really knew me. And because of that, I was very vulnerable and susceptible to getting deeper into my sin and struggle. I'm just challenging guys to find a safe place as a leader, as a student, and press those around you to be honest, authentic, and real in relationships. It doesn't get easier, and I wish someone had challenged me as a seminary student, working on my M.Div., because I think that a lot would have been different in my ministry."

Now, in leading fallen leaders to restoration, Troy points to five areas that must be whole. These areas of spiritual health are significant not only for those seeking restoration but also for those guarding their ministry against assault.

Haas lists the five key relationships in this order:

1. A right relationship with yourself.
2. A right relationship with God.
3. A right relationship with your spouse and immediate family.
4. A right relationship with the church.
5. A right relationship with ministry.

"If you're not right with the first four relationships, then one's relationship with ministry will never be right," Troy said.

Chapter 12

Wrong Answer. Try Again.

Compulsive sexual behaviors may be common,
but that doesn't make them any less painful and destructive.
Joann Condie, professional counselor and author of
Aftershock, Overcoming His Secret Life with Pornography

S arah felt her body shaking and wondered if her pastor noticed. Maybe the cushions of his office guest chair absorbed the earthquake of emotions that seemed to rattle her bones. Reassured by his sermons and his trustworthy demeanor, she had finally built the courage to ask for help. This could be the turning point, she hoped, because the pain and hiding had continued too long.

She had rehearsed how she would describe the brokenness she felt in her marriage, how her husband Andy's pornography use sliced at her heart and tormented her mind with questions about her worth. She tried to be supportive, even sympathetic, when Andy apologized for the parade of porn on his phone and computer, but as quick as a whip, his apologies would turn to blame and how she was overreacting. They had been faithful members of the church for a decade, and their pastor called pornography unequivocal sin. But then what? Why couldn't Andy stop looking at porn? When they had sex, why did he seem to be somewhere else? Why was she not enough? Who could help them?

The empathy and reassurance Sarah's pastor offered soothed her heart. She didn't know if anyone would understand her pain and roller coaster of emotions, but her pastor had listened. He had really listened. He asked questions. "How long had this been going on? What did Andy say about his porn use? Does anyone else know?" The pastor would call Andy and pray with him. Surely, this was the long-awaited fresh start that she and Andy so desperately needed.

The next day, the pastor's wife texted and asked Sarah if she could stop by to chat. Though she gave her approval, Sarah wondered if her pastor told his wife about her husband's porn use? Was that okay? Would others now know? When the pastor's wife arrived, she was accompanied by the assistant pastor's wife as well, and they each carried a small box. Receiving each box in wonder, she felt her gut punched when she opened the first lid. Lingerie. Each box provided sexy outfits for her to wear. She got the message: it was her fault that her husband looked at porn. She wasn't enough. Her pastor believed it and, apparently, so did the pastor's wife, and assistant pastor's wife, and likely the assistant pastor, and who knows who else.

Focus on the Family counselor Rob Jackson recalls this story during a roundtable interview with counselors in Colorado Springs. Dr. Russ Rainey nods his head and pipes up: "I probably have dozens of these stories." Dr. John Thorington joins the discussion, and the three counselors tell one story after another of how pastors are heaping spiritual harm and bad advice on the gaping wounds of wives wounded by their husband's porn use.

This chapter and the next might be tough for many pastors to read, especially if the story above sounds familiar. By no means do I aim to throw anyone under the bus. Simply put, most pastors receive little preparation to address the legitimate needs of spouses betrayed by porn strongholds. Pastors often rely on personal intuition, discussions within their spheres, and the general marriage books they have read, and, unfortunately, they have often been misled. How a husband's porn use impacts a wife are details pastors didn't learn in seminary, and it's extremely rare to hear a discussion on how porn use impacts wives at a denominational conference or pastors' retreat.

I aspire to better equip you for conversations with both men and women whose spouses struggle with porn. In this chapter, I focus on men and sex and why sex is not the answer to finding freedom from porn. I'll also recommend time-tested resources for additional support and study. In the next chapter, I have asked a trusted colleague and author, Dr. Sheri Keffer, to take you on a deeper dive. She knows the pain that pornography causes to a marriage firsthand, and as a professional Christian counselor, speaker, radio host, and author, she is among the very best in her field.

But first, let's return to my roundtable interview with three Christian counselors. The stories they tell are commonplace among those I've heard from counselors across North America. It's important to review these stories because the advice given might resemble that from a member of your pastoral team or denomination. You can serve as an agent of change within your range of influence, and these stories may assist you as you teach others.

Dr. Rainey remembers one wife who came to him for advice. She had first gone to her pastor because he shared a close friendship with her husband, who was also a leader in the church. She described her husband's ongoing pornography use to the pastor and wondered if he could mentor and help him. The pastor responded simply; she needed to take better care of her husband sexually and pray for him.

It was soon discovered that the husband was sexting with a woman on the praise team and also hid a private profile on a dating site. Despite these issues and the risk of STDs to her, she was supposed to pray and deliver more sex. A few months later, the husband left his wife and their three kids, and he also left the church.

"Now, the pastor will rarely speak to this woman when he passes her in a church hallway," Dr. Rainey said. "The pastor completely took his friend's part and gave her what I would call a 'good-old-boy' approach, 'Honey, you just need to take better care of him sexually.'

"I had to say to her, 'Do you think this is a form of spiritual abuse?'" Dr. Rainey said. "That was the first time she broke down and just wept. She knew her husband was abusing her in a sexual way. But she never connected the dots to say, 'My pastor has now spiritually abused me.'"

Jackson recalled a situation where a husband frequented massage parlors and gorged on pornography for years. When he and his wife dined at restaurants, his wife noticed how his eyes wandered over the bodies of the waitresses that served them and how he flirted. She told multiple stories to her pastor about immoral and inappropriate behavior.

"The pastor's advice was for her to ask her husband with some regularity, 'Are we okay?' That's it. And she is supposed to take her husband's word. This is without the husband confessing, repenting, or without the husband going into treatment. Just ask, 'Are we okay?'" Jackson said.

After hearing similar stories from women he counseled, Dr. Thorington began asking women if he could speak to their pastors. One pastor was defensive initially but agreed to meet. With just a little review and training, the pastor repented of the advice he offered and invited Dr. Thorington to teach at his church and start programs to fight the impact of porn in marriages.

"A lot of pastors don't understand the nature of addiction, and more sex isn't the answer," Thorington said. "It's like saying to a wife whose husband has a problem with alcohol, 'Just give him some more alcohol.' It's ridiculous."

Reframing the More Sex Bias

As we dive in, please allow me to relay some basic facts to make everyone mad at me at once. In this stanza, I'm walking barefoot on the broken glass of political correctness.

Hear me out.

Most people serving in pastoral and church leadership today are men.[93] It's a simple fact. (I am not raising a biblical or theological debate. I'll leave that to your denomination or church.) As men, we often see our world through our male perspectives. Further, besides my wife, my closest friends and the majority of my deepest discussions happen with other men. I suspect that, for the men reading, we share this in common. And thus, teaching and views among pastoral leaders and even lay leaders often weigh unevenly on male experiences and perspectives.

In play with this truth, overall men show greater sexual desire than women, and countless scientific studies confirm this truth.[94] Yes, women crave sex, too, and sometimes, more than their husbands. But, in general, men carry a bolder appetite for sex. Another simple truth: the vast majority of male pastors and leaders, like most men, have experienced the desire for sex when their wives lacked interest or were unavailable. Yes, I've been there too. When the timing and emotions were finally right, we enjoyed sex, and we as men felt a release of sexual tension.

So far, all facts, no judgments or additional explanations.

Now, let's cut to the crux of the problem. As male leaders in the church, we have often allowed our experiences of sexual desire, rejection, and release to cloud our judgment and our responsibilities, not only as men but also as followers of Christ. This has led to a false equation used widely in many churches that sex on tap is the simple answer to many marital issues, including defeating pornography use.

This false equation might have been reinforced in Christian marriage seminars or books. But even some of those authors and speakers are reevaluating and correcting misleading advice. For instance, Steve Arterburn told me that he revised *Every Man's Battle* in 2020 and will make more changes because the original version wrongly advised that a wife's sexuality can be used similarly to how methadone is used for a heroin addict. He also removed a section that described how a man craves sex every seventy-two hours because it was misleading. Though the book has sold five million copies since its release in 2000 and has helped many men create change, Arterburn said he is humble enough to admit where he and Fred Stoeker got it wrong.

Here are a few reasons why sex is not a prescriptive antidote for porn use, compulsive or not.

1. Prescribing sex for compulsive porn use and sexual behaviors pours gasoline on a house on fire. Sex doesn't satiate the porn user's desire for porn. Instead, he has sex and uses porn too.
2. This advice misdirects the responsibility of sin from the sinner. It even allows the porn user to say, "I wanted sex. I didn't get it, so I'm justified in using porn."
3. It fails to tell the one sinning to receive help for healing, accept discipline, and learn self-control (2 Peter 1:5–7, 1 Corinthians 9:25).

Here's the skinny. The vast majority of men who struggle habitually with porn began using porn at a young age, and they gave it lots of practice. If a wife tells you she discovered porn on her husband's devices a couple of times, rest assured, he watched porn many more times than she knows. Why? Because he's not stupid and usually covers his tracks. Through my journey and in hearing the personal stories of more than a thousand struggling men while serving at Covenant Eyes, I see a common theme. Before he was dating, he was using porn; while he was dating, he was using porn; if he had sex before marriage, he used porn as well; he proposed to his wife and used porn, and he entered marriage using porn. He's ashamed of his porn use and will lie about it if asked for details unless he has a safe place to tell his story. Even if there are periods of abstinence from using porn, it likely didn't last for as long as he says it did. He uses porn the same day or the same week when his wife says yes to sex, and he uses porn when she says no or is unavailable.

His use of porn isn't her fault. And her providing more sex won't solve his struggle with sin.

Dr. Keffer recalled discovering phone sex charges on a credit card statement during the first year of her marriage to a pastor. She was shocked by the February 13 date for the charge.

"Valentine's weekend—are you kidding me?" Keffer wrote in *Intimate Deception, Healing the Wounds of Sexual Betrayal.* "That was the time I taped red hearts to the wall, cooked Cornish game hens for the first time, and surprised him at the door dressed in hot-pink lingerie. It didn't matter what I did, how I cooked, or what I wore. It was never enough."[95]

Sex or Abstinence?

When porn and sexual behavior rip apart the seams of a marriage, most Christian counselors and Christian sex addiction ministries will prescribe a period of abstinence rather than more sex. That period of abstinence from self-sex and marital sex might last thirty, sixty, or ninety days, depending on the severity of the behavior and the damage done to the marriage.

For example, Faithful and True, founded by Mark and Debbie Laaser, requires patients to sign a ninety-day abstinence contract. Bethesda Workshops in Nashville maintains that ninety days of abstinence (and often longer) is crucial for marital healing. Pure Desire Ministries and Be Broken Ministries will qualify a period of abstinence, based on the individual and might suggest a commitment of thirty to ninety days during their sex addiction recovery programs.

The abstinence contract on the front end is entirely about neurochemical detox, counselors agree. The brain needs a reset of sexual expectations. Thirst for porn and sex may feel agonizing during the first fourteen to eighteen days, but after this period, the perceived torment lessens. After thirty days, men often say they gain confidence, feel greater focus in their daily lives, and grow more energetic.

So if it takes fourteen days to detox and thirty days to begin gaining confidence, why do sex addiction counselors commonly focus on ninety days of sexual abstinence? It has much to do with cultivating a mind focused on genuine intimacy. The porn user trained his brain to pine for personal and immediate gratification. He consumes the people in porn and bestows nothing in return. Especially for men, porn use becomes a selfish ritual that often extends to their marital life. Compulsive porn users commonly replay porn in their minds while having marital sex. At Covenant Eyes, we speak with many wives who erred or were coerced into allowing porn into their marital bedroom because these husbands can only reach climax while watching porn. While such activity isn't the norm, many men indeed practice sex just as they exploit porn to regulate their moods, feelings, and compulsive neurology. Recovery circles coined the term "vaginal masturbation" to describe how sex with one's spouse is used rather than given in intimacy. This sexual selfishness includes the overemphasis men can have on their sexual performance, pride, or fear about their prowess, and where sexual performance is equated to their manliness. Porn teaches these delusions emphatically.

Ministries and counselors that establish periods of abstinence also argue that the compulsive person has equated sex as equal to love and intimacy, and he needs to learn that sex conveys only one form of intimacy and love. The compulsive porn and sex user must learn to give, receive, and enjoy emotional and spiritual intimacy. Even if a person knows the mechanics of how to give these, emotional and spiritual intimacy might only be offered as currency in a down payment for sex. In other words, he only gives to manipulate his wife toward sex. Manipulation and coercion are opposites of the affection, bonding, and communion for which God designed sex.

Also, during a period of abstinence, be it thirty, sixty, or ninety days, a man discovers he won't die without sex or masturbation. He learns self-control through practice and with the support of a process guided by a mentor. He learns patience and manages sexual abstinence while giving his wife time to collect her bearings and physical and emotional safety. This patience and self-control are imperative for his future sobriety. In the past, he likely watched porn when his wife was on her period, was ill, or when one of them was apart from the other. In the past, he watched porn when he was angry, anxious, frustrated, or experienced other negative emotions. With time and a mapped recovery process, he discovers healthy habits to cope with life and manage his moods. He learns to express love through non-sexual touch, to bond through conversation or a long walk, and to express affection through a growing variety of means that are valued not only by his wife but also by himself. In living a porn-free life, he presents his wife with a gift of protection, safety, love, and honor.

While I've explained several benefits of a period of marital abstinence, a variety of counselors toss the abstinence contract aside in some cases. A minority of sex addiction counselors never require marital sexual abstinence for their recovery methods. They contend that a wife should have a say in whether she wants to have sex with her husband. Requiring her abstinence without consent robs her of her sexual voice. She might not want sex because of the trauma caused by her husband, and she should never be coerced, chastised, or made to feel guilty about her decision. Either way, these counselors say she deserves a voice.

Under the right circumstances and parameters, some counselors believe sex can help recovery and restoration through neurological and psychological bonding and attachment. It is often said that what you feed grows and what you starve dies. Under this neurological premise, brain pathways for porn are starved and intimate and caring sexual pathways are fed and grow.

But this model isn't without pitfalls. First, earlier paragraphs illustrate the value of a period of abstinence. Reengaging in sex immediately allows a man, who still owns a pornified brain, to use sex to regulate his moods, thoughts, and emotions. Second, sometimes women become hyper-sexual to manage their husband's compulsive behavior, but this isn't healthy for her or the marriage because it can last only so long before she becomes emotionally drained.

In either scenario, many counselors use polygraphs. Initially, the tool is used for a man to disclose his past behaviors well and with guidance, so as not to cause ongoing trauma to his wife. Additional polygraphs might be used to ascertain if he is honest about porn, masturbation, or sex with others, and the polygraphs can also provide his wife reassurance. She's been living with ongoing lies and deceit, and a polygraph might become her first step in knowing what is true and lay the groundwork for restored honesty. As well, if acting out escalated from porn to physical acts with other people, testing for STDs is required.

Not Done Yet

I hope you receive this chapter with the grace intended. While I've provided an overview of why sex isn't the answer, in the next chapter, Dr. Keffer writes with experience and precision why pornography tears at a spouse's heart. She provides a framework of the relational damage and why it's more impactful than you might suspect.

Chapter 13

When We Have the Right to Say, "Enough is Enough"

Chapter by Dr. Sheri Keffer

Healing is hard work. It's not for the faint of heart or the weak-willed.
Nancy Houston, Christian sex addiction counselor

There was standing room only.

That was no surprise since a deeply loved and respected world-renowned pastor, Chuck Swindoll, was leading a pastors' forum on *Doing Ministry, the Right Way for the Right Reason.* His captivatingly straight-as-an-arrow style of teaching peeled back the pages of 2 Corinthians 4. Quoting R.V.G. Tasker, he revealed three primary actions that must be rejected if any ministry is going to thrive with integrity and grow:

1. Hiding things that are shameful.
2. Doing things that are deceitful.
3. Corrupting things that are sacred.

He strikingly continued, "If you are living a lie, you're hurting your ministry. If you hear nothing else this morning, hear this: the greatest gift you can give your congregation is authenticity. Aside from Christ, the greatest gift you have to offer is your-self—the authentic person. Ministry is not about pretense, it is not about playing a role, it is not about looking good, it is not about appearing better than we are. That's a croc; that's nonsense, it's double-speak. Don't let yourself fall into that trap."[96]

The air in the room was motionless. Not a cough, recoil, or sigh. Eyes straight. Knees front-and-center, squared to the chair. Like being girded into an ill-fitting tuxedo, people barely breathed. It wasn't long before his transparency, stories, and playful anecdotes filled the room again. That's what happens when an audience comes to listen and a speaker comes to love them well.

As I listened, my mind drifted back to fourteen years earlier when my former husband Conner (not his real name) served as a pastor. We had lived for years with secrets, and it wasn't a surprise that porn and the pulpit didn't mix. We lost our church community and friends. People scattered—like crickets. We may as well have gotten leprosy. Conner and I were too ashamed to tell people what *really* happened. We continued in isolation as we blindly tried to keep food on the table and a roof over our heads. Hoping it would go away over time didn't help. It just got worse. Painfully, our marriage ended in divorce.

A New Pair of Glasses

After betrayed partners discover pornography, we often garner enough courage to reach out to our faith community and trusted spiritual leaders for support. Our pastor, priest, rabbi, or bishop often becomes our first call for help. We've been noticing our spouse or significant other has been spending hours on their phone, iPad, or computer and end up discovering they've been looking at pornography. We arrive at our place of worship looking for comfort and hoping no one will recognize us. Some of us report feeling seen and understood by clergy who "get it," while others describe being sorely misunderstood, deeply hurt, or dropped without further follow-up or support.

Well-meaning spiritual leaders often ask questions, like "What's been going on at home?" "How busy were you with your children before all this happened?" Or with a raised eyebrow they might say, "Maybe having more sex or buying new lingerie might help." The partner is bleeding out—and the subtle question behind the question is, *What's your part in this betrayal story? What have you been doing (or not doing) to make him feel like he needs to go elsewhere?*

I get it. For many of us, we're looking through the lens from which we've been trained. As a former pastor's wife, betrayed spouse, and counselor, I've apologized to partners I've worked with for using phrases like, "You're two heat-seeking missiles that found each other," or "stop snooper-vising" to describe their behavior. It even hurts today, as I say it. Yet when pornography compromises safety and trust, betrayed partners intuitively go on a truth-seeking mission to figure out what's going on. It's what we do when someone has taken something from us.

Imagine for a moment what it would be like if a trusted staff member stole money from your church's bank account? You wouldn't sit on your hands, wait, or wonder. You'd stop what you were doing and do some research. You'd call the bank and start looking for a money trail. You'd naturally wonder how much money had been taken and for how long. When it comes to ongoing pornography use, we feel the same way. How else can we find out what's true, when lying, hiding, and defensiveness are in the mix?

It Only Takes a Spark

Pornography is not merely glossy images in a magazine as it was decades ago. One of the largest virtual porn sites has 2,273 pages, hosting over half a million live HD videos. It's free content for anyone who's looking. Like an unwelcomed spark decimates a house by fire, it takes less than three seconds to get onto this porn site on a phone or computer. *There's no condom for the internet*, and sadly it's not a secret. The porn industry hosts an endless array of mortifying acts that are active, forceful, dehumanizing, and very dark. The fingerprints of a sworn enemy appear all over this unending pit. Abaddon, better known as the angel of the bottomless pit, Satan, the deceiver, a lawless one, the father of lies, tempter, and thief are common names for this spiritual force of darkness who's aimed at robbing our souls. What better way to assault the church, the *bride* of Christ, than through pornography, a stealth mission of mass destruction aimed at taking out women and children, *first*? What better way to infiltrate a congregation and successfully plunder its lifeblood, leadership, purpose, and personal callings?

It's impossible for men to authentically lead without integrity. Porn keeps them under siege, spiritually impotent, and compromised in their leadership. Sadly, their self-deception gets the best of them as they tell themselves, "No one will know what I'm doing," or "I need to protect my wife by keeping this to myself," or "I will take this to my grave." That's what deception does; its bloated belly of sexual duplicity eats you alive from the inside out. Those who sexually act out hide things that are shameful, do things that are deceitful, and corrupt things that are sacred. Marriages and churches fail. The porn industry and its contents are constructed for war—against men and women, their families, and generations to follow.

I See You

The pain is real. According to my research with betrayed women, 76 percent of them showed clinical symptoms of posttraumatic stress. These aren't soldiers returning from war or survivors of a devastating tornado or earthquake. They are our parishioners, friends, elders, pastor's wives, family members, colleagues, and neighbors. It may even be your story.

Seeing the impact that pornography has on partners is like getting a new pair of glasses. Today, when I meet a betrayed partner, I listen to their immediate need for safety and imagine them on a gurney in an intensive care unit (ICU). I'm taking note as they describe symptoms of shock, confusion, ruminating thoughts, difficulty sleeping, panic attacks, hypervigilance, and depression—signs often associated with posttraumatic stress. They desperately need our help. Their families need intervention, recovery, and support. Treating betrayed clients from the lens of crisis care first is much like being in an ICU ward and saying, "I see you."

A Secret Basement Under the House

According to Dr. Frank Seekins, the term *betrayal* dates back to ancient Hebrew, in which much like the ancient Chinese, Egyptian, and Arabic languages, every word is formed by adding pictures and sounds together to paint or illustrate the meaning of the word. The word betrayal conveys two ideas: to betray (*reema*), "what comes from a person of chaos;"[97] and to deceive (*bagad*), "to hide, cover, offend, or deal unfaithfully."[98] Betrayal is a deliberate act of disloyalty intended to dupe or cheat by lying and breaking someone's trust. There must be limitations between the one who's sexually acting out and the betrayed.

Fidelity becomes more difficult when one person in the relationship constructs a virtual secret sexual basement underneath their family home. It's not a basement built with brick and mortar but a metaphor Dr. Omar Minwalla uses to describe a virtual sexual space undetectable by family members.[99]

A husband comes home, throws his jacket over a chair, kisses his wife, and greets his kids after walking through the front door. The idea is—he's home, we're safe, and all is well. Later, the husband retreats into his secret sexual basement where he acts out (pornography, virtual sex chat rooms, porn videos, cybersex, social media sex sites, and more) without his wife's knowledge. He might come up from his secret basement just in time for dinner, to help the kids with homework, fix a leaky faucet, or even cook a meal. There's likely a whole other world the rest of the family doesn't know about. In addition to pornography, it might also include other people, affairs, excessive time and money spent, co-workers, massage parlors, children born outside of marriage, or deceptive sex acts with friends or family members.

The Covenant of Consent

Consent between two parties means that both individuals "allow, approve, or accept" what's happening within the relationship. It gives both individuals a choice. At the heart of marriage, there's a covenant of mutual consent, a commitment to mutual exclusivity by forsaking all others in exchange for loyalty and truth.

Having a secret sexual basement not only violates a couple's sex life but one's commitment as well. If one person wants consent to use pornography, it means we go to our significant other and say, "Hey, I just wanted you to know that I'm going to be looking at porn in our home office today," or "I'm taking my phone into the bathroom so I can look at porn behind closed doors." It's a very simple solution. Be honest; just tell us. Don't hide it. I've offered this solution to hundreds of couples I've spoken with over the past twenty years. I have yet to have one porn user take me up on my simple idea. Why?

While many believe pornography is harmless and private, they know it hurts us, and that's why they hide it. They may feel entitled to look at it when they're mad at us, not getting enough sex or the kind of sex they want, or because it's just what "all guys do." Typically, it's *not* done in broad daylight or in the family room where their spouse and children walk by. It's behind closed doors. When I ask porn users, "What if your children were to see you looking at porn? Or your partner was to find you? What if your boss or HR director were looking over your shoulder or tracking your porn use at work, what then?" Most porn users shrug their shoulders, look away from my eyes, and say, "I wouldn't want that. I love my family," or "I wouldn't want to risk my job." Porn is a soul-eater. Porn and love don't mix. Porn and spirituality don't mix. Porn and integrity don't mix.

Six Ways Pornography Harms Us

Pornography, as a silent killer, is sweeping our globe and continues to take its prisoners by deceit. It is not just men who get hooked on porn, women do too. While my current research is with betrayed women, pornography use crosses all boundaries, touching every socioeconomic line, gender, and faith. Because current statistics show that one-third of the visitors to sexually-oriented websites are female, I hope all betrayed partners, both men and women, receive the help and support they need.[100] Regardless of the relationship status, when deception, lies, and sleight of hand manipulations become a part of our relationships, our sense of safety is shattered, and we begin to question who we are.

Thanks to research, there's more to this story. There's a new way of understanding how betrayed partners have been deeply hurt through the framework of a multi-dimensional trauma model.[101] In my book, *Intimate Deception: Healing the Wounds of Sexual Betrayal*, I call these layers of impact the Dirty Dozen.[102] For this chapter, I've chosen to highlight six layers of harmful impact that specifically surface with non-consenting porn use within an intimate partnership.

1. Impact on Spirituality and Faith

Faith-based helping professionals often become the first line of care after a wife has discovered her husband has been looking at pornography on his laptop or phone. After mentioning how devastated she is by the pornography, many times, clergy will normalize, dismiss, minimize, or even worse, blame the porn use on the betrayed partner.

Sadly, pornography is commonly introduced into someone's life during their childhood or teenage years. Many people start looking at pornography even before they're married. Wrongly transferring the responsibility for the origin of the porn, the ongoing use of porn, or a responsibility to shoulder the solution for the porn use places an unfair burden on us as the betrayed partner and causes tremendous harm. As a result, many of us experience a spiritual/faith trauma that results in anger at God, separation from our faith community, and disconnection from our once trusted spiritual leader with whom we initially sought help.

Additionally, when well-intentioned helping professionals practice outside their area of training, especially with the updated models for treating sex addiction, porn addiction, or betrayal trauma, parishioners can be either missed or

THE TRAUMATIC
RELATIONAL IMPACT OF **PORNOGRAPHY**

IMPACT TO SPIRITUALITY & FAITH

The spiritual disillusionment and disconnect from one's faith in God, place of worship, or spiritual leaders, when porn use is normalized, dismissed, minimized, or blamed on the betrayed partner by a once trusted clergy in whom they originally sought help.

IMPACT TO IDENTITY

The painful turmoil caused by internalized shame beliefs such as "I'm not enough", "I'm ugly/unlovable", or "I can't trust anyone". These are the direct results of porn use. The betrayed partner is placed into a crisis of belief, unrelenting comparisons, and shattered self-confidence.

IMPACT TO LOVE & RELATIONSHIP

The devastating experience when fidelity, intimacy, and companionship within an exclusive relationship are violated by non-consensual porn use, which damages relational safety, vulnerability, and trust.

IMPACT TO PERSONAL HEALTH

Whether porn use discoveries are ongoing or intermittent, prolonged stress impacts the betrayed partner's brain and body health. This can result, in issues with anxiety, depression, sleep disturbances, and ailments such as diabetes, heart disease, adrenal exhaustion, chronic fatigue, and cancer.

IMPACT TO SEXUALITY

Injury to the partner's sexual safety, sensuality, passion, pleasure, spontaneity, and sexuality, due to their significant others pornographic objectification, deceptive sexuality, toxic fantasy, sexual entitlement, sexual aggression, coercion, and sexual abuse.

EMOTIONAL INJURY & PSYCHOLOGICAL ABUSE

The disorientation and psychological abuse caused by intimate deception, lies, anger, manipulation, blame, control, gaslighting, and defensiveness, due to desperate and deliberate attempts to hide secret sexual behaviors.

Visit BraveOne.com for more information
Copyright © 2021 Dr. Sheri Keffer. All Rights Reserved.

deeply misunderstood. And devastatingly, when helping professionals minimize the amount of hiding and deception commonly used to cover up pornography or illicit sex acts—or encourage forgiveness too soon—clergy can unknowingly collude with deception.

> *My husband started erasing the history on his computer after I found porn. My pastor told me that it didn't sound like my husband was doing anything inappropriate because I couldn't prove anything. I should forgive him just like Jesus does. Several months later, my husband was arrested for child porn.* (Pamela)

> *I was told I must forgive my husband. I believe in forgiveness yet felt shame for not being able to forgive him right away. There were too many false confessions, dishonest disclosures, fake apologies, and guilt trips because my husband said, "You're unforgiving and keep bringing up the past." I wasn't sure what was true. When I told the pastor I thought he still might be looking at porn, the pastor told me to let it go and immediately led me in a forgiveness prayer. I was expected to "pray, hurry up, and get over it."* (Brenda)

Statements like these hurt us and can make us feel responsible for another's deceptive sexual acts. While there's no guarantee for how a spouse who's sexually acting out will move through their recovery process, it can be overwhelming to treat chronic sexual problems or sexual addictions, especially when it's not an area of specialty. Organizations such as the International Institute of Trauma and Addiction Professionals (IITAP) and The Association of Partners of Sex Addicts Trauma Specialists (APSATS) welcome, train, and certify clergy to better understand what's happening with members of their congregation.

2. Impact on Identity

It's been said that some pieces of art are "priceless" and "a picture is worth a thousand words." But we as human beings are masterpieces that hold great dignity and surpass any other works of art. Once we discover that the person we love is looking at pornography or engaging in virtual cybersex, our identity quickly shifts for the worse. It creates a crisis of self-confidence and injects shame into our bloodstream.

Ask any woman if she felt like a good enough wife or decent mother before she discovered her husband had been looking at porn or involved in virtual sex chat rooms, and she'll probably say something like, "I wasn't perfect, but I felt a whole lot better than I do now," or "Who are these women? Why is he doing this, and what's wrong with me?"

Ask a man whose wife has been frequenting sexually-oriented websites, and he'll say, "No matter what I've done to love her, nothing has worked. I'm at the end of my rope. What have I done wrong?" One man shared, "The pastor handed me a book and challenged me to do the Love Dare with her. My wife is addicted to porn. Painfully, it only pushed her further away."

Shame is the splat within our soul that tells us something is terribly wrong with us. I often ask betrayed partners one simple question, "What's the negative belief about yourself in light of the pornography you've discovered?" Shame beliefs surface that often sound something like this:

- "I'll never be enough."
- "I'm unlovable, and quite frankly, I don't matter."
- "I'm ugly. From what I've seen, my body will never keep my spouse happy."
- "I'm not safe and can't trust any man."

This stinkin' thinkin' from shame causes us to pull away from others, feel unloved, and struggle to even get up in the morning. Our best attempts to "be" around others often include presenting a false self or fake smile to hide what's really going on. It's our way of trying to protect ourselves from the shame and messiness we feel inside.

3. Impact on Love and Relationship

Relationship integrity, honesty, authenticity, and trust are foundational stones of an intimate partnership. It's what is set in place to support love. When pornography invades our most intimate relationships, it destroys safety and healthy companionship.

I remember the day Conner and I vowed to forsake all others. We loved each other, and I knew he had my back. Five hundred people who joined our marriage celebration witnessed as we became one. People wrapped around the inside of the church banquet hall to give us hugs and wish us well. We were poor as church mice—our best plan was a potluck and cake reception. Time flew and people waited as we never moved from our reception line. You can imagine my confusion and shock after discovering Conner had exchanged me for thousands of pornographic images and illicit phone sex conversations within our first year of marriage. It's no surprise that it created an "attachment injury" in our relationship.

Pornography made it impossible for me to inhale intimacy or breathe out love. I was incredibly lonely. We avoided touch and healthy sexual banter. More often than not, Conner and I would fall asleep back-to-back as silent tears dampened my pillow. I remember asking myself:

- How could I have missed this?
- Who am I married to?
- How could I have been so stupid?

Among the women I surveyed, 95 percent of them said, "I felt safe with my partner until I discovered their sexual behaviors." Even though we know what safety feels like, our relationship is no longer trustworthy.

My husband told me he had those images in his mind even when he hadn't looked at porn that day. He told me that no matter how well our relationship seemed to be going, he'd sneak off to see "the other women" every chance he got. I can't even look at myself in the mirror now without feeling ugly and noticing everything that's wrong with me. (Sandra)

When my wife's been viewing pornography and reading her romance novels, I feel like she's bringing other men into our bedroom. I feel used while she's acting out her sexual fantasies. I can tell she's distant, and I don't know what to do. It's clear; I'm not enough. (Mike)

Pornography not only erodes love, but it exchanges integrity for duplicity, honesty for lies, authenticity for a counterfeit, and trust for unfaithfulness. If pornography is in the mix, love doesn't have a chance to grow.

4. Impact on Personal Health

I was married to a pastor, a man of the cloth. No one told me that being married to a pastor could feel lethal, especially when the cloth was laced with something much like arsenic—pornography. The longer I breathed it in, the worse I felt. I became clinically depressed. The shock, surprise, and pain from keeping his secret not only impacted my relationship with Conner but my brain and body as well.

The strain from long-term relational stress is like sitting on a powder keg of what we don't yet know. We hold our breath in fear, waiting for something to explode. Our observations open the door to suspicions as our minds wonder what *really* happened. Was that woman truly a part of a business deal? Or did the iPad he purchased to help make his "job easier" become another device to hide porn? Our gut tells us something's wrong. We can either trust our gut or the one who says he's not lying to us. We second-guess ourselves. Pornography impacts our physical and mental health, making us susceptible to serious diseases and immune disorders, such as diabetes, heart disease, thyroid problems, adrenal exhaustion, chronic fatigue, and cancer.[103,104,105,106]

5. Impact on Sexuality

Today's porn is changing the way people treat people. At the click of a finger, virtual sex on the internet, social media, or smartphones, is more like sexual menus reminiscent of the 1974 Burger King jingle, "Have it Your Way."[107] While technology has its benefits and is here to stay, the porn industry holds a vast range of consequences to one's sexuality.

When we discover pornography on our spouse's device, we often feel horror-struck, unattractive, dishonored, and cheap. Here's how the one hundred women I researched said it directly impacted their sexuality:

- "I feel violated due to my partner's sexual behaviors." (100 percent)
- "Since learning about my partner's sexual behaviors, I find it difficult to undress in front of him/her." (88 percent)
- "Due to my partner's sexual behaviors, I have become concerned that I might contract a sexually transmitted disease." (67 percent)
- "I've been pressured to perform sexually in ways that were uncomfortable for me" (e.g., forced painful sex, being watched while having sex with others, anal sex, sexual domination, being filmed." (22 percent)

Porn has become increasingly violent, and, as a result, a mind steeped in porn projects its intentions onto us. My research showed how nearly one in five Christian women felt coerced, forced, or pressured to perform sexually in ways that were uncomfortable for them. It's no surprise that aggression is a direct result of watching porn as well.[108] The more a woman feels like an object, the less she wants to be with her significant other.

It's crazy how we, as women, pick up on subtle changes and even not-so-subtle sexual demands. We feel it. We sense it in the way our spouse touches us, interacts with us, and looks at us. Many women who've grown up in faith-based settings have been led to believe they are to sexually serve their spouse regardless of their comfort level with the sex act or type of sexual request. When a husband has been influenced by toxic fantasy or the "skies the limit" pornographic objectification, the lives of men, women, teens, and children are destroyed. There's absolutely no place for healthy sexuality where human dignity is shattered.

Porn also inhibits sexual intimacy.

> When I found porn on his laptop, I'd never seen anything like it before. I slammed the lid down and, within minutes, opened it back up again. I couldn't believe my eyes. I felt my body shut down and couldn't undress in front of him for months. He wondered what happened to me. I was in shock and didn't say a word. (Marsha)

With ongoing use, pornography becomes an unwanted "third party" in our relationships. Like a sexual revolving door, porn devastates our sense of sexual safety and directly undermines our sensuality, passion, pleasure, and spontaneity within the relationship.

6. Emotional Injury & Psychological Abuse

After we confront the pornography we've discovered, more often than not, our husbands push back and say things like, "I don't know what you're talking about." We're hurt, angered, and scared. We do what comes naturally, we ask questions. We make desperate attempts to figure out what's true to restore safety within the relationship. To avoid exposure, the spouse who's sexually acting out practices deception, which often causes emotional injury and psychological abuse to the partner.

- Denying, justifying, and minimizing.
- Representing themselves as innocent.
- Gaslighting (psychological manipulation).
- Blaming the spouse as a form of cover-up.
- Lying and twisting the truth to cover up the facts.
- Emotional, financial, spiritual, physical, sexual, and psychological abuse.
- Smear campaign (gathering allies while making the spouse look bad to others).

Many times, pleas to stop from the wounded spouse are met with entitlement. It's not that the one who's sexually acting out can't take steps to control what they're doing. The real issue is sexual entitlement. It sounds something like, "I don't want to stop. I'm actually not invested in doing what's needed to change." It's about choice. And because they're making choices to lie, blame, and cover up what they're doing, it's a problem with integrity. According to Barbara Steffens in *Your Sexually Addicted Spouse*, strategically using ongoing lies, gaslighting, and sexual deception to keep their world, home life, profession, and reputation intact hurts us. As we're exposed to ongoing emotional harm, abuse, violations of trust, and integrity disorders, we often experience problems, such as acute, posttraumatic, and complex posttraumatic stress.[109]

Things That Hurt and Help Us

When I was invited to write this chapter rather than merely expressing my perspective, I emailed 7,000 betrayed partners and asked them to share their thoughts about what their faith leaders have done that have either helped or hurt them.[110] Who better to ask than the ones who've experienced pain from non-consenting porn use?

Examples of experiences that hurt us:

- The pastor wasn't very supportive and never checked back with me to see how I was doing. The silence was the thing that hurt the most, especially after they knew what was going on.
- My church has recovery groups for men but absolutely nothing for women. I offered to start a support group for betrayed partners and was told there wasn't enough interest.

- The thing that hurt me most was being told, "Men are drawn to beautiful things. It could have been worse if he'd been with a real woman." It put my husband's acting out to porn on me and caused me great shame.

- After telling my priest about the porn, he said, "You are both broken people and need to deal with it. Before I left his office, he gave me suggestions: "Go on a date night once a week, have more sex, let him be the leader he needs to be." I've never been back.

- My husband was an elder in the church. He told the pastor he looked at porn, and it would never happen again. When I went back because my husband had locked all his devices with new passwords, my pastor said I was making things up and (was) on a witch-hunt. He told me it was my duty to stop looking and stay in the marriage.

- After I was hit by a car during a cycling accident, my pastor came to my home, prayed for me, and sent meals to my home. After I got hit by my husband's pornography, the pastor did nothing. How can I sit in church each week and wonder why a high number of Christian men are sitting in the pews objectifying women, and it's not even being talked about?

- The most hurtful thing a pastor said to me was that if I divorced my husband after years of porn use and clear requests for change, I'd be the one committing adultery.

Here are some examples of things that helped us:

- One of the pastors agreed to read things I sent to him on betrayal trauma. A few weeks later, with great empathy, he said, "Thank you for the resources. . . . I had no idea how much you'd been going through."

- My pastor said, "I don't feel qualified to counsel your husband on sexual addiction issues, but we'll support you any way we can. You are welcome here." Even though he didn't know how to fix the issue—just being there was so important.

- They were awesome. The first question they asked me was, "Do you feel safe?" I can't tell you how seen I felt at that point.

- After discovering the years of hidden porn use and emotional affairs, my priest listened and believed me. He said, "It wasn't your fault." That was incredibly healing. I've never forgotten his words.

- Listening and validating me by saying that porn is not God's plan for my marriage. They were willing to wade into the mess with us. They prayed with us and sat with us. We were also told that my husband needed to do the heavy lifting by getting into recovery and earning my trust back.

- We are both involved in church leadership. Our pastors contacted my husband directly to ask him if he'd been looking at pornography and involved in cybersex sites. They asked my husband to step down from his leadership position and encouraged us to get into counseling. They also made sure to let me know I was loved and that this wasn't my fault. My pastor told us that there are no lost causes (something we say at our church) and that he wanted my husband to win, get help, change, and get better.

- When I discovered my husband had been looking at porn for twenty-plus years of our marriage, my pastor and his wife acknowledged that long-term porn use was as damaging to our relationship as having an affair. It's exactly what I'd been feeling. They supported me and offered to find me help.

Enough Is Enough

As clergy and helping professionals, we're most often the first line of defense. It's time to join forces by saying, "Enough is enough." Our cultural paradigm for Christian leadership must shift to change the devastation caused by the porn industry and its impact on the families we serve.

As faith leaders, we fight for what's right. As people of God, we despise injustice and are defenders of those who are being oppressed. Now more than ever, we're seeing what's happening to families from the onslaught of pornography. Sexual deception and infidelity damage us. As Dietrich Bonhoeffer said, "We are not to simply bandage the wounds of victims beneath the wheels of injustice; we are to drive a spoke into the wheel itself."[111]

We can't do it by ourselves, but we can do it by locking arms with those around us. I'm asking clergy from all denominations, as well as para-church ministries, to take seriously the problems caused by sexual deception and the impact of pornography on the emotional and sexual wellbeing of those under our care. We can rise up. We need to make changes. The future health of our families and the effectiveness of our churches depend on it.

Chapter 14

A Sinner's Guide to ~~Accountability~~ Ally Relationships

Honesty is often very hard. The truth is often painful.
But the freedom it can bring is worth the trying.

Fred Rogers

"Luke, I know you have a secret," Shawn began. "And you don't like to tell anybody what it is. You don't like to tell anybody how bad it's getting. But I want you to know I'm willing to listen if you are willing to tell me."

Luke's mask cracked, and tears began to fall. The guise he wore at church and his campus ministry meetings crumbled between the forces of crushing shame and the power of hope. As he fought for composure, his admissions flooded out. Seeing Luke's distress, Shawn suggested a more private location for Luke's confessions and took him to his house. Luke took a risk on his newly found mentor. He told him how porn had steamed through his life and rolled over his heart, flattening any hope of being free.

When Luke finished his story, Shawn told Luke he would like to pray for him. Luke's face darkened, and he scooted to the edge of his seat, bringing his stare close to the face of his friend.

"Hold on. Stop," Luke said. "I have walked down the aisles of a lot of churches, and I've asked a lot of people to pray for me. What in the world is going to be any different about this?"

Shawn smiled and said, "Because the difference is, Luke, after I'm done praying, I'm not going to leave you. Luke, I know you believe there is no hope and that you can't change, and I want you to know that's okay because I am going to believe it for you until you do."

Shawn's obedience to the Spirit that day would eventually lead thousands of people to a deeper understanding of repentance through accountability relationships.

While taking ever deeper steps into authenticity and recovery, Luke Gilkerson joined the Covenant Eyes team in December of 2007, and God used his gifts as a writer and teacher to start the Covenant Eyes blog and create several of the free ebooks and other resources that Covenant Eyes provides. Our blog receives hundreds of thousands of unique visits each month, and our ebooks have been downloaded hundreds of thousands of times. Luke served at Covenant Eyes for eight years before starting Intoxicated on Life with his wife to serve fellow homeschool families. Shortly after his departure, we invited Luke to speak on the topic of accountability at a church leaders' training event called the Set Free Summit produced by Covenant Eyes and Josh McDowell Ministry. After a standing ovation from the crowd, one couple asked if Luke would sign their marriage certificate because his writing had such an impact on their relationship.

Accountability relationships are a key part of the recovery process. Pastors, support groups, twelve-step groups, counselors, and everyday Christians testify to the value of having a personal accountability relationship, but so often, we as Christians make a mess of it.

I'm grateful to call Luke a friend. As fellow writers, Luke and I hit it off immediately when he joined the Covenant Eyes team. We argued . . . mostly for fun. I poked at him on purpose. Our debates prompted new thoughts and insights and challenged our stances.

Throughout this chapter, you will benefit from our arguments, the insights I learned from Luke, the people we interviewed, the writing produced at Covenant Eyes, and the constant feedback we received from Covenant Eyes members. Of course, you will also benefit from my personal experiences with accountability relationships, including my mistakes.

Having made so many mistakes with accountability relationships, how to do accountability poorly might be a personal expertise of mine. An influential pastor in my teen years, Jerry Reliford, offered a personal proverb for guidance: "A wise man learns from his mistakes, but a wiser man learns from those of another." Consider portions of this chapter as your golden ticket to learning from another person's blunders.

I Tried It, and It Didn't Work

After years of living as an agnostic, I found a powerful new desire to serve and love God when I humored my wife and attended a small, rural church with her. Pastor Dr. David Fulks seemed to ignore everyone else and focus on every single struggle, hurt, and sin in my life. Soon, my wife and I began attending a marriage class taught by Roger and Cathy Baker, who both overflowed with Christ's joy and acceptance. Roger was a recovering prescription drug addict, and Cathy was on her own recovery journey. It turned out that several in the class were also in recovery groups outside of the church, and they were a magnetic bunch.

I wanted what they had. I just didn't know how to get it. They could be so real, authentic, and vulnerable. Cathy and Roger would start the class by saying, "This is a safe place, and what is said here stays here." And everybody, including the newbies like my wife and me, never said a word of what was spoken outside that class. Sometimes, a class member would confess something horrible they felt or said to their spouse, and Roger and Cathy would nod their heads and say, "Thank you for sharing that."

I wanted to correct everybody because I had Scriptures buried in my head from my youth. Isn't that what good teachers did? And who says these kinds of unholy admissions in front of others at church? Isn't confession supposed to be a secret between you and God? But Roger and Cathy were different from me. The gospel was buried in their hearts, and they never judged, corrected, or admonished a person in front of the group. They listened and showed love. (I later discovered several people in the class visited Roger or Cathy in their home, where they were discipled.)

How could these druggies and alcoholics be so patient and happy! I wondered. They talked about "Jesus with skin on" and other nutty phrases. I'd never been an alcoholic or a drug addict, so why wasn't I better at conquering sin than they were?

Through my journey, I began to understand what set them apart. They were authentic because they practiced authenticity, humility, and genuine care. I had grown up in a home and churches where we said the right things, flipped switches to turn a frown upside down, and "acted" like Christians. These twelve-steppers went to meetings each week to pour out their souls, met or called a mentor where they went even deeper, declared their weakness unabashedly, studied fervently, and saw Jesus Christ and the power of the Holy Spirit as their only strength.

But I'm a slow learner. I saw others, both in a twelve-step program and outside of that sphere, practicing accountability, and I hoped it would help me just be a better Christian. At this point, I didn't understand compulsive behavior or strongholds. I wanted to please my savior. My heart hurt over my sin, and I would pray that God would strip any desire for porn from my life. Since then, I have heard thousands of men describe the same prayer with the same lackluster results.

My first experiences with accountability relationships were the equivalent of dipping a toe into a bath and expecting my whole body to get clean. Fear and shame gave me a stiff upper lip. I developed friendships at church, and we would get together and read lists of questions that were published by a men's ministry. The last question was the zinger. "Did you lie to me about any of the earlier questions?" I discovered that if anyone lies along the way, they are going to lie in responding to the final question as well.

I was selective with the sins I confessed. Often, they were sins that didn't seem so bad. If another guy said he saw something provocative on TV that made him look twice, I might say, "Yeah, I know what you mean." Typically, we deferred to talking about what we read in Scripture or our recent Bible study, and then we meandered to sports, work, or our family activities.

Luke told me that he dove a bit deeper. He would confess to seeing porn on Friday to one friend, confess to another he watched porn on Saturday, and then he might confess another sin to a third friend. He calls this musical chair accountability.

"If you asked any one of my accountability partners about me, each would have said, 'Yeah, Luke has a little struggle with lust, but he's doing okay," Luke said. "But if you got them all in the same room at the same time, they would compare notes and discover I had a big problem."

These fledgling and guarded efforts are among many reasons why accountability fails. In brief, here are a few common pitfalls:

- **Hierarchal accountability is ineffective**. For example, Covenant Eyes serves many churches, missionary organizations, and other groups, and using accountability software on all devices can be very beneficial—but only when individual team members are encouraged to have safe and personal friends or mentors receive their Covenant Eyes activity feed. I recall one organization had everyone's activity go to a human resources manager. Separately, a megachurch had every staff member's report go to the senior pastor, even though he wasn't personally engaged with those under him. In both cases, the effort was a disaster because the effort was about catching problems instead of carrying each other's burdens and struggles (Galatians 6:2).

- **Top-tier leaders are often unaccountable.** The higher you are on the organizational chart, the lower the number of people willing to hold you accountable. This is true in even small churches. In some circles, it is expected that leaders are simply above the fray, that they never struggle with temptation, or that they have exceptional powers unavailable to the common Christian. When that leader falls, partly because he had such a poor support system, that's when people start talking too late about the need for accountability.

- **Performance doesn't bring wholeness.** Stopping the porn binge is imperative in a person's recovery because it creates distance between ongoing sin and the shame and relational devastation it creates. Unfortunately, when control over porn is the only point of accountability, it doesn't bring true healing. I was guilty of stopping behavior before exploring greater emotional and spiritual health. That added time to my recovery journey. God doesn't just want us to act good. He wants to restore our hearts, our lives, and our relationships.

Let's explore several tenants for strong ally relationships and poke at more of my mistakes. In addition to this chapter, I encourage you to download The Victory App by Covenant Eyes for additional support and guides to godly accountability.

Ally Relationships

Accountability has gotten a bad rap for many of the reasons we've already discussed. The term is commonly used in business or law enforcement as an event that happens after failure, an exacting of consequences as in, "He will be held accountable for his actions." Years ago, I ordered at least a dozen of the best-selling secular and Christian books on accountability, and they failed to help or even describe my authentic relationships. If I saw an article in a Christian magazine, I would snatch it up only to be disappointed.

Let's reframe the conversation.

I've grown to prefer the term *ally relationship*. You trust allies. They have your back. When under attack, an ally comes to your aid. They bind your spiritual wounds when you're bleeding and feed you gospel-centered nourishment when you're starving and thirsty. Because they have your best interests in mind, they guide and correct, extol and encourage, admonish and exhort. An ally doesn't control your life, and that means they can't do the work for you, but they often hold you up, which is helpful when you're broken. Within our Christian experience, the Holy Spirit in them works through the Holy Spirit in you.

An ally relationship is fragile as glass and hard as nails. It requires vulnerability to expose our deepest scars as well as the harms we have committed. Our sin is laid bare, its ugliest parts showing, and with anyone else, we would anticipate rejection, knowing just how much we deserve disdain. But within these safe relationships, we experience the Father's love.

In my formative years, I had not seen examples of vulnerability or discussions of how one ally confesses to another. I witnessed many altar calls, where tears and laments flowed. I heard about confessing to God in a 1 John 1:9 context, but James 5:16 seemed to focus on the second sentence of the verse (the prayers of the righteous) rather than the first (confessing sin to one another). When we want freedom from our nagging habitual sins, we often want a private solution to our private problems. We don't want to involve anyone else. But the Bible doesn't point us to private solutions. Deep Christian relationships are one of God's means of changing us from the inside out.

Today, my ally relationships look much different than the accountability question groups where I started. At this writing, I meet on Thursday nights with four other men I met through the Samson Society. We use a specific process, called the FASTER Scale, to check in each week.[112] Check-ins might be short for one man and detailed with stories for another guy. We go through the curriculum together to focus on our continued healing and growth as Christian men. In some ways, it's not unlike an ongoing Bible study, but it's far more honest, vulnerable, and insightful than the Bible studies I have attended.

While I can call on any of the men in this group, my closest ally is Pastor Danny Bledsoe. When I'm talking about a struggle, he has this knack for listening patiently and then letting the Holy Spirit do the talking. He provides remarkable discernment. I often find myself asking, *Can you say that again? Tell me more about that? Where did you get that?* He shrugs, "I don't know, it's just the Holy Spirit speaking through me."

Here's a simple example. For nearly a week, I watched hours of videos where people talked about their recovery from sexual brokenness. The videos were used for an online Covenant Eyes program. I reviewed the videos for editing purposes, and I cut segments that were too descriptive or might be triggering for someone else watching. One day, I just didn't feel right. I didn't feel triggered, exactly. My mind didn't wander to a lustful place, but something wasn't right. So I left my desk, stepped outside, and called Danny while I walked a few blocks.

"It's like distant gravity," Danny says.

"Distant gravity? What's that?" I reply.

"Like a star is pulling at a distant object," He said. "You haven't slipped; you're not even thinking about acting out, but there is a distant tug on your heart."

Nailed it.

Accountability Is Biblical

The Apostle Paul provides one of the most concise bits of advice in the Bible about how to fight back. "So flee youthful passions and pursue righteousness, faith, love, and peace, along with those who call on the Lord from a pure heart" (2 Timothy 2:22).

Paul gives us three steps: (1) run from, (2) run toward, and (3) run with.

First, run from sinful passions like pornography. This includes physically fleeing, running away from tempting situations. This includes visually fleeing, shifting our eyes away from pornographic media. This includes mentally fleeing, directing our thoughts away from lustful imaginations.

Second, run toward a life of righteousness, faith, love, and peace. Our hearts were not meant to be devoid of passion; the opposite is

The Association for Talent Development did a study on accountability and found the following statistics.

The probability of completing a goal if:

- You have an idea or a goal: 10 percent
- You consciously decide you will do it: 25 percent
- You decide when you will do it: 40 percent
- You plan how you will do it: 50 percent
- You commit to someone you will do it: 65 percent
- You have a specific accountability appointment with a person you've committed to: 95 percent[144]

true. In Philippians 4:8, Paul tells us to seek out things that are pure, excellent, and praiseworthy.

Third, run with those who call on the Lord from a pure heart. Don't go it alone. Have Christian companions, real ones, who have your back and who walk with you in your fight for purity.

Ya Gotta Want It

You can't force accountability on someone else.

Sometimes, people enter accountability discussions because they've been pressured to do so, but their hearts aren't in it. Men, especially, are taught to be self-sufficient. They don't want to talk about how they feel or their hidden desires, let alone talk about the last time they used porn. Often, people use phrases to evade accountability, such as, "I'm sort of a private person," or "I'm accountable to God."

A man or woman who doesn't see anything wrong with their pornography use will avoid accountability relationships. If they identify as a Christian, they may simply lie about their pornography use, and they might even be confrontational about porn discussions. "Never attempt to teach a pig to sing; it wastes your time and annoys the pig," Robert Heinlein wrote.[113]

Before a fruitful ally relationship can begin, men and women have to understand their brokenness and their need for relationships. Sometimes, they come to grips with that brokenness on their own or with supportive instruction. At other times, it is a result of consequences, such as a loss of a job or those imposed by a spouse.

Regardless, there has to be a desire, even if it is a desire to mend a wounded marriage or relationship. An ally relationship is like love; you can't force it into someone's life. Having an ally requires a desire for true and honest repentance. An unrepentant heart has no room for an ally.

You Gotta Own It

The biggest mistake of many accountability efforts is that too much of it rides on the accountability partner or accountability group. Accountability relationships often start with good intentions. A person may say to his friend, "I give you permission to ask me at any time how I am doing." Often, this isn't specific, and it's a recipe for failure. If the accountability partner didn't ask the right question, no confession is given. If they didn't call or text that week, they let it slide. If the pair or group didn't meet last week, then there is no reason to bring up last week's sins and slips this week.

There is a common guiding phrase in recovery circles: "You own your own recovery." In other words, I can only work on the problems that I own. It's not the job of my allies to seek me out—although, that is extremely helpful. It's my job to call those who have agreed to hear my sin and my struggles or just to check in. My allies should know my goals, weaknesses, and biggest potential pitfalls. They won't know unless I tell them.

In the end, it is not your ally's job to change your life or reach your goals for you. You must completely own your mistakes, your messes, your weaknesses, your habits, and your character. Many end up looking to accountability partners as scapegoats. "I didn't see any change in my life because my accountability partners fell through." Wrong. I am the one who fell through. I must be willing to take ownership of my sins. Only then can others help, guide, exhort, and pray with me.

Within recovery circles, it's not uncommon for a mentor to fire his or her mentee after a period of evasiveness and inaction. If the person seeking recovery isn't broken enough to do the work, then the ally relationship isn't worth the effort. When relational accountability is divorced from personal responsibility, then little progress can be made.

Be Proactive

We should provide no pause for confession to each other because the Bible requires us to be doers of the Word and not just hearers (James 1:22). Christians fighting for freedom from a stronghold shouldn't wait for sin to happen. They should pre-plan their ally discussions.

"In Christianity, most often (if ever) we confess our sin reactively. That is, *after* the sin has already been committed," John Elmore writes in *Freedom Starts Today*. "Reactive confession is good, biblical, and right, but at the same time, the sin has already happened. If you want to overcome addictive behavior, waiting until the behavior has occurred yet again can leave you feeling stuck in a defeating cycle. But what if you both confessed sin and decided to go on the offensive (the theological term is *repent*, or turning from sin by turning toward God)? We do this by making a *proactive* decision by God's strength not to do/use/say/go/

act upon 'xyz' over the next 24 hours. Then, let another person know about your commitment, and plan to follow up with them 24 hours later and let them know you abstained."[114]

The value of pre-committing to a goal and confession with someone else cannot be understated. Temptations will come, but when they do, we remember our commitment to check in the next day. Being reminded of our commitments prompts opportunities for prayer, to set up guardrails, and to reach out to a brother in Christ (for men) or a sister in Christ (for women).

Freedom is a journey, and its path is worth walking every single day.

Eureka!

Finding a eureka moment of decision comes with a stark realization and clarity of purpose. Recovery from porn needs a eureka moment, a splash of cold water, a wake-up call, a line drawn in the sand. Thought, knowledge, and understanding are needed to understand porn is a problem and that escape is paramount.

This "aha" moment may come amid a crisis. When a person's secret love affair with porn is discovered by loved ones, it can cause heartbreak, disappointment, and anger. In 56 percent of divorce cases, pornography is listed as a major contributing factor to the split.[115] The knowledge that one's marriage can be part of such a dismal statistic can be highly motivating and can spark a new point of clarity.

For others, they may simply recognize how far they have sunk into their secret life. They review the lies they tell, the time they lose, and how hopeless they feel, and then understand they are no longer in control over this area of their life. A man may discover his porn use has resulted in erectile dysfunction when having sex with his spouse. A person may discover that porn is destroying marital intimacy both in and out of the bedroom. The porn user may recognize how porn is harming society. Porn hurts the people who consume it and the people they love, but it also hurts the people who are trapped in the pornography industry, including the women and children who are trafficked.

Meanwhile, Christian (and other religious) tenants denounce pornography and the abuse to which it contributes. To adhere to one's faith and draw from its principles can be a major motivator and asset to recovery.

Moments of clarity about pornography are everywhere. Finding one or several to cling to is a first step to escaping porn and must be shared with an ally.

Though she writes to food addicts in *The Hunger Fix*, Dr. Pam Peeke calls this moment of clarity an EpiphaME, personalizing the word epiphany.[116] She says that people will recognize when their EpiphaME has occurred because they will stop making excuses to others and themselves. They will start a 180-degree attitude change toward recovery. To help people get a sense of their current attitude, she encourages them to write down every excuse that comes to them for twenty-four hours. "When that excuse maker is gone, you're home," she writes. "That dopamine receptor is yours—you own it [. . .] Feed your soul, not your addictive beast."

Two or Three Better Than One

People fight porn on their own and get beat up. Because they've adapted to cycles of being beat up (the addiction and shame cycles), they don't heal. Because they don't heal, they are weak and stuck with getting beat up, possibly every month, every week, or even every day. Getting beat up stinks, and the Church body has to step up to protect its own from the bully.

Scripture shows us how not to get beat up. Ecclesiastes 4:9–12 says, "Two are better than one, because they have a good reward for their toil. For if they fall, one will lift up his fellow. But woe to him who is alone when he falls and has not another to lift him up! Again, if two lie together, they keep warm, but how can one keep warm alone? And though a man might prevail against one who is alone, two will withstand him—a threefold cord is not quickly broken."

Simply stated, Satan loves to find people trapped, alone, and without anyone to pull them from the trap. He whispers lies: "You should be so ashamed that you never seek help from anyone. If they knew what you watch on your phone, they wouldn't love you anymore. They would reject you."

Satan lays the trap and elates in people struggling alone in weakness.

Honesty and Vulnerability

In an ally relationship, lying is self-defeating. Unfortunately, people do it and for reasons you might not suspect.

People lie even when they pay money for the conversation. A 2015 study showed that 93 percent of people admitted to consciously lying to their therapist, and 84 percent of patients said they lied regularly. Think about it. A therapist isn't relationally involved with their client. They are sworn to secrecy and legally liable for breaking confidence, yet their patients still lie. Only 3.5 percent fessed up to their lies, and only 9 percent of therapists uncovered the truth.[117]

More importantly, what did people lie about? Here are a few things they lied about:

- How bad I really feel: 54 percent
- The severity of my symptoms: 39 percent
- My thoughts about suicide: 31 percent
- My insecurities and doubts about myself: 31 percent
- Why I missed appointments or was late: 29 percent
- Pretending to be more hopeful than I am: 27 percent
- Things I have done or regret: 26 percent

The lying stems from shame, fear of being judged, angst about consequences, not wanting to upset someone else, and dread of being misunderstood. Most people who have never explored a recovery journey feel they are singularly defective, that they would be rejected for their failures, sin, and behavior.

Honesty requires vulnerability, and vulnerability demands safety and grace. For the person who truly desires freedom, a common anecdote to unleash vulnerability is the gift of someone else going first. He receives the gift of going next. He gets the opportunity to say, "Me too."

A perfect example happened when I joined my friend David Zailer, the author of *Our Journey Home,* for a twelve-step meeting at an Orange County, California church. Men arrive in construction boots, sneakers, and hand-crafted dress shoes, but they are all walking the same road. On this night, two new men joined the room for their first meeting. Unknown to these newcomers, the men conspire to offer a gift wrapped in courage and honesty. Before the night's lesson, each man takes a turn sharing their personal story in brief. Though the men know each other's stories, when they hear a struggle, emotion, or false belief that they have experienced, they sound out "Me too." They say those two simple words over and over. These guys don't just talk about their long past struggles, they also discuss the temptations and misgivings they felt the prior week and the ones they felt that day. "Me too" affirms each other that they are understood and not judged, heard, and not disdained. By the time the newcomers are given the floor, they have witnessed men from every walk of life be vulnerable, honest, and authentic. Their fears set aside, they tell their stories for the first time. And, in turn, one day these newcomers will give the same gift to others, remembering how alone they once felt.

CPR: Confession, Prayer, and Repentance

Christian leaders know the ally trifecta well—how confession, prayer, and repentance, lead to God's healing. They know James 5:16 by heart. I find that each of us needs reminding more than we need fresh instruction. We need to remember more than we need to be told.

Many accountability relationships focus on giving an account, which can be helpful, but the practice falls short. Several Christian men told me they didn't find their secular support meetings helpful because the truth-telling didn't lead to change in their lives. They knew in their hearts that just saying what was true about their lives wasn't enough. Feeling bad about their behavior wasn't sufficient. But similar issues happen in Christian circles as well. For some accountability relationships and groups, the whole point can be confession to ease one's conscience.

After a night of intense truth-telling, re:generation recovery leader Lauri Lueck recognized something was missing from her meeting with other women. "Thank you for sharing" seemed an inadequate response to hearing a woman talk about watching porn, clicking through a hookup app, and learning that her spouse left. Now what?

When her group met the next week at Hope City Church in Macomb, Michigan, the assembly agreed to switch up the time of sharing. After women shared the truth about their lives, each was bathed in prayer. The recovery manual didn't say to do it, but the manual to life did, and the switch made an immediate impact.

As Lauri recounted the change to other re:generation recovery group leaders at a national meetup in Dallas, it turned out her group wasn't unique. Other leaders chimed in to say they made the same change to their meetings as well.

"We were confessing, but there was no prayer," said Watermark teaching pastor John Elmore, who was a former re:generation director. "It's a good exercise, but it lacks God's power. At Watermark re:generation, every time someone confesses or shares, we wrap them up in grace and prayer."

In his ninety-day recovery guide, *Freedom Starts Today*, Elmore uses a biblical equation when considering the truth of James 5:16: Confession (your part) + Prayer (their part) = Healing (God's part).[118] This isn't just a duty to confess. It's God's prescription for getting well, for crushing the sin that so easily entangles (Hebrews 12:1–3).

Confess in New Testament Greek translates "to speak the same as." Confession brings us into alignment with what God already knows so we can experience His forgiveness. Water will not flow through pipes that are disconnected. When our hearts and minds are aligned with the truth and with each other, we can experience the healing flow God has for us through the work of the Holy Spirit (1 John 1:7).

At the core of the Christian ally relationship is not only giving an account but also repentance and prayer. Our sanctification is a symbiotic process between God and Christians (Philippians 2:12–13). Christ and His finished work redeem even the youngest believers (1 Corinthians 2), but we face an incremental process throughout life to be more like Christ, to be renewed and transformed (1 Corinthians 11:1, Romans 12:1–2, Philippians 1:6).

True repentance comes not from the Pharisees who wear phylacteries on their heads, but from the broken who draw water from the Well of eternal life.

"When you are loved as a disobedient son or daughter, it hurts, doesn't it? And it hurts in the best way you can imagine," Luke Gilkerson said.[119] "When you get loved when you're not living in the way you ought, it hurts, but it changes you. This is the ultimate motivation for repentance as it says in Romans 2:4—not that the fear of shame leads to repentance but God's kindness. It is God's kindness that leads to repentance."

Good allies understand this, and their demeanor reflects it. These times of prayer are not miniature sermons and condemnations; rather, they are cries, affirmations, and requests from brothers and sisters to our Savior. Though the sin is real, God does not condemn me and neither does my ally. Christian allies use their presence as a window to see the love of God and even the loving discipline he gives (Hebrews 12).

The practical application of James 5:16 illustrates a simple truth: The lion's share of our hurts and wounds came through others or in relationships. We were wounded in community, and it created fear, animosity, anger, self-doubt, isolation, and more.

God uses His body, His community, to create healing. We were wounded in community, and we are restored in community. When we are honest about our sin with allies, they listen in love and help us expose our hearts for the Great Physician to do His work. Within the company of prayerful allies, we grow in peace, joy, faithfulness, self-control, and so much more (Galatians 5:22–23).

Ally Selection, Part 1: Not Your Spouse

Let me start by stating the obvious . . . or possibly not-so-obvious. Men need men and women need other women for positive ally relationships. Otherwise, despite good intentions, there are just too many opportunities for confusion. Married, single? Yes, especially when dealing with pornography and unwanted sexual behaviors.

Many spouses, and in my experience many pastors, first think of their husbands or wives as accountability partners, but I stick by the above paragraph. I'm not alone in offering this advice to married couples. I'm backed by my numerous recovery leaders and counselors.

First, depending on the depth of the porn use, the struggler might need to check in daily or more often about emotions, temptations, thoughts, and a history of such struggles. That puts a terrible burden on the spouse and the marriage relationship. The spouse deserves guided disclosure and honest updates—I'm not advocating secrecy—but the day-to-day accountability must be borne by someone other than a spouse. As well, a spouse should have a final say in whether a specific person is trusted to be an ally. A wife might think one of her husband's friends is a little too chummy, and even worldly, but another may meet her personal gauge of trustworthiness.

Second, a strong voice outside the marriage provides greater clarity. A struggler may have unequal power in a marriage. A struggler may gaslight, berate, and blame their spouse to shut down their questions and maintain control. A strong outside voice isn't pushed around.

Many people lack deep friendships outside of marriage, and unfortunately, this can be very true of men. A wife may be the one person with whom a man expresses vulnerability. He may have many friends to share sports, hunting, and even religious activities, but he often avoids discussions that show perceived weakness and, heaven forbid, his intense feelings of shame and fear of rejection. At Covenant Eyes, we commonly hear wives tell us, "He says he doesn't have a close friend at church that can be his ally."

This is sad and unfortunate, but with guidance, a person can learn to open up their heart and mind to another.

Ally relationships often become intense and bonding—emotionally and spiritually. Psalms 18:24 describes how I have felt my allies as being like "a friend who sticks closer than a brother." Every David needs a Jonathan.

Ally Selection, Part 2: Partner Selection

As a pastor or church leader, you know men and women in your congregation who could mentor others. Being an ally is a great honor. I see Galatians 6:1 not only as a call to gently correct but also as a command and calling to those who are spiritually mature. The spiritually mature meet the woman at the well, they eat with sinners, and they recognize the sick need healing (rather than the healthy, Mark 2:17).

Though not required, a guide who has walked his or her own journey to recovery can be especially helpful. Depending on the size of your congregation, you may or may not know such a person. If you don't know of someone with experience, then arm individuals with the training and education from the resources offered in this book. Covenant Eyes continually offers new resources to train allies. Reading and training create empathy and understanding and provide a path for ongoing support.

Commonly, ally relationships start as friendships. Encourage your parishioner to make a list of anyone with whom they feel a genuine connection, both personally and spiritually. They don't have to be close friends. They could be old friends, church acquaintances, neighbors, or someone to whom they look up. Have them make a long list.

Then have them narrow their list based on certain character traits. Is there anyone on the list that is disengaged with their faith? Anyone who seems untrustworthy or has been known to be a gossip? Anyone who is known to be legalistic or harsh? Ideally, a strong ally is spiritually engaged, trustworthy, and gracious.

Ally Selection, Part 3: Support Groups

Possibly, one of the best ways for people to find an ally is through a support group. Samson Society, re:generation recovery, Celebrate Recovery, Pure Desire Groups, SHE Recovery, and many other types of support groups provide guidance not only for healing and life change, but they also guide and urge each member to have an ally, which they may call an accountability partner, a sponsor, or some other name.

For instance, every Samson Society member is urged to have a Silas, taking the name of the Apostle Paul's early traveling companion. A Silas isn't a guru; he's just another guy willing to listen in confidence and who will provide feedback, opportunities for reflection, and prayer. He isn't perfect, and he is on his own journey of repentance and healing. This Silas relationship is not a forever friend, most likely; instead, it is a strategic companionship for a season of life.

Because Samson Society groups meet in person as well as online, men have multiple opportunities to seek a Silas.

Support groups are especially helpful to the ally relationship because they enhance focus and growth. Many support groups have a curriculum to study, or at minimum, discussions on a specific topic. The lessons and discussions provide greater opportunities for ongoing learning, growth, and commitments to change. Also, the group adds another layer of accountability because each person in the group is expected to complete a lesson and share with the group what they have learned. As part of a group, each member may also keep a journal or write answers to specific questions that require deeper thought and reflection. Often, these groups require a check-in at the beginning of a meeting, encouraging each member to talk about their temptations, struggles, slips, and victories.

The self-reflection, spiritual disciplines, and other learning provided through a support group can supercharge ally discussions because the individual is "working his own recovery." The struggler is less dependent on his ally for his next spurt of growth; rather, the struggler is sharing about what he has learned, how he is applying it to his life, and how his ally can pray for his ongoing journey. Yes, confession and repentance are part of the equation, but now, the ally relationship is better equipped to examine relapses and prepare for greater freedom.

Be the Ally You Want for Yourself

"There is an old saying, 'Be the kind of friend you would like to have,'" Danny muses in one of our conversations about ally relationships. "If you are searching for a great ally, be a great ally for others."

Being a good ally for others does three things for you.

First, it causes you to check your actions and behavior. That's right! You will be more successful in your journey by being a great ally to someone else.

Second, being a good ally bolsters your own resolve. The advice, the reading you do, and the prayers you give all have an impact on your own walk with Christ when it's done with the humility of a servant's heart. Being a great partner for someone else helps you speak truth into your own life.

Third, by modeling how a great ally acts, you can develop mutual accountability relationships. You help teach your partner how they can support you well, as you do for them.

Here's the bonus: In short, we get to keep the freedom and growth we give away.

Ally relationships are one of the means God uses to bring about solid growth and maturity. In a society that has become more individualistic, God reminds us to care for one another. In closing, let me leave you with a guiding principle that Luke Gilkerson taught me. An ally's primary purpose is not to call me out on my sin, but to call me up to the man I am in Christ.

Chapter 15

No Need to Lift Alone

Discipleship is making copies of Jesus Christ.
Tony Evans

Procrastination kills good intentions.

Ron DeHaas, the founder of Covenant Eyes, has a habit of saying, "When is *now* a good time?" It means there is no time like the present to take the first step because it doesn't take long to lose energy and allow an actionable step to be lost to everyday tasks. Six months or a year later, leaders look back and say, "Weren't we going to do something?"

Perfectionism kills good intentions too.

Most churches don't need a perfect solution to address pornography; they need a first step. After that first step, even a baby step, leaders can improve, iterate, and build on their efforts. And a first step, small or large, for one church might be much different than that of another church.

The point is to do something now.

Let's break initiatives into four categories in terms of effort, whether it's a simple referral or to get a program up and running. Let's classify endeavors into how much time, energy, and effort are required for pastors and leaders to take action.

- **Easy Lift.** These trusted action steps are easy handoffs, such as software or educational recommendations.
- **Small Lift.** Plug in and play these programs to get the conversation started in your church. Or do your homework to provide counseling referrals.
- **Medium Lift.** Help a leader do the basic training, help people engage, and encourage commitment to a course of study.
- **Large Lift.** Within three to nine months, your church can host a full-fledged recovery/discipleship ministry that deals with a wide variety of issues.

Most important to note: The Easy-Lift category is no less important than a Large-Lift program. Each level can play into the next where people learn and grow. A small or medium-sized church can start with an Easy Lift so that it can progress to a Medium- or Large-Lift initiative. These efforts not only have an impact on the individual or the group involved but can also have an impact on your church culture.

In each section, I will provide examples of resources, most of which I have mentioned elsewhere in this book. By no means is this an exhaustive list. More and more excellent resources are being created because the need is so great.

The Easy Lift: Trusted Programs for an Easy Handoff

Whether you have thirty people or 3,000 or more at your church, Easy-Lift options provide staples for recovery and life change. If you are committed to helping people with basic support or you have a full-blown recovery ministry in place, these resources enhance and aid your efforts. For many people set free from porn, these are the tools they have used.

Using the Easy Button doesn't mean life change is a cinch for the person trapped by porn. Don't confuse that an effort that is easy for the pastor or the church to implement is an easier recovery for the individual. Instead, these programs are easy to engage in and can serve two purposes: 1) Enhance and support other efforts, including Small-, Medium-, and Large-Lift programs, and 2) help a church act now when they don't have support programs or personnel ready to help.

About 44 percent of churches in the United States have one or fewer full-time staff members and those leaders are preaching, visiting the sick, and doing most other shepherding tasks.[120] That often means pastors' plates feel full—and they are.

The church might lack prepared mentors to disciple others, let alone trained facilitators to lead support groups. Nonetheless, small churches carry no immunity to the porn pandemic. Porn struggles cross demographics too; older and younger people, men, women, boys, and girls struggle.

But a shortage of mentors and facilitators isn't just a small church problem. Larger churches experience the same dilemma. These Easy-Lift options help any church, regardless of size, act now to help an individual who has confessed after a convicting sermon, during a counseling session, when a marriage is in meltdown, or in some other fashion.

Covenant Eyes

Since 2000, Covenant Eyes has provided software and educational resources to help people quit porn. Covenant Eyes provides accountability and filtering software for phones, tablets, and computers. More than 1.5 million people have used the software as part of their healing journey and to protect the people they love. The focus of the software is to create ongoing ally relationships, where people become transparent about their lives and how they use their devices.

Covenant Eyes also antes up a plethora of educational resources to enhance ally relationships and to support men, women, and teens in their journeys to healing and freedom. Covenant Eyes continually launches free and paid courses, daily challenges, and other tools to help people understand how they became ensnared by pornography and how to break free. All of the recovery courses are peer-reviewed by Christian counselors so you can feel confident the content is sound and adheres to biblical principles. Discover a growing list of tools from Covenant Eyes at our website or contact the **Covenant Eyes Church Support Team** at ChurchSupport@ covenanteyes.com or at 989-720-8000.

Samson Society for Men

Men find godly relationships, support, and a home base for their freedom journeys by visiting the Samson Society website and registering for a newcomer meeting. Everything a man needs to know is explained in the newcomer meeting by a volunteer like me.

The Society encourages and helps its members find a traveling companion— what the Society calls a Silas, borrowing the name of the Apostle Paul's aide in his initial ministry, as described in an earlier chapter. A Silas listens, provides guidance and encouragement, and prays with his sojourner, and it's common for him to receive accountability activity from Covenant Eyes or a similar service.

When it comes to attending or hosting a support meeting, it doesn't get more simple than the Samson Society. Every portion of the meeting is scripted, except for the gut-wrenching and freeing honesty that pours out when men talk. There is no curriculum for meetings, but there is a strong online community for members only, where men share links to the books they read, the podcasts they listen to, and the devotionals and Bible studies they use. Spin-off groups happen often, where men use curricula and books for support in addition to Samson Society meetings.

Meetings are held both online and in person. To become a member, a person must understand that this is a fellowship of Christian men where Scripture and prayer are part of every meeting. Like any group, there are rules and etiquette for the meetings, and the guys keep each other in check, including an agreement of strictest confidence to support a safe environment. (Strictest confidence does not apply to breaking the law or putting oneself or others in danger.)

After becoming a member, your parishioner might be inspired to host a Samson Society meeting in your church. Anyone who becomes a member of the Samson Society can host a meeting at any time in their local church, home, or garage. The Society only asks that meetings are registered so they can be listed on the website so other men can attend.

Online meetings happen multiple times a day each day of the week. This can be especially helpful for men who have odd work schedules. Also, many men use Samson Society meetings for support between the recovery meetings held at their churches. In other words, a man might attend re:generation recovery or Celebrate Recovery each week at his church and attend Samson Society meetings as a supplement or when he is feeling triggered to act out.

SheRecovery for Women

SheRecovery offers a safe and Christian online community where women can learn to grow in freedom from compulsive sex and porn behaviors. Led by trained facilitators, SheRecovery Virtual Meetings provide women with accountability, recovery tools, spiritual growth, prayer, and more. Women are encouraged to attend virtual meetings at least weekly, seek an accountability partner for daily connection, and join the **SheRecovery online community** for further support.

Crystal Renaud Day founded the SheRecovery Virtual Meetings because rarely do women find support meetings at their churches. Crystal hosts the SheRecovery podcast and is the author of several Christ-centered recovery books for women.

Crystal is a trusted partner of Covenant Eyes. She and the Covenant Eyes team worked together to produce the first SHE Virtual Recovery Summit in 2020. The video from that online event is available for free through Covenant Eyes. And Crystal co-wrote, with Covenant Eyes team member Lisa Eldred, a free ebook for women, called *New Fruit: A Woman's Guide to Porn Recovery*.

The Small Lift: Minimal Homework and Study Required

Examples of small lifts are additional handoffs, but they require review and even investigation by church leaders. If the Easy Lifts are no-brainers, this category of Small Lifts deserves more of your attention for deeper understanding and possible involvement. These effective resources assist your church in providing meaningful care to people, especially if they are in crisis.

Counselor Referrals

First, discover the Christian counselors in your region that are certified to address porn and sexual behaviors. CSAT (certified sex addiction therapist) and C-SASI (Christian Sex Addiction Specialists International) are the two most common certifications that Christian therapists pursue. Search online or visit these organizations' websites to find a certified counselor. In addition to providing training for clinicians, C-SASI also provides training to coaches, clergy, group facilitators, and lay leaders who may serve in your area.

Dr. Doug Weiss founded the American Association for Sex Addiction Therapy, and he provides certification and training to counselors, coaches, therapists, and pastors. Find a counselor at their website.

Intensives

Christian intensive workshops and programs hosted by counseling and coaching ministries provide a deep and quick immersion into the recovery process. Intensives provide deep focus to provide people a fast track toward life change and healing. It's a head start toward getting well.

Bethesda Workshops in Nashville, Tennessee, estimates people receive the equivalent of eight to twelve months of weekly counseling within its four-day workshop. Many workshops are three to five days, and it's common for people to travel across the country to the hosting venues. Boulder Recovery offers a fourteen-day intensive in Boulder, Colorado, where men create deep bonds during those two weeks. Some counseling centers, like HopeQuest Ministry Group near Atlanta, Georgia, provide twelve-week programs, both residential treatment and outpatient intensives. There are likely Christian intensives in your state, but this is a very brief list among many organizations that have deep experience in providing intensive workshops.

- Bethesda Workshops
- Faithful and True
- HopeQuest Ministry Group
- Be Broken Ministries
- Heart to Heart Counseling Center
- Boulder Recovery

Support Ministries

More and more ministries provide support for people struggling with porn and unwanted sexual behaviors. Many of these ministries are founded by people who have walked out of darkness themselves, and they want to share the freedom they have found. Sometimes, they are small and support people within their region, while others serve on a national scale.

Michael and Christine Leahy are co-CEOs of **BraveHearts**, a ministry whose mission since 2002 has been to lead men and women to freedom from porn and sex addiction as well as betrayal trauma. BraveHearts provides online, instructor-led recovery resources to those who request help. BraveHearts also provides a comprehensive Mentor Training and Certification Program to help equip people in your church to guide others in a healing process.

Another example is **Be Broken Ministries,** which provides courses and support for men, women, wives, and parents. Their team offers personal consultations for men and delivers three-day intensives for men wanting to leave porn and unwanted behaviors behind. Their team also offers one-on-one coaching for men via audio or video calls as well as online small groups for both men and women.

The dedicated professionals of the **Covenant Eyes Church Support Team** connect pastors to a variety of resources and training. Covenant Eyes continues to add to a series of free ebooks, online app courses, and other resources aimed at pastors and church leaders. Because we work with so many ministries, this team can point leaders to vetted and trusted partners that provide exceptional resources. If you're unsure of your next steps to support people in your church, call 989-720-8000 and ask for our church support team. Or send an email request to ChurchSupport@covenanteyes.com.

The Medium Lift: Time-Framed Programs That Lead to More

Typically, Medium-Lift programs have a beginning and an end, and these studies and groups might be provided by a church on a rotating basis. Often, they fit within school semesters so they easily fit within program periods you may already have in place. In some cases, a book or workbook study might be used for an existing small group.

These studies help people understand how they got stuck and why they stay stuck and establish a trajectory for living in freedom. People learn what it means to have deeper accountability and stronger relationships, how to set boundaries for recovery, how to start the healing process, and what's needed to live well in God's provision.

While the amount of preparation varies to do these programs well, leaders should have a good overview of the material and recruit facilitators to run a group for men or women to attend. Many of the leading programs for men and women come with training for facilitators. If you have someone in your church who has walked through a recovery program, they can be a prime candidate to facilitate a group. These types of programs work best when leaders, including lay leaders, from your church get involved in promoting them. Imperative for these programs to take root in your church is for senior leaders to embrace the need for them, create a safe space for the groups to meet, and speak unabashedly about their value.

Here are just two examples.

Pure Desire Ministries

Pure Desire offers a deep library of books, workbooks, and video courses on sexual integrity that can be used by individuals or a group. For a pastor or a church leader,

Pure Desire is a trusted source for the easy hand-off for a man or woman, but these studies and resources are also easily implemented at your church.

Known best among church leaders for Ted Roberts's participation in the Conquer Series, Pure Desire also offers the eight-week *Sexual Integrity 101* course, the *Seven Pillars of Freedom* kit, and other resources for people seeking to escape sexual brokenness. They offer studies and groups for spouses who have been betrayed, including the *Betrayal & Beyond* study. They even have a study for young women called *Behind the Mask*. Once you establish a group at your church, it can be listed on the Pure Desire website so people in your region can join your church's group.

Covenant Eyes, Life Change

Dr. James Reeves, who is also known for speaking in the Conquer Series, wrote a twelve-week workbook study with accompanying videos for Covenant Eyes called *Life Change: A Biblical Journey to Freedom*. Though I list it as a Medium Lift, this course is simple to employ and can even be a resource for an individual and his or her ally. This is likely one of the easiest courses your church can start.

Within this course for quitting porn, Pastor James focuses on a Christ-centered process to help people overcome the wounds in their lives and the lies they believe. People discover the importance of community, repentance, honesty, and learning how to forgive. Course participants are also directed to give away the freedom they have received, which can bring new volunteers to a church's ranks. Request group or bulk copies and supporting resources through the **Covenant Eyes Church Support Team** at ChurchSupport@covenanteyes.com or at 989-720-8000.

The Large Lift: Support Groups for Ministry and Recovery

With staff or volunteers and readily available training, your church can have its own full-fledged recovery ministry up and running in three months to one year. These year-round programs are not porn or sex addiction specific; rather, they deal with a broad variety of struggles. I call this a Large Lift and not a "Heavy Lift" because once it's going, it can become a self-perpetuating living program that generates new leaders, strengthens disciples, and invests in servants who give back in multiple ways to your congregation and community.

Many churches create their own Christ-centric programs to introduce people to deeper support groups, including twelve-step groups. For instance, Mariners Church in Irvine, California, developed *The Bridge,* and City on a Hill in Fort Worth, Texas, created *Life Change for Every Christian* to provide biblical introductions to the twelve-step or other recovery processes at their churches. These introductory programs help people participate in self-discovery before diving into additional support for concerns like recovering from a divorce, living with chronic pain, coping with grief, overcoming chemical dependency, and even porn and sex. Once people move through these programs, they have a firmer footing to join a specific support group.

Some leaders in porn and sex addiction recovery circles are wary of overarching programs like Celebrate Recovery because in our broader culture, chemical addictions are viewed with less shame than compulsive behavior with porn or sex. It's up to each local recovery chapter to create a safe environment for everyone asking for help, and I have found many churches use these larger programs to do just that.

Celebrate Recovery

Over the past thirty years, Celebrate Recovery (often called CR by its members) made the phrase "hurts, hang-ups, and habits" familiar. It was the first well-known program to take the twelve-step process back to its biblical roots. The original twelve-steppers were called The James Club in 1857 because its foundations were built on the book of James, Jesus's Sermon on the Mount, and 1 Corinthians 13, Paul's chapter on love. With 37,000 churches hosting groups in the United States in 2022, Celebrate Recovery is the best-known Christian recovery organization in America.

In a nutshell, the agenda of a Celebrate Recovery meeting has three main components:

1. A large group session where members participate in praise and worship and hear a recovery-centered teaching or a personal testimony. This instruction might be taught by a pastor, CR facilitator, or volunteer. Groups also use recorded teachings available through the Celebrate Recovery store.

2. Open Share is a time when the large group separates into smaller gender and issue-specific groups, where each person should feel safe to share their struggles and victories. Rules require people to share only about themselves, to listen and not give others advice, to maintain confidentiality and anonymity, and to keep their language clean.

3. Step Study is the third component. Within gender-specific breakout groups, people use Celebrate Recovery resources to follow a weekly study of Jesus-centered principles for recovery.

Churches are encouraged to host meetings on a night when the church building isn't otherwise being used so people feel a sense of safety about coming for support. Childcare is provided by volunteers at many Celebrate Recovery meetings, and it's common for children to be trained not to say, "Hey, it was great to see you at CR," when they see members at church on Sunday morning or in the community.

"Anonymity and confidentiality—that's part of the DNA of Celebrate Recovery," said Meagan Grider, the director of CR at Saddleback Church, where the first CR group was formed.

People often think recovery is only for chemical dependency, Grider said, so CR groups do their best to promote a common statistic of CR members: one in three are seeking recovery from chemical dependency. Two-thirds of its members are seeking support for a broad variety of issues, including anger, shame, food issues, pornography, grief over an abortion, divorce, and many more issues.

Over the years, to help people with this broad set of struggles, CR has created a ton of content for its members and leaders. Through a paid subscription service called Celebrate Recovery Connected, CR members have access to a library of inspirational and educational videos, readings, and more. Members of CR Connected also have access to a private Facebook group for an extended community of support.

While many people are familiar with the main Celebrate Recovery program, there are several complementary programs under CR, including:

- **The Landing.** A student ministry geared toward junior high and high school students. The curriculum mirrors the adult program but is packaged for students to help them live emotionally and spiritually healthy lives and point them toward freedom in Christ.
- **Welcome Home.** This is CR's tool to help veterans cope with pain, overwhelming emotions, and other issues in their lives. It's for veterans and is led by veterans.
- Resources for several other accompanying programs can be found at Celebrate Recovery's website or pastor.com.

Most churches, small and large, can start a CR group in about ninety days, and CR hosts regional trainings to help churches get started. Church leaders also receive help by visiting the Celebrate Recovery Store.

re:generation recovery

From its founding in 1999, Watermark Community Church in Dallas created small close-knit community groups of its members to support one another and live authentically as followers of Christ. Living authentically quickly reveals that all Christians struggle with something, and the church launched Celebrate Recovery in 2002 to help its members care for each other. With pastors and leaders working the steps and preaching the precepts to the congregation, the CR group bloomed quickly, and by 2011, more than 700 people attended weekly.

Though it had become one of the largest Celebrate Recovery groups in the nation, the team at Watermark felt like it needed to create a new ministry to further develop participants' spiritual growth to align with the discipleship philosophy of the church.

Re:generation recovery launched in 2013 with a daily curriculum for its members, and by 2018, more than 1,200 people were attending the recovery program at the Dallas campus alone. By mid-2022, re:generation chapters were established at 150 churches across the United States with sixty-five more in development.

Re:generation offers several distinctions worth noting.

First, members are called to do more work and more reading than in most recovery programs. While other recovery programs offer weekly lessons, re:generation participants complete daily lessons, Scripture reading, and practices in spiritual formation. Nate Graybill, the primary author of the content, knew that people desperate for healing are willing to do difficult work to get well, which created an environment for discipleship rarely available elsewhere in the Church.

"Often, when you ask someone desperate for healing to do something to get well, they will do it. So we ask a lot of them because we want Christ to heal and grow every part of their lives," Graybill said. "To shift the emphasis off weekly meetings to a daily relationship with Jesus, we created daily content. And because the [twelve] steps really outline a Christian's sanctification process, this daily interaction with Christ becomes a spiritual formation journey for the participants."

Some people are quickly put off by the fifteen minutes of daily work and drop out during the early phase, called Groundwork. In fact, two-thirds of people don't complete this stage on their first try. People are still welcome to participate, but they can't advance into a closed step group until they complete Groundwork.

"Sometimes, people just aren't ready to work on recovery daily. We actually want it to be difficult for people to get through the early phase of the ministry. We want everyone who makes it to the closed groups to be committed to working on their relationship with God and recovery every day," Graybill said. "It really makes a solid group going forward. And the people that don't make it on their first try often come back when they are ready."

Once people finish Groundwork, 75 percent complete the year-long course.

This work and the focus on discipleship usher people toward a deeper understanding of Christ and biblical teaching, Graybill said. Members learn about Christian apologetics, individual giftedness, the purpose of the Church, and memorize Scripture. They learn practical and meaningful Christian lessons about growing in their identities in Christ, forgiveness and conflict resolution, how to engage in serving in the local church, and how to share the gospel.

Second, unlike many recovery groups where people might attend for the rest of their lives, re:generation recovery hosts commencement for participants after they complete all twelve steps. Men and women are welcome to repeat re:generation, but the aim is for participants to take what they have learned about Christ, themselves, and authentic relationships to serve others in their own communities. That labor might be mentoring other members in re:generation or some other area of service where God has gifted them, and they are growing in the use of that ability.

Third, launching re:generation requires more time and effort. During the planning and pilot phase, key leaders from your church go through the program for themselves. This is important for many reasons. First, re:generation blends recovery, spiritual formation, and discipleship, and that can be a unique experience for facilitators, even if they have been through other recovery or discipleship programs. Since re:generation can serve the health of the entire church (not just those with addictions), this pilot phase is an excellent time for church elders and senior ministry leaders to experience the program their churches will host and promote. Mature Christians will find the material impactful in their own lives, and it will affect how they think about re:generation in connection with their other small groups, the counseling they provide, and even the culture of their church.

Fourth, re:generation doesn't offer anonymity or confidentiality, but it guards against gossip. The manual covers this in careful detail with more instruction than I have room to provide here, but here is one part:

> Re:generation is not a safe harbor to confess guilt while protecting sin, but rather a safe place to bring sin into the light in order to deal with it biblically. Because the Bible instructs us to sometimes widen the circle, we cannot promise to keep secrets, but will pledge to not gossip, and commit to counsel one another according to Scripture with those who are a part of the problem or a part of the solution for purpose of healing (James 5:16).
>
> What is shared in the group will only go outside the group if additional steps are needed per biblical commands and never without the involvement of group leadership.

Finally, re:generation can be used in a broad spectrum of Protestant churches, but churches must align with the ministry's statement of faith to use the re:generation name and be listed on their website. Some churches that do not align doctrinally are allowed to use an unbranded version of the ministry. More information can be found online at Watermark's Resources page.

Equipping Your Church

I hope you noticed that none of the tools and programs listed require the senior pastor to have sustained engagement. Pastors simply don't have time to provide ongoing one-on-one counseling and discipleship; however, pastors must engage to create a culture of safety and grace and equip the body to do the continuing work.

Employing tools and programs in your church might face resistance from any number of fronts. It requires courage to extend grace and resolve to address such a formidable enemy to the spiritual life of your congregation.

Chapter 16

Guarding the Next Generation

It is easier to build strong children than to repair broken [people].
Frederick Douglass

When it comes to porn and kids, there is so much gloom on the topic, so let's start with a happy story.

I had just finished setting up a Covenant Eyes booth at a Florida homeschool conference when I heard a woman shriek. I looked over my shoulder and saw a mom bolting in my direction. She plodded up to me and exclaimed, "I attended your session last year, did exactly what you said, and my seven-year-old son was exposed to porn!"

I hoped not to be hit with a purse. Tammy introduced herself and was grinning from ear to ear, so maybe I would escape unscathed.

Tammy went on to explain how she had used the software, training tools, and conversation guides with her son that I had recommended. My talk explained parental awareness and how parents can prepare kids for the day they are exposed to porn so that young children know what porn is and how to turn away and let a parent know what happened.

Her son was playing with their seven-year-old neighbor who had just received a tablet for his birthday. Unfortunately, this young lad quickly found pornography with his new device, which he thrust into the face of his friend with the exclamation, "Look what I found!"

Tammy's son turned his head immediately, thrust his hand in front of the screen, and said, "No, that's pornography!" And then he turned, ran, and told his mom and dad what happened. Tammy praised her son for doing exactly as she had taught him. But she also let the neighboring parents know what had transpired.

The neighbor parents were taken aback, shocked that their son would even be curious about sex at age seven. When they dug deeper, the parents discovered their son had shown pornography to kids (ages seven through eleven) throughout their neighborhood.

The neighborhood kids kept the porn a secret. Some had been shocked by what they saw, not knowing what to do. Likely, some felt shame or feared they would get in trouble. Others might have seen porn before and corroborated with their young friend. Whatever the reasons, these kids were mum to adults.

Tammy's son, the only youngster who had been trained by his parents, was the lone child who told a parent.

This is the truth I have found. We can equip our young children to be resilient to porn. We can sharpen them to be bold, daring, and brave, but it will require courage from each of us.

Innocence Lost

When you greet families in your church next Sunday, notice the beautiful young faces looking up at you. Many of those kids eight and older have been exposed to porn. Some of the five- and six-year-olds have been exposed as well. Keep in mind that today's kids aren't just seeing nudity, they are seeing hardcore, violent, demeaning, and explicit sex. In a flash, many kids go from knowing nothing about sex to hardcore porn.

Not just the kids who attend church without their parents, but also the good kids from great families have seen hardcore porn too. In the years around 2010, when my son was young, I collected smartphones from eight- to ten-year-old church-going friends that were soaked in porn when they entered my house.

Approximately 53 percent of eleven- to sixteen-year-olds have seen explicit material online, and 94 percent of these kids had been exposed by the age of fourteen, according to a Middlesex University study released in 2017.[121] Secular organizations like Culture Reframed provide Western culture research from several countries that place the average age of first exposure at twelve years old, "and anecdotal evidence as young as 8."[122]

But surely our good Christian boys and girls are not so susceptible, or are they? In 2019, I led a team to speak at twenty-seven homeschool conferences, where parents are among the most protective of what their children see and hear. The vast majority of those attending were Christians, and I heard repeated stories of six- to eight-year-olds being exposed to porn. In a follow-up email survey with parents who had visited our booth or attended a speaking session, I found that:

- 40 percent of these homeschool parents knew their child had seen porn. Of those kids,
  - 2 percent were ages two to four.
  - More than 21 percent of kids were ages five and eight.
  - 37.3 percent of the kids were nine to twelve years old.
  - 31 percent were thirteen to fifteen.

There is another caveat to this scenario. A 2012 Tru Research survey found that 71 percent of kids hide portions of what they do online from their parents.[123] So if 40 percent of these homeschool parents were aware their child or teen had been exposed to porn, how many more kids had been exposed without their parents' knowledge? Did children see porn earlier than their parents' discovery?

While 26 percent of these parents said their child was exposed by a peer or family member, about 60 percent of these parents said their child found porn on their own.

Porn Hijacks Kids' Brains Too

I often find that parents believe five myths about their child and porn.

1. My child is a good kid and wouldn't be curious about sex and would never look at porn.
2. If my child saw it, he would just look away.
3. The measures I have in place are good enough. (This typically means occasionally looking over a shoulder to see what is on a screen.)

4. Boys are the only ones who struggle. I don't need to worry about my girls.
5. If I talk to my child about pornography, they will become curious and search for it.

As a homeschooled child growing up in a Christian home, Sarah had many advantages in avoiding inappropriate content online. She didn't ride a school bus packed with kids watching cell phones, and she missed the naughty jokes on the playground. But at eight years old, she overheard some boys saying words she just didn't know, so she petitioned her dad for his phone and asked Google what the words meant.

Each search produced a parade of images and videos that shocked and confused her and ignited feelings she didn't understand. Like every child, she was curious about what people looked like naked, but this was so much more than that. And each image and video led to another, and only the sound of her parents' footsteps could break the trance.

Like most parents, simple over-the-shoulder glances were the only way Sarah's parents filtered and monitored devices in their home because they expected the best from their child. However, week after week, month after month, Sarah watched porn for two years before her parents discovered her habit and provided help.

Only 39 percent of parents use parental controls to block, filter, or monitor their teens' online activities.[124]

At fifteen, Sarah brought her dad to our Covenant Eyes conference booth to sign up for our services, and she grabbed a handful of Covenant Eyes flyers to take home. "So many of my friends are struggling too," she said.

Sarah's story is common. Children today, who know little to nothing about sex, stumble into hardcore and deviant porn. Because they are unprepared for what they see, they fall headlong into its neurologically stimulating trap. Often, they have the sense that this must be wrong, but their brains won't turn away. Feelings of shame, secrecy, and fear help them keep their secret from their parents, yet they are less reserved about sharing their discoveries with other children. And thus, pornography is being spread from child to child like the secret handshake of an exclusive club, except the membership is sadly broad and destructive.

Parents shudder at this thought. Surely, their beautiful, sweet, and playful child would never be curious (like you and I were curious at that age). And even if they did see pornography, wouldn't they just look away? It wouldn't dig its claws into them, right? If they did see porn, wouldn't it be better to just ignore it because talking to them about it might make them more curious, right?

Let me pause here and address the curiosity question first. I have never found that children seek porn because their parents provided meaningful information on the topic. The opposite is true. When parents withhold training, they are putting their kids at higher risk for porn discovery and ongoing secretive use. Many Christian counselors and parenting professionals confirm my experience too.

In the following sections, let's review why it's so hard for an untrained child to look away from porn.

Holy Smokes. What's That?

God designed our amazing bodies and our amazing brains. He created sex and sex is good. And what has a more intense impact on the brain than sex? Not much.

Porn is not sex. Porn is a hijacking of what God created.

Today's graphic online pornography commandeers the brain's neurology with what neurologists call supernormal stimuli. In basic scientific terms, supernormal stimuli are artificially enhanced. They subvert and hijack our natural appetites and motivational systems and overstimulate our neural pathways.

In common terms, porn can light up a brain, including an unsuspecting and inexperienced child's brain.

Since the 1950s, a myriad of studies by Niko Tinbergen and others have shown songbirds choosing to feed fake babies who had wider and redder mouths, peacocks preferring exaggerated dummies for mating, and butterflies trying to mate with bright cardboard replicas and ignoring other real butterflies.

We see supernormal stimuli affecting people today as they choose saltier, sweeter, and fattier processed foods. Our senses are artificially stimulated far above what we find in nature. If those supernormal stimuli change behavior, they pale in comparison to today's pornography, which activates a fireworks show in the arousal and rewards systems of the brain.

Online, a person can surf through dozens, even hundreds, of images and videos at a time. Seeing so much pornography, which is often shocking, violent, and even bizarre, isn't normal. And a child's brain, as well as an adult's brain, can become hijacked.

One night while doing her homework, eleven-year-old Janeen clicked a pop-up ad that flooded her screen and her mind with images and videos she wasn't prepared to see. Instead of looking away, she looked for more. Instead of telling an adult, she was ashamed and kept her secret.

Janeen—an honor roll student, soccer player, and active church kid—kept her secret for eleven months until her mom discovered her activity. Janeen is not unique among the kids treated at Capstone Counseling, which has offices in six cities in Georgia. Especially since the advent of the smartphone, Clinical Director Dr. Richard Blankenship said that compulsive pornography use among teens is becoming prevalent and the ages are becoming ever younger.

"I have treated children as young as five," Blankenship said. "A five-year-old was brought to treatment with me after charging $700 to the family credit card."

Supernormal stimulus is just the first step. Cravings and seeking behavior for porn come with repetition, and most adults who struggle deeply with pornography were exposed during their formative years of development.

Neurology Special to Youthful Brains

Earlier chapters discussed the neurology correlated with porn use, but there are facets important for children specifically.

First, one reason that children learn faster than adults is that they have many more mirror neurons. Simply explained, mirror neurons allow you to see something, and it feels like you are doing it. It's why you recoil when you see a batter get hit with a baseball or your heart races when you see runners cross a finish line. And mirror neurons are at work when watching porn, helping ignite the arousal and rewards centers of the brain.

Second, a young brain is in conflict. This conflict arises from a more robust rewards center versus underdeveloped executive functioning. You've likely heard of the marshmallow test, invented by Dr. Walter Mischel in the early 1970s, where a child is presented with a marshmallow. The child can choose to eat the marshmallow immediately for an instant reward or he can wait for some time and receive extra marshmallows. Overwhelmingly, children gobble the first marshmallow.

The prefrontal cortex is responsible for managing impulse control, making decisions, weighing risks, and making other executive decisions. But the prefrontal cortex doesn't develop fully until a person is in his mid-twenties. Meanwhile, the limbic system, the emotional center of the brain, which is responsible for basic functions like hunger, thirst, anger, fear, and even sex, gets a big head start over the prefrontal cortex. The limbic system is sensitive to possibly rewarding behavior and impatient for the reward. It is also sensitive to adrenaline and enjoys risk-taking behaviors. For example, car insurance for teens is more expensive because their brains are prone to enjoy risky driving behaviors and are more likely to fail at weighing the consequences of driving too fast.

Now, let's add to this conflict the neurochemical dopamine. You'll recall that dopamine focuses attention, gives a spritz of reward, and helps us remember how to respond to a stimulus in the future. Dopamine loves new experiences and novelty.

Let's put this together for a child encountering porn for the first time or seeing the ongoing and endless novelty of online porn. A child, who is naturally curious about what people look like naked, sees the supernormal stimuli of today's porn and receives a hit of dopamine. The child may feel shock but also gets a surprising dose of good feelings within the rewards center. Dopamine focuses his attention to the point of tunnel vision. Even if there is a part of the child that says they should turn away, the limbic system typically overpowers the weaker prefrontal cortex.

This perspective helped a mom understand why her eleven-year-old son was so entranced when he was discovered watching porn on the family computer. "I knew it was wrong," the boy told his mom. "I just couldn't stop clicking. I don't know why, but I just couldn't stop clicking."

As well, dopamine and norepinephrine solidify the memory of porn exposure for future excursions. Mirror neurons can make a child feel like he is part of the video being watched, and he might mimic the behaviors he sees in porn even before his body is physically capable.

"A seven-year-old boy was brought to our office, having been exposed to porn online by older boys in his neighborhood," Blankenship said. "This boy graphically described sexual activity he had experienced with a seven-year-old relative. He explained that 'I did with her what I saw in the sex movies.'"

Should the Church Provide Help?

As a church leader, I hope you are concerned about what you've read so far in this chapter. But you might be saying to yourself, "Protecting kids from porn is a job for parents, not my church." You're not wrong, but ignoring the issue as a pastor or church leader will damage the future of your church. Pastors and church leaders impact the parents in their church by both action and inaction. Albert Einstein once said, "Doing nothing is very destructive."[125]

A modern-day proverb describes a village set on the banks of a river. One day, a villager spots a person flailing about in the water and pleading for help as he floats downstream. The villagers rush to the man's aid and pull him from the river. In the following days, weeks, and months, more and more people are rescued from the swift-moving current—so much so that the villagers set up rescue training seminars and build a hospital for all of the poor souls who are rescued from the current. Then one day, someone suggests they walk upstream to find out why so many people are being caught in the flow.

There are multiple versions of what happens next, but suffice to say, the downstream villagers work at prevention efforts upstream: a bridge is repaired, a railing is placed on a cliff, and children are taught how to avoid falling into the river.

Helping adults with porn struggles is like dragging people from the river; protecting kids from porn and training kids to be resilient to porn is the equivalent of protecting people from falling in the river in the first place. What Walter Mischel discovered with the Marshmallow Test is that kids can be trained to resist taking the marshmallow for a better reward. Likewise, children can be taught to know what pornography is before they see it and learn to turn away.

"I would rather put a fence at the top of the cliff than an ambulance at the bottom," Josh McDowell told church leaders at the Set Free Summit.[126]

Here are seven reasons you should host an annual online safety and pornography training night for parents.

1. Training parents to protect their kids is a comfortable segue to talking about porn at your church in general.
2. By helping kids in your church, you may be protecting your own kids and grandkids from child-to-child exposure.
3. Parents will learn and take action.

4. Your actions may prevent child-on-child sexual assault.

5. The biblical training provided in Sunday school, mission trips, church camps, and other youth efforts are undermined by porn habits. If you want your youth efforts to be impactful, don't miss the opportunity to help children avoid porn.

6. The training will impact future generations of the Church body.

7. Pornography issues in marriages will rise to the surface so they can be addressed too.

What Parents Need to Know

The myths and facts in this chapter, as well as the stories of adults found in this book, are good fodder for an evening or series to train parents. Churches need to prompt and prepare parents to have ongoing discussions with their kids and protect the devices in their homes. This isn't rocket science, but parents will need to invest time and patience.

When it comes to parents teaching their kids, here are two important steps.

First, you need to help parents dispel the myths that we discussed earlier in this chapter that paralyze parents from taking action. I regularly hear parents tell me about how they don't need to worry about their kids seeing porn yet because their kids are only twelve or thirteen. They often delay this conversation until the teen years, but it doesn't get far because parents haven't practiced difficult and even embarrassing conversations with their kids in general. What often happens is the parent tries to talk about porn with the teen and their son or daughter becomes embarrassed and defensive, and then the parent is embarrassed, and the whole conversation comes to an abrupt halt.

Parents need to have formative conversations with their kids early and consistently. These guiding conversations about pornography can be part of the normal and developmental discussions parents have with their kids about their bodies and how they should be protected.

Second, neither pastors nor parents have to figure this out on their own. A strong contingent of resources is available to help parents train their kids and more are becoming available, including books and websites.

In this chapter's opening story, a mom described how her son learned to turn, run, and tell. She used a book that I highly recommend for four- to seven-year-olds. It's called *Good Pictures, Bad Pictures Jr.,* and it has three awesome attributes.

1. It's a read-along book that is fun, and neither the child nor the parents will be embarrassed. I've heard many parents describe how their children ask to read this book as a bedtime story.
2. It teaches a child where their bathing suit area is and that it is private, which is also valuable to prevent child sexual abuse.
3. It gives children action steps to turn, run, and tell when they see an image or video where the bathing suit area isn't covered.

The original book, *Good Pictures, Bad Pictures* is aimed at kids from eight to twelve years old. This small chapter book explains what pornography is and details how a child can use their thinking brain to overcome their feeling brain to turn, run, and tell.

I encourage you to order a copy for yourself. Review it, and then buy a copy for each family in your church based on the ages of their kids. If your church can't afford that, urge your parents to buy it. I recognize I am putting a strong emphasis on this book, but I receive nothing for doing so. I just know it's part of a plan that's effective.

Several websites are churning out consistently strong support for parents and kids. I recommend, in no specific order, the following, and you'll likely know of others.

ProtectYoungEyes.com was founded by Covenant Eyes team member Chris McKenna, who has testified before Congress on protecting children online. This site provides outstanding training for conversations, details on the latest technologies and apps, as well as how to use parental controls on specific devices. Chris is also a sought-after speaker at schools and churches.

Axis.org has a motto of "Connecting parents, teens and Jesus in a disconnected world," and it fits their mission well. This is a subscription educational service that provides a strong library of guides, video, and audio training for parents with helpful plans that instruct parents in discipling their kids in a digital world.

Focus on the Family is a longtime favorite of pastors and parents. It continues to provide outstanding support, not only for parenting in general but also for parenting in a smartphone world. Their hotlines can help people find resources for specific situations, a free consultation with a counselor, and counseling referrals.

CovenantEyes.com is focused on accountability with adults, but it also offers educational resources to families who want to teach the value of accountability to their teens and young adolescents. In support of this effort, Covenant Eyes created resources just for churches. For example, Safe Haven Sunday (with specific versions for Protestant churches and Catholic parishes) is a program that provides special training events for the families of your church. The program includes a guide and assets to promote and launch the event, family conversation guides, and other educational materials for families.

A Parting Positive Note

Just as we started this chapter, let's end this chapter on a positive note. This is a true story from a Covenant Eyes member and dad who prepared his son for a world confronting him with porn.

One day after soccer practice, an eighth-grade boy got into the family car and said, "Dad, guys are dumb." Any parent can recognize what is bound to be a good conversation.

"Okay, I'll bite," the dad said. "Why are guys dumb?"

"Today after soccer practice, the guys were standing around talking about their favorite porn to watch. They're talking about the acts they like to see and the sites they go to. They notice I'm not saying anything, so somebody says, 'C'mon Andrew, what's your favorite porn?' I said, 'I don't watch porn.'"

"They are like, 'What? You don't watch porn?'"

"I told them the first reason I don't watch porn is that I'm a Christian. And some are like, 'Okay, that's your thing.' And others were like, 'Yeah, we go to church too. What's the big deal?'"

"Then I said, 'Guys, did you know it's addictive?'"

"They were like, 'No way, porn's not addictive. I can stop anytime I want.'"

"'Well, it is addictive. That's why there are so many people seeking therapy for porn addiction and sex addiction. What about guys like Tiger Woods, who was married to a supermodel, yet that wasn't enough?'"

The boys had no comeback for this, and so Andrew said, "What does it say about you if you get excited by watching a slave?" (He didn't say excited. I cleaned it up for you.)

The boys were at a loss. "What are you talking about?"

Andrew replied, "Pornography contributes to sex trafficking and sex trafficking contributes to porn. If you do a Google search for porn, you're likely going to be looking at a slave. What does that say about you?"

Picture this thirteen-year-old boy surrounded by his peers, all of whom have been sucked in by porn. He is a lone voice. He is the minority. Yet he is educated enough, courageous enough, and bold enough to look other boys in the eye and say, "I don't look at porn, and it's wrong."

Who do you want the children of your church to be? Do you want them to be the ones comparing porn notes with friends? Or do you want your parents to raise kids who can stand in a world awash in porn and say, "Pornography is wrong, and I will protect my purity because it matters to God, it matters to me, it matters to a world that is enslaved, and it will matter to my future spouse and children."

It is our time as parents, as communities, and as churches to raise courageous kids. But it will require courage from each of us. We can prepare our kids to confront our sexualized culture. We can help them exercise and train their hearts and minds to be skillful and daring and brave.

Chapter 17
Culture Eats Strategy for Lunch

The bigger the change we hope for,
the longer we must be willing to invest, work for, and wait for it.

Andy Crouch

his is the big deal. This is the secret sauce.

Remember Brandon, Darlene, and Nate Graybill? Their churches share something brilliant.

Yes, all three people struggled with porn or unwanted sexual behavior. Yes, all three found freedom. Yes, all three now mentor others. But none of that is my focus in this chapter.

All three people found individual churches that strive for an overarching culture. Those cultures are focused on creating disciples who love God, live in authentic community, love one another, and serve and share their joy with others. It permeates everything these churches do, and their leaders are passionate about it. This brand of discipleship doesn't fall to charismatic personalities at these churches. The champions, the inciters of change, are ordinary staff members, volunteers, and church members who have walked this journey themselves.

You might be saying to yourself, "Don't we have that in our church?"

Pause for a moment and ask yourself the following questions about your church body: Would my church welcome the old sinful Darlene when she asked for help?

197

Would the culture in my church want Brandon to confess and tell his story? Would people in my church not only pray *for* Nate but also pray *with* him and walk with him daily as his guides toward freedom? Would members at my church be equipped with the knowledge and processes to help an addict? Could Nate ever be restored as a fallen Christian leader and serve in ministry?"

Notice that I didn't ask if *you* would do this. I asked if your *church body* would do this work. If you just said, "No," that's okay. It's a good place to start. If you said, "Yes," great! I hope you will pluck golden nuggets from these pages too.

Let's pull the steeples off of a few churches to look under the roofs at their cultures. What makes their staff and congregational culture special? Why are they so good, not only at helping people escape porn habits, but also at helping people drop other habitual sins and focus their affections on God? We'll learn from their mistakes too. We'll discover why they do hard things well. We'll unlock how leaders crafted their cultures and strategic focus with intention. We'll also review unexpected opportunities and trials that tested and strengthened their resolve. I am not asking you to mimic or attempt to duplicate the values, activities, and cultures of the churches in this chapter; rather, I hope to provide you with examples that inspire you to spend more time, effort, and emphasis on your own church culture.

"Culture eats strategy for lunch," is a common phrase in business circles. It's no less important for your church. A church may claim to reach the lost and disciple followers of Christ, but if the culture doesn't support those efforts, the staff and church members will weaken or undermine any strategy you set in place to accomplish such goals. Often, it's not intentional; they will simply be distracted by shiny objects—campaigns, programs, and other efforts—that may not fit the vision set by your church.

As you go through this chapter, here are a few questions to keep in mind.

- Is my church culture intentional or accidental? (In other words, do you and the leaders in your church focus on creating culture?)
- Do the leaders in my church and I nurture the culture we have envisioned? Or do we just have a mission statement that isn't practiced?
- How much time (weekly) do I spend reinforcing the values and mission of my church?
- Are our values both written and spoken? Do I repeat them often?

- What would you change first about your church culture?
- If my church culture could address pornography well, how much more could we do for the Kingdom?

Within this small space, I hope to help you address these questions and more because creating culture is pragmatic and not abstract. Because it deserves further study, I will also include a list of resources for deeper review.

Every organization and every church has a culture whether it's recognized as such or not. It might be passed down through tradition or established within a church plant. Whatever your culture, it may support your efforts or defeat your aims, or even create lots of activity with little progress.

Culture is a multiplier. Whatever your culture, you will see a multiplying effect.

Accidental Culture

Sometimes, the culture within a church or organization happens by accident and grows from the behaviors of leaders and individuals within. For instance, a church with competing programs and visions might create a culture with silos of activity that miss the stated vision of the church.

Accidental culture isn't always bad, necessarily. Have you ever had a dynamic small group teacher or couple in your church, and that small group seemed to be alight with joy and service to others and the church? But when those leaders moved to a different city, the small group dried up, and it did so because no one else could match how they defined the group's culture. Their vocabulary, conduct, ceremonies, and goals weren't codified and weren't passed on.

When it comes to addressing the issue of pornography and other strong-holds, accidental culture is common and typically detrimental to helping people find healing.

Here is an example. We have discussed the devastating impact of shame in several chapters of this book and how it exacerbates a cycle of compulsive behav-ior. Shame is not only a personal barrier, it's also a cultural phenomenon in many churches. On one Sunday morning, a pastor announced from the pulpit that he would like to offer a well-known video series and workbook study on porn for the men of the church. Any man interested need only fill out a card and place it in a basket found in the sanctuary foyer. As about 200 people filed out of the building, the basket remained empty. Though well-intended, the pastor underestimated the lack of vulnerability in his church. Unless you address shame directly and publicly, an underlying shaming culture will undermine your efforts to address pornography.

A church that hosts support and recovery groups might deny the undertow of a shaming culture. Unfortunately, many churches have created a cultural chasm between recovery groups and the main body of the church, and people won't cross the bridge to find support until the consequences overwhelm them.

For instance, the church staff might talk about the value of a support group in the church, but they won't attend themselves or even teach a lesson for the group. This can happen for many reasons, but here are two: First, staff often don't participate in order to support anonymity for people attending. Second, church culture has claimed staff members are too mature to have weaknesses and are somehow better off than the Apostle Paul in Romans 7. Church attendees who want to look good in the eyes of their pastors and others follow the examples they see, trying to work out their struggles without a good process or mentors.

This distance results in a caste system, said Dr. James Reeves. Those support groups and programs become reserved for the "sickos." A person may need the help offered, but he wears a mask. As a member of the general congregation caste, he would never attend a support group for fear of being placed in a lower caste of Christians. Recovery is for "*those people.*" *That* workbook and video series are for the misfits.

Missional vs. Permissional

Permissional may not be a word, but it makes sense when Nate Graybill uses it to describe how many local churches implement recovery ministry.

When work and ministry garner missional importance, it becomes woven into the fabric of the church. Pastors and church leaders have a vested interest. It's entwined into a variety of activities and efforts across a spectrum of the congregation. Examples would include a church's missionary objectives or teaching focus. Likely, you carry a passion for areas where God has granted you spiritual gifts, and those gifts might focus your attention on specific priorities. All of that is good.

Permissional ministry lacks this integration. Pastors and church leaders might agree to host a recovery ministry at their church, but it's an adjunct ministry at best, and it's possibly an accessory that wouldn't be missed if the undertaking folded.

Many pastors know they need to provide help, but they are often unsure of what kind of resource is the right fit for their church. Is it as simple as a sermon or a guest speaker at a men's, women's, or singles' night? Should staff members refer a confessing porn struggler to a Christian counselor or to a church that hosts a Celebrate Recovery meeting? Maybe the church could offer to its attendees a program or Bible study on overcoming lust?

Often, pastors see recovery ministry through a clouded lens for several valid reasons. First, in an effort to provide safety, most twelve-step models and support groups offer their members a secure location where non-attendees don't meander past. What's said within the group, stays in the group, and the pastor might wonder, "Is Jim (or Jane) making progress? What goes on at those meetings anyway?"

Sometimes, recovery ministry is viewed through the lens as a program for the underling, second-best Christians. It's not for a broad spectrum of people, just a few who struggle abnormally.

Finally, the term "twelve-step" might conflict with a pastor's view of sanctification. It might collide with church theology. If this is true for you, would you consider a different premise for recovery ministry? What if recovery became another tool for discipleship?

Discipleship Recovery

When Nate was restored in community at Watermark, he didn't just find freedom from a nagging problem with porn. He also found healing that impacted every part of his life as a father, as a husband, as a layman, as a man, and as a Christian.

Looking back, Graybill said his journey to freedom followed the Twelve Steps even though none in his small group realized it. They were simply using the Bible as a guide to surrender in faith, mortify sin, and bring healing through fellowship. After a year of discipleship, sobriety, and recovery, Pastor Todd Wagner asked Nate and his wife Teresa to share their story before their still-growing congregation of about 500 people. While a video of their story played on the screen, Nate and Teresa were surrounded by their community group who had walked with them through the grim details, the wounds, and the journey to freedom.

Some attendees were shocked that words like pornography were used openly during a Sunday morning worship service, and they looked down their noses and pursed their lips. Some people left the church. Many people were quiet.

But overwhelmingly, authenticity won the day. People caught a vision of how the Body of Christ could love, care, and restore its wounded.

That day sparked a movement that brought people with many struggles out of hiding and into groups that supported life change. To this day, fresh stories of God's grace are celebrated in Watermark's newsletters, videos, and live testimonies. Watermark Church members speak about a process of restoration with the support of a community that cares more about sinners than their sins. By leaning into people's lives, the church more than ever began to live up to its nine core values:

- Biblically-based.
- Fully devoted to Christ.
- Grounded in grace.
- Passionate about prayer.
- Authentic in our walk.
- Committed to the uncommitted.
- Relevant and innovative.
- Committed to community.
- Focused on ministry and service.[127]

Testimonies, support, and other exercises illustrated a grace-based culture, which became a magnet, drawing the unsaved, the broken, and the curious. At this writing, more than 12,000 people attend this Dallas church on a typical Sunday morning, a far cry from its humble beginning of 150 people. Watermark's practices and cultural innovations are shared across the nation through its annual Church Leadership Conference and its restorative programs, such as re:engage (for marriage support) and re:generation.

Recovery as discipleship is what sets Watermark, Mariners Church, City on a Hill, Grace Church, and other churches like them apart. Recovery ministry is simply part of helping Christians—veterans and new believers alike—live authentic lives and be restored and transformed.

A man stuck in compulsive porn behavior can't express a full love for God when porn remains an idol in his life. He can't love his wife to his full ability when he compromises his attention and affections for pixels. When he is fully known and fully loved, he becomes free to welcome God into every room of his house. With freedom and the support of a loving community, he experiences a joy that must be given away. That's the biblical call to go and make disciples, and it's also the Twelfth Step.

Safe Community

Honesty demands vulnerability and vulnerability requires safety. Within a safe space honesty blooms. Through a safe process, people dig deeply, discovering their personal inventory and the roots of their struggles. They learn to live in the light and have fellowship with others where healing begins and the blood of Jesus cleanses sin (1 John 1:7).

Achieving a safe culture in your church might look different than it does for another church. It depends greatly on the values practiced and the behaviors reinforced for the staff and congregation.

Traditionally, recovery groups meet at churches on nights when nothing else is going on. People can attend without the greater church community or the public knowing that they are struggling or addicted. When newcomers first attend, they are relieved to know they only need to say their first names when participating. In essence, safety is secured by providing the opportunity of anonymity both within the group and the greater community.

Veteran members of recovery groups know each other well and even claim membership proudly in public. You've likely seen Alcoholics Anonymous and Celebrate Recovery members proudly displaying their chips (signifying years of sobriety) on social media. Men and women living free of porn are often more reserved because of lesser public acceptance. Nonetheless, they eagerly share the home they've found with others in the church and help newcomers feel safe at meetings. Not all support groups are twelve-step groups, but the vast majority lay claim to something resembling the Twelfth Step: You give away what you have received.

Declarations of safety provide guidelines for newcomers and security for everyone. Within Samson Society meetings, which happen in-person at churches and online, this statement is part of the liturgy:

> We tell the truth about ourselves, knowing that our brothers will listen to
> us in love and will hold whatever we say in **strictest confidence**. We try to
> keep our comments brief, taking care to leave plenty of time for others. We
> address our statements to the group as a whole rather than directing them

toward any one person. As a rule, we refrain from giving advice to others or instructing them during the meeting, believing that such conversations are best reserved for private moments between friends.

Of course, this kind of safety can be achieved in a less formal setting than in a typical support group. For a small group study, it might be as simple as reading a statement about how the members will not repeat the honest discussions outside of the group study. Attendees might even sign a written agreement.

Still, other churches take a bold, straightforward approach. Churches like Watermark and City on a Hill secure safety through authenticity. Let's return to Watermark's early story of discipleship recovery.

From its founding, Watermark focused on connecting members in small, close-knit community groups where imperfect people live in authenticity, carry one another's burdens, and exhort one another to follow Christ. Belonging to a community group is mandatory for church membership. When people deal with strongholds, pastoral care and community groups work in tandem to restore and support members. With this premise, and more people seeking help after Nate's testimony, adding a formal recovery ministry seemed like a natural progression.

With a missional directive from the elder board, Nate and other Watermark Church members launched a chapter of Celebrate Recovery; however, early implementation missed the stated values set by church elders. One night as the elder board convened in the office building that served as the church's home at the time, the women's ministry director burst in to shoo them out. The elders were told they couldn't be in the vicinity where Celebrate Recovery attendees were entering for the night's meeting.

That didn't sit well with Todd Wagner, at that time the senior pastor (and now author of *Come & See*). He thought, if people needed to enter a back door to a secret room to feel safe, that meant Watermark wasn't a safe church.

Leaning on their stated values, the elders began to work more diligently on creating a safe congregation and not just a safe group within the church. Todd and the elders told their personal stories of life change at Sunday morning services and other venues. They preached on the destructive nature of shame and described how those who attended Celebrate Recovery were the healthiest people in the church because they were focused on tearing down barriers in their relationship with Jesus. Elders, staff, and respected lay leaders worked from the top down, while the Celebrate Recovery leaders and community group shepherds worked from the bottom up.

A prime ingredient of this culture shift came through the power of stories. Stories change lessons into roadmaps. Stories make the ethereal undeniable. Stories provide an example of someone who is a lot like me, and if they can do it, maybe I can too. The stories came slowly at first—painfully so. For a few years, it was mainly leaders who were telling their stories, but they were consistent and patient. The elders, staff, and church leaders concluded they were not only shaping culture at the church, but they were also overcoming years of shame and secrecy that members had learned outside the church.

One Christmas season it became evident that the consistent strategy was working. Elders and other leaders taught a series on hurts, hang-ups, and bad habits. Christmastime might seem an odd time to start such a series, but think about it. For many people, the holidays bring a period of heightened stress, conflict, and emotions. The prevalent triggers that push people to bad coping behaviors are common. Instead of pleasant cantatas and cute Christmas plays, the Watermark team pressed into people's pain. As part of the series, they asked if ninety people would volunteer to give cardboard testimonies, which are very simple. A person stands on the stage with a large card. On one side a card might say, "Addicted to pornography," then the card is flipped, and it might read, "Free from addiction!" No talking required.

Within ten minutes, all ninety slots filled up. Thirty people stood on stage at each of three services, acknowledging their biggest struggles and proclaiming victory. Nate recognized at least eighty of the people on stage had gone through Celebrate Recovery, and they were taking a bolder stride in working the Twelfth Step.

That Christmas sermon series flipped a switch at Watermark. Suddenly, the leaders weren't the only ones telling their stories of life change and recovery. The dynamic provided ongoing opportunities for video testimonies that were paired with sermons. The weekly church bulletin includes a segment called the Watermark News, where a member tells the story of their freedom journey.

A new phrase also entered the vocabulary of the church body, and it's still used today—"the healthiest people." It refers to those who faithfully attend or complete the recovery program born out of Watermark's experiences, called re:generation recovery. "The healthiest people" is a phrase repeated at every opportunity: in sermons, in small group discussions and Bible studies, in pastoral care and community group discussions. When people go to a staff member with a habitual struggle re:-generation recovery is part of the process.

Keys to Creating Culture

So far, you likely picked up pieces about creating culture. With these examples in place, let's boil it down to six imperative steps that you can put into action.

1. Document Your Values

Unwritten values ebb and flow with time and circumstances. Watermark elders could have accepted being shooed from their meeting. Instead, the written values of the church are aimed at higher principles. It reminded and guided the elders' choices and responses. If your written values don't hold enough weight to sway and guide your leaders and congregation, then revisit, recommit, or rewrite them.

Pastor Jonathan Pokluda rewrote the mission statement of Harris Creek Baptist Church in McGregor, Texas, because the prior one didn't describe what the church was actually doing. The new mission statement is emblazoned in bold type on the church's homepage: "Harris Creek exists to help everyone follow Jesus by engaging the lost, equipping the saints, and empowering members for service." Any effort or program that doesn't meet that guideline receives a swift ax.

2. Repeat Like a Broken Record

If your values truly matter, then say them out loud so often that they become a reflex for your choices and behaviors and that of your staff and volunteers.

Managers and executives at Covenant Eyes start the vast majority of our weekly meetings with a recitation of what we call our Organizational Clarity. Most employees memorize them. It describes 1) Why do we exist? 2) How do we behave? 3) What do we do? 4) How will we succeed? These principles govern not only our work and projects, they also guide our interactions with our members, partners, and within our staff.

For purposes of being succinct. Here are the first two for our employee-owned company:

Why do we exist?
Pornography is corrupting hundreds of millions of people. We exist to change the course of history by enabling the world to overcome porn and be restored and transformed.

How do we behave?
- Honor God.
- Optimism.
- Passion for excellence.
- Service to others.

Here's one example of how these values guide costly choices. Several times, financial and business advisors have protested that we spend too much money staffing our Member Care Center to respond to more than 90 percent of our calls and chats within one minute. That is our goal because we are passionate about excellence and service to others. People are struggling deeply with pornography, so our Member Care specialists not only help people with our software, they also introduce our members to educational resources to help them in their journey and protect their homes. Notice that the department isn't called "tech support." It's called Member Care. We nurture people who bear the image of God, and 96 percent of our members say they use Covenant Eyes to draw closer to God.

When advisors point to overhead, we smile and repeat the values that guide our mission.

3. Lead by Example
As the Apostle Paul told believers to follow him as he followed Christ (1 Cor. 11:1), good leaders model the culture they want to see. A culture that rises from the bottom typically hits a low ceiling. When culture is orchestrated from the top down, modeled values become more inspirational and important.

At City on a Hill, every ministry leader has been through a twelve-step group of some kind, including their base-level class called "Life Change for Every Christian." At Watermark, about 60 percent of the staff, including many elders and teaching staff, have been through their one-year program, re:generation recovery.

When a pastoral team does this deep dive, it strips any shame for the newcomer. It took modeling and repetition by leaders for church members to accept that Watermark was a safe church.

If that's too big of a step for you, a common way that pastors create safety is by speaking and preaching with authenticity. Lead with a limp. Speak with vulnerability about your struggles, both past and present, as much as you feel you can. It may be a progressive effort. If you don't have a trusted ally relationship, get one soon, and talk to your congregation about the healing power of living in authentic relationships. Model the relationships and community you want for your church.

4. Build Trust

People often think of trust as a predictive sense—in that, if you know someone, you can trust how they might react or behave in a certain situation, wrote business expert Patrick Lencioni in *The Advantage*.[128] But that's not the kind of trust that builds cohesive teams, which is what he calls vulnerability-based trust.

"This is what happens when members get to a point where they are completely comfortable being transparent, honest, and naked with one another, where they say and genuinely mean things like 'I [messed] up,' 'I need help,' 'Your idea is better than mine,' 'I wish I could learn to do that as well as you do,' and even, 'I'm sorry,'" Lencioni wrote.

This kind of trust must be taught because it doesn't come naturally in our larger culture. More importantly, it must be modeled and valued and praised when team members do it well.

Trust allows teams to cooperate better, achieve goals faster, and creates ongoing opportunities for learning and growth. A culture that provides helpful feedback is a good example of a trusting culture. At Watermark and Covenant Eyes, asking for feedback is routine. People want to know, "How well did I run that meeting so I can make it better the next time?" "What did I do well and how can I improve in running a project?" Modeling requires leaders to ask for feedback as well. When you or a member of a team has feedback to offer, ask permission to give it and make it constructive. Mistakes and failures are good opportunities for learning and growth.

The Watermark "Owner's Manual" for its team has a section to instruct staff members on how to give feedback well. "Our feedback culture doesn't only impact the staff, it impacts the entire church," the manual states. "We often provide feedback to our members as part of shepherding them, caring for them and at times correcting them. We do this because we love them and we believe this is part of our role as pastors and shepherds. Giving feedback is a skill, so work hard at it and observe and learn from those who do this well."

5. Fun and Rewards

Creating a great culture is a gas. If you're not having fun, you're doing it wrong because laughter reduces anxiety, boosts participation, and focuses attention. This might sound bizarre because life-saving recovery ministry is serious business. And that's why laughter is so important; hard and stressful work needs a double dose of joy.

At Covenant Eyes, we do some bizarre things. One example is Marmot Day, where we celebrate woodchucks, groundhogs, and their near relatives with huge amounts of food, a wood-chucking contest, a dunk tank for executives, and many other games and activities. It's a half-day celebration for employees and their families to build camaraderie and blow off steam from diligent work.

At Watermark, they often play Farkle. The whole point of Farkle is that everyone has an equal opportunity to lose. It's a game of chance where your strength, skill, or knowledge prove worthless. Winners receive a prize but remain largely ignored; instead, the losers reap all the attention. For example, losers of Farkle might have to announce themselves with a boisterous voice whenever they enter or exit a room for the day, such as "David is here!" Or, they might take a swim in the pond outside the church while eating a gifted lunch.

"I'm asking you to take fun seriously. As leaders, we owe it to ourselves. We owe it to our teams to give them laughter, to give them humility, and to build unity," David Penuel, a Watermark pastor, told leaders with a smirk at an annual Church Leadership Conference.

As well, provide fitting accolades to your teams, including support staff, volunteers, and others. Recognition inspires and builds confidence, especially as people take their first steps in a new venture or push the limits of their abilities. Reward the often overlooked people who do boring yet necessary tasks ongoing. But don't use a one-size-fits-all model. For some, public recognition is welcome, but others will find it humiliating. You might handwrite a personal note and include a gift card. Be specific and describe why they are deserving of recognition.

At Covenant Eyes, if "you're caught" doing great work or serving others, a manager or other leader might present you with a quartz crystal (our founder, Ron DeHaas, is a geologist). This chunk may be delivered to our accounting department in exchange for thirty bucks, but often, employees choose to display their troves in their workspace instead.

6. Hire for Culture

In his investigations, Lencioni finds the best teams aren't made up of superstars with expensive degrees and notoriety. Instead, the healthiest organizations (Lencioni helps churches and non-profits too) maintain cohesive teams. These teams maintain a high degree of trust, master conflict, embrace accountability, and focus on results. They provide helpful feedback to each other, work to support each other's successes, and reflect on completed projects to learn from their mistakes.

Core values become more important than resumes in the hiring process because the team is hiring not only for competence but also for chemistry and attitudes. Watermark even created a staff "Owner's Manual" for new staff members, and it describes why they were chosen.

"We did not hire you because you are a 'strategic fit,' we hired you because we believe you are a person of character, you are competent, you are a good chemistry fit and because we believe you are going to help preserve and improve our staff culture. Since we believe the culture is more important than the strategy, it is not a stretch to say maintaining and strengthening the staff culture is our strategy. Everything we do as a local church flows from our staff culture . . ."

7. Less Work for the Pastor, Not More

Recovery ministry might scare you, especially if you've provided pastoral counseling to someone caught in a stronghold. I remember a pastor telling me how he spent three hours with a man struggling with compulsive porn use. I asked, "So do you have time to do that again next week?" He shook his head. Of course not. What pastor can afford to provide one-on-one counseling week after week to the same person? None.

Pastor James Reeves doesn't even try and hasn't provided that kind of counseling for two decades. When other pastors ask how he gets all these people to lead and care for people in his church. His answer is simple. "We turn drunks into elders, and we turn addicts into staff members—people who are willing to turn their malady into ministry and then shepherd others," Pastor James said. "The group recovery leaders are men and women who have been through recovery. This work is done by the body; it's not done by the staff. It can't be.

"I tell pastors, if you do this kind of work, it will not add things to your plate, it will take them off because you will have an army of people who will say, 'Call me, I'm ready to give back,'" Pastor James said. "We move people to a point where they can give away more than they have to receive."

Culture Multiplier

In reading this book, you're reminded that people and their problems can be complex. Can you imagine trying to create special programs or setting aside time for pastoral counseling to fit the needs of each individual? You'd never be done.

Discipleship is a process and not a program. In other words, programs support the process of godly growth, change, and sanctification. But the discipleship process will never reach its potential without a culture that embraces and supports it.

A church that can address and disciple people struggling with pornography and unwanted sexual behaviors is a church that can help people through many more issues. Professional Christian counselors provide amazing support, no doubt. But I hope you've begun to capture a vision of how your church can create a culture that embraces a holistic process of discipleship. Instead of simply referring people to support resources outside the church, your church members become the hands and feet of Jesus. Your staff and members know the mission of your church, and they have gone through a process themselves to guide people to the freedom they have received.

In starting this chapter, I told you culture has a multiplying effect, and it's pragmatic and not abstract. Let me finish with a concrete example.

Remember Darlene? Pharisees would have stoned her for sure; and she left her church because she knew if she confessed her sexual sin, she would be stoned there too—socially and spiritually. Yes, she was a hypocrite of the highest order. She knew that. She pled guilty. But at City on a Hill, a church of about 800 in Fort Worth, she learned that God's grace is sufficient. She walked through a process and was guided by mentors that taught her how to surrender every part of her life to Jesus. God healed her marriage, and she hasn't acted out in thirty years.

Darlene thrives. After years of personal change and growth, she began serving as the women's ministry director. Not just full, her cup overflows and spills on those around her. She's grateful to share a path to redemption and wholeness through Christ with other women, regardless of their struggles. And their struggles are diverse.

One day, while I was writing this book, Darlene listened to two women who had heard about City on a Hill's culture of safety and support.

- After Sarah was raped at work, she was asked not to come back to her former church because its members feared the publicity. Sarah had played piano at that church for a decade, and when she needed them most, her fellow church members ostracized her. After her conversation with Darlene, Sarah knew she had a new church family that would care for her.
- Kari is a former prostitute who was sexually trafficked from a young age. Desperate for hope, she sought and found Jesus at a church near her home. As her faith deepened, so did her recognition of how people gossip about others at the church. She knows she has trauma, coping behaviors, and serious issues to deal with, but she also knows her church isn't a safe place to seek help. She is taking her first steps toward healing with Darlene and other women, who are teaching her a safe process for healing and discipleship in a safe place.

One day, Darlene knows, when Kari and Sarah receive the restoration they so desperately need, they will take the next step in their healing journey and give back the love and support they have received. The gift of freedom never stops giving.

Chapter 18

The Sum of Small Steps

Most times, the way isn't clear, but you want to start anyway.
It is in starting . . . that other steps become clearer.

Israelmore Ayivor, inspirational writer and entrepreneur

Long-distance hikers and marathon runners often recite an axiom that the longest journeys begin with the first step. They are not referring to the first stride in running the Chicago Marathon or walking the Appalachian Trail. No, the first step happens months before—in training.

In enjoying both of these recreations, I can tell you they did not come to me easily. It wasn't until my forties that I ran my first marathon. Through the inspiration of friends, I caught a vision of the joy of running, something I hadn't done since high school. I confessed to a running club's members, "I can't run two blocks, let alone a 5K!" Their advice was to take the first step and to run and walk intermittently. Early on, I spent more time walking than running. Soon, I could run a mile, then a 5K, then a 10K, then a half-marathon, and so on. The progress was slow, but my body and brain began to react differently to each challenge. Several things happened that I didn't understand until much later. First, I trusted guides who had run the distance before me. Second, my body became conditioned to the stress and pounding of running for long periods. Third, through consistent training, my body grew in its capacity to store more glycogen and regulate oxygen, which gave me greater endurance. Fourth, I discovered better self-care, by eating better and treating injuries. Fifth, I grew in overcoming the mind games that would urge me to give up.

Had I shown up to my first marathon without taking the right steps first, I would have given up quickly and failed to reach the end.

Similar applications can be applied to the compulsive porn user and the church aimed at providing restoration. Those who live in freedom tell me consistently that their recovery from porn was a marathon and not a sprint. The churches and organizations that are providing long-term change have a marathon mentality.

That might leave you asking, "Okay, what's the first step our church can take?" And that's the right question, but it might look different from one church to the next. The most important thing you can do is take the first step.

Davin Granroth, the COO of Covenant Eyes, has a habit of telling stories and even fables to help our teams capture ideals and philosophies and create culture. Here's one fable he recited to our company that I hope will help you take the first leap.

Once upon a time, two frogs enjoyed their lives in a shallow fifty-acre lake. They were great friends and did everything together, but they were quite different from each other. The younger of the two was a hard worker, and you could tell this by the wear and tear on his gloves and the sweat stains that circled the base of his wide-brimmed hat. The other frog was older and wiser, and he studied every detail found on the shores of their great pond, asking questions and learning from the other frogs who lived in the nearby marshes.

The two frogs enjoyed their familiar muddy banks that were shaded by enormous oaks and swarmed with the easy meals of plentiful flies. But in the great distance, near the center of their lake, floated a prize they wanted to see in person: the Golden Lily Pad.

It was heard in a legend that frogs who reached the Golden Lily Pad found greater insight, and their work produced greater value. This intrigued both the hard-working frog and his wise friend. So one day, sitting atop the shaded and gnarled roots of an oak, they shook webbed hands in a pact to see the wonder of the Golden Lily Pad.

In preparation for their trip, the wise frog consulted with other knowledgeable creatures about the journey ahead. He learned from a dragonfly that just past the shallows, wide-mouth bass lay in wait for insects and small creatures that move among the matted weeds and devour their prey in a single gulp. To get past the bass, the wise frog learned from the dragonfly how others had built bridges on the tops of cattails to escape the reach of the hungry bass.

With plans in hand, the hard-working frog went to work right away on building the bridge. The first bridge he built wouldn't hold their weight; it crumbled soon after he climbed aboard. Thus, he reviewed the plans with his wise friend, and after a few changes, the hard-working frog tried again. With each effort, the bridges from one cattail to the next became stronger, so much so that the pair could travel together.

Once past the cattails, the wise frog committed to an ongoing study of the landscape for the safest route, and the hardworking frog built continued means for their travels. From one lily pad to another, they leaped over each other toward their common goal of the immaculate Golden Lilly Pad. One could not continue without the other—the wise frog needing the grinding work of his diligent friend, and the hard-working frog needing the guidance of his keen companion.

"The lesson is this: The Golden Lily pad represents mastery of a subject, and the frogs represent two kinds of knowledge—experiential knowledge and theoretical knowledge," Davin told our team. "I believe every one of us can see this pattern in mastering our efforts, and we need to ask ourselves, 'In my next step, do I need to put the hardworking frog in action? Or, do I need the wise frog to study, learn, and discover to gain perspective."

Sometimes, I find myself doing, doing, doing, and wondering why my progress is so slim. In the same way, I can study a subject in great detail, but until I put the theory to work, I show no outcome.

The same is true in our efforts to address pornography within the Church, where the theoretical often trumps action or action trumps the truth of God's Word. The book of James teaches that we need both understanding and action, faith and works.

Within these pages, you've learned how several churches are taking James's advice. They learned how people became trapped in strongholds and why they remained chained. Within a grace-filled culture, they disciple both the lost and the struggling Christians through a safe process with personal mentors to lead the way. Leaders train the body, and the body becomes a kingdom of priests, who declare the gospel to others.

Helping your fellow leaders and your members grow in understanding takes instruction. Implementing programs that help people leave their strongholds and run toward Jesus takes time and patience. Right now, you likely don't have all of the pieces in place to create the kind of culture where honesty is enticing, where a mentor is sought, and where a Christ-centered process leads to wholeness. You might be asking, *what should I do now?*

The right step is the first step. Start now. Start small. Set a realistic first goal and achieve it. Don't attempt to do everything at once.

Similar to the marathon runner, achieving goals for your church requires the first step.

In Chapter 15, you learned about initiatives, organizations, and programs that can help you get started in supporting people who want to find freedom from strongholds. You can't implement them all, but you can start with an effort that you believe fits your church. In Chapter 17, you reviewed how churches are looking at their cultures to provide a safe place for meaningful change and restoration. You can't mimic everything they do, but you can borrow aspects that can create change in the culture of your church.

My purpose in writing *The Healing Church* is not to tell you what to do, but to urge you to take the first step, which leads to the second, and so on. Play leapfrog by learning and doing. Use your experiences and gained knowledge to grow the outreach of your church.

I hope this book has brought to you an awareness of how people become trapped, why they stay stuck, and how they can begin a journey to a life of integrity and lasting freedom. Awareness and aspiration are the first steps to creating change.

I pray that awareness inspires you with a desire to tackle today's strongholds with new knowledge of the support systems available. And I urge you to take action and run with perseverance because this effort tests the strong and resilient. "Therefore lift your drooping hands and strengthen your weak knees, and make straight paths for your feet, so that what is lame may not be put out of joint but rather be healed" (Hebrews 12:12–13).

Acknowledgments

T hank you, Father, for enriching my life with amazing people who showed me your love, kindness, and grace. Your mercy endures forever.

To my wife Amy, who encouraged me and prayed for me even as I worked nights and weekends on this book. Her sacrifice and support as I wrangled words and ideas were invaluable.

To my son Ben and daughter Hannah, who rooted for this effort. I am a proud dad and so very blessed by both of you.

Thank you to Covenant Eyes Founder Ron DeHaas for his consistent and godly leadership. He is among the best Christian men I have ever met.

To Covenant Eyes leaders Scott McClurg and Davin Granroth, this book would not have been possible without their patience, guidance, encouragement, and belief.

To the countless pastors, counselors, coaches, and mentors from whom I have learned so much. Your patient instruction fills these pages. I cannot possibly thank all of you. I'm especially grateful to Christian counselors Troy and Melissa Haas, Marnie Ferree, Jim Cress, Jay Stringer, Sheri Keffer, and Geremy Keeton. The late Dr. Mark Laaser is a lasting influence on me and so many others. Thank you, Doug Weiss, for your ongoing texts of encouragement as I wrote. Thank you to the many pastors who gave me godly teaching, including Jack West, John Elmore, Dr. James Reeves, Brian Duncan, Steve Gladen, Dr. Gerald Reliford, Dr. Jay Dennis, Dr. Michael McCarty, Danny Bledsoe, and Dr. David Fulks. This list of pastors could go on and on. Thank you to the coaches, mentors, and co-conspirators in this fight, including Nate Larkin and the fellows of Samson Society, Jonathan Daugherty and the team at Be Broken, Nick Stumbo and the team at Pure Desire Ministries, Michael and Christine Leahy and the mentors of BraveHearts, David Zailer, and Nate Graybill and the teams of re:generation.

Special thanks to Roger and Cathy Baker, who showed me what authenticity and the first steps of freedom look like.

Thank you to Josh McDowell whose words of encouragement inspired me as I wrote.

Super special thanks to the men and women who shared their stories with me so that together we could bring greater understanding to church leaders. Your vulnerability, authenticity, and redemption give hope to others.

Thank you to my editor, Cortney Donelson, for her excellent guidance, experience, and patience. She has been a thoughtful guide and cared deeply about this work. I'm grateful for the initial editorial feedback from Steve Lawson and so appreciative to Donald Lindsey for his proofreading.

I am so grateful to the team at Morgan James Publishing, including Jim and Chris Howard, the publications board, and the pastors review board for believing in this book and seeing its value for the greater Church.

Finally, I am so grateful for my Thursday night book study group of Samson Society brothers. Rob Chenoweth, Daniel Swanson, and Mike Page hear my check-ins, confessions, and ponderings with grace, encouragement, and insight. We are growing together.

About the Author

S am Black serves as the director of recovery education for Covenant Eyes (covenanteyes.com). Having walked his own grace-filled journey to healing with the support of allies, Sam is passionate about helping people live free from pornography. He knows you keep what you give away. He is the author of *The Porn Circuit,* which reviews the neurological impact of pornography and is available through Covenant Eyes. He joined the Covenant Eyes team in 2007 after eighteen years as a journalist. He has edited seventeen books on the impact of pornography and speaks at parenting, men's and leaders events. He has been married since 1995 and is the father of two adult children.

Appendix A
Defining Porn Over Time

I t's difficult to understand how people think about porn today without looking back to understand the present. While we didn't arrive at a crisis overnight, your congregation is fed a modern cultural narrative that today's porn is a natural expression that has been displayed through the ages.

Porn proponents often say that porn has been with people since they were drawing sexual depictions on cave walls and argue that today's porn is nothing new. Indeed, people have expressed adoration for the human body and sex for millennia.

Ancient figurines, like the Venus of Willendorf, depict nudes and may have been used as fertility figures, good luck totems, or might be ancient porn.

The ancient Venus of Willendorf features a nude woman carved from limestone. Though she was found in 1908 with other fragments in Willendorf, Austria, scientists don't know what to make of her. She is obese with large breasts and wears a braided cap. Is she ancient porn, a fertility figurine, a totem of good luck? No one knows.

Though adultery was punishable by beatings and even death in ancient Egypt, the infamous Turin Erotic Papyrus depicts people and animals in different sexual positions. Some scholars argue the depictions are satire and a mockery of the upper class while others consider it drawn pornography. The famed Kama Sutra was roughly translated into English in the nineteenth century from 2,000-year-old Sanskrit texts, and among other lessons, it shows a variety of sexual positions, yet Hindu and Indian culture overall has remained sexually conservative. The frescoes and statues unearthed at Pompeii were scandalous when discovered in 1748 by Europeans who were accustomed to the comparatively modest nudes of the Sistine Chapel. People throughout the ages from a variety of cultures have drawn, molded, and sculpted the sexually provocative.

In more modern times, especially over the last 180 years, pornographers not only adopted the latest technology but were the driving force behind advances. In the 1840s, the earliest photographs, called daguerreotypes were quickly used to create nude displays of women in risqué poses. Twenty years after the Cinématographe debuted in France in 1895, short and silent stag films were produced in Europe and the United States and shown in brothels, fraternities, and other secret locales.

Mainstream nudity came to American capitalism with the advent of *Playboy* magazine in 1953. For $50, cash-strapped, jobless, and not-yet-famous Marilyn Monroe posed nude showing her side and breasts with the photographer's promise that she would be unrecognizable. Hugh Hefner purchased the photo rights for $500 and made millions when he published the photo in the debut edition without her permission. About a decade later, *Penthouse* and *Hustler* magazines followed and pushed the envelope of acceptability under American laws.[129]

Porn in America and the rest of the world took a major turn with the VCR, and its success is directly linked to the pornography industry. In 1978, fewer than 1 percent of American homes had VCRs, and more than 75 percent of VHS tapes sold were pornographic. One of the reasons why VHS became so popular over other video formats is because video rental stores helped drive the VHS market, and the first video rental businesses sold primarily pornography.

The internet changed everything. People no longer need to drive to the seedy shop in an urban area to buy magazines or videos. You can have porn pumped into your home at high speeds. The reason we have internet technologies such as streaming audio and video, pop-up windows, high-speed internet connections, and security improvements for online payment services is that pornography investors pumped money into them.

In June 2007, Apple launched the iPhone, and though it banned porn from its app store, porn producers lauded the new larger phone screen as "the porn-friendliest phone" on the market.[130] By September 2008, Android phones with display screens similar to iPhone joined the fray, and in 2014, Google also kicked porn apps from the Play Store. But browsers and social media apps filled in the porn gaps.

Courts and Porn

While the purveyors of porn adapted new technologies, the US Supreme Court was attempting to define what was legal and illegal porn.

The courts didn't care about porn.

"Pornography is a generic, not a legal term," said Patrick Truman, president and CEO of the National Center on Sexual Exploitation. The Supreme Court aimed to protect our culture from "obscenity."

While most people today believe this is all a matter of free speech, obscenity isn't protected speech. In addition to obscenity, there are several forms of speech for which a person may be fined or jailed. For, instance it's illegal to scream "fire" in a crowded theater when there is no fire. You can go to jail for perjury, true threats, blackmail, defamation, child pornography, and more.

Throughout most of the United States' history, the Supreme Court said little about obscenity, because although pornography was available in New York, back alleys, and brothels, the overall culture pushed nudity away from public forums. Though pin-up girls, covered from neck to toe in blooming pants and boots, first appeared in the early 1800s, World War II was the golden age of the pin-up girl.[131] These pin-ups were typically artists' drawings, but from 1949 to 1957, Bettie Page[132] and others posed for photos for cards, calendars, and posters. This broader acceptance ushered in public offerings of sexual innuendo in advertising, allowed Playboy's launch, and a greater appetite for underground porn.

As underground nudity and hardcore porn moved toward a more public display, the Supreme Court sought to halt the progress of obscenity's march into the American marketplace.

In 1957, the Supreme Court in Roth vs. the United States created the following definition of obscenity: Speech which ". . . to the average person, applying contemporary **community standards**, the dominant theme of the material, **taken as a whole**, appeals to **prurient interest**" and which is "**utterly without redeeming social importance . . .**"[133]

For Justice Byron White no erections and no insertions equaled no obscenity. Justice William Brennan also said no erections were allowed. Justice Potter Stewart was open to nudity but willing to ban hardcore pornography as obscenity, where he famously said, "I know it when I see it," in a 1964 case, *Jacobellis vs. Ohio*.

During the 1950s and '60s, pornographers attempted to overcome obscenity rules by adding odd segments that discussed values, clinical discussions, and even lines of Shakespeare. These were poor attempts to pose porn films as also educational works. When clerks and justices watched "Vixen," a soft-core film that ended with a discussion of the merits of Communist and Western societies, Justice Thurgood Marshall quipped, "Ah, the redeeming social value."

In *Miller vs. California*, the Supreme Court established in 1973 a three-pronged test for determining whether a "work" (i.e., material or performance) is obscene and therefore unprotected by the First Amendment, Truman said.

To be obscene, a judge or a jury must determine:

- First, that the "average person, applying contemporary community standards," would find the work, taken as a whole, appeals to the "prurient interest," meaning a "shameful or morbid interests" in sex or watching others have sex. The Court found that sadistic porn fell into this category.
- Second, that the work depicts or describes in a patently offensive way, as measured by contemporary community standards, "hardcore" sexual conduct specifically defined by the applicable law.
- And third, that a reasonable person would find that the work, taken as a whole, lacks serious literary, artistic, political, and scientific value.[134]

Soon after the Court further clarified obscenity:

(a) Patently offensive representations or descriptions of ultimate sexual acts, normal or perverted, actual or simulated.
(b) Patently offensive representations or descriptions of masturbation, excretory functions, and lewd exhibition of the genitals.[135]

During the 1970s to 1990s, porn producers and even store clerks were prosecuted successfully under the Supreme Court's guidelines. But the prosecutions and fines and jail time were just a cost of doing big business and happened more in some states and rarely in others. More porn was produced, more family video stores kept a backroom to pedal the genre, and in 1994, President Bill Clinton came to office. More importantly, Janet Reno took her post as Attorney General, and she had no interest in prosecuting obscenity cases.

During the Clinton years, says (prominent obscenity prosecutor Bruce) Taylor, porn producers were "flying high . . . [thinking] we're invincible, nobody's prosecuting us. The Justice Department doesn't care what we do. We can rape, pillage, and plunder, and use everybody up."[136]

When George W. Bush took office, obscenity fighters cheered Attorney General John Ashcroft's proclamation in 2002: "The Department of Justice is committed unequivocally to the task of prosecuting obscenity." Porn fighters and church leaders hailed the renewed resolve.[137]

But despite Ashcroft's resolute statements, a mere ten obscenity cases were prosecuted over the next four years.[138] It is possible that outside forces contributed to this lackluster effort. First, the attacks on the World Trade Center on Sept. 11, 2001, set more pressing matters for the Bush administration, and second, the internet was rife with pornography, and what was once considered "prurient" and obscene seemed less so in many communities and states.

Prurient is a word most people didn't understand in the decades before the internet, and today, it seems nearly irrelevant to our changed culture. Even when people know the word, they can't clearly define its meaning.[139]

As magazines pushed the envelope, as the VCR made porn more available, as the internet and smartphones delivered it everywhere, people were exposed to more and more porn. "Contemporary community standards," a key component in establishing obscenity, simply changed. Once the internet took hold with little to no regulation, "extreme porn" became commonplace. The definition of obscenity shifted both individually and as a society from decade to decade. The pornography industry slowly co-opted what people describe as obscenity and obscenity became the new commonly streamed product of the internet.

The law remains, but prosecutors simply stopped prosecuting. "The U.S. Supreme Court has repeatedly upheld obscenity laws against First Amendment challenges, explaining that obscenity is not protected speech," Dani Porter wrote for NCOSE. "Even so, the U.S. Department of Justice (DOJ) refuses to enforce existing federal obscenity laws."[140]

Though President-elect Donald Trump signed a pledge from Enough is Enough, few expected the man who appeared on Playboy's cover to enforce obscenity laws beyond addressing child pornography. Reminding of the president's pledge, four Republican Congressional lawmakers called on Trump's Attorney General William Barr in 2019 to enforce obscenity laws and drag hardcore pornographers to court, but nothing became of it.[141]

Safe Disclosure With a Safe Process

By Troy and Melissa Haas

He who conceals his sins does not prosper,
but whoever confesses and renounces them finds mercy.
Proverbs 28:13

Because of fear and shame, sexual sins usually involve secrecy, deception, and lies—behaviors that betray the trust of those we love. Repairing our relationships is a three-part process in which we disclose the sinful behaviors we have done, make amends to those we have hurt, and work to rebuild trust to move toward reconciliation. The first part of the process is dependent on us and us alone. The second and third parts of the repair process require a joint effort between our loved ones and us.

Let's begin with the first part of the repair process: disclosure. In the context of mending relationships, disclosure means telling others about sinful behaviors that have affected your relationship with them. It means bringing all secrets to light and exposing the ways you have betrayed trust and broken promises. Hopefully, you have already been disclosing your sexual behaviors to the people in your small group and to a counselor or mentor as well. If you are married, you must be honest with your spouse about your behaviors. When and how you disclose, however, is very important.

While disclosure is always a challenging and painful process, there are three guidelines you should follow to make it as safe as possible for both you and your spouse. Your disclosure to your spouse should be ***planned*** and ***mediated*** in a ***safe place.***

A time of disclosure needs to be ***planned*** to allow both husband and wife to prepare emotionally and spiritually for a very difficult conversation. It needs to be ***mediated*** (preferably by a counselor) so both spouses can be guided and supported as painful information is shared. Disclosing in a ***neutral/safe place*** protects you and your spouse from painful associations and unintentional exposure (such as having a disclosure being overheard) while allowing you both to be on equal ground. The best-case scenario for disclosure is a planned time with a counselor in the counselor's office.

The timing of disclosure is also important. If you are actively working on your recovery, full disclosure to your spouse should take place approximately a month after you have fully disclosed to a counselor. This gives you time to talk about and process your sexual history from childhood to the present and creates space for God to remind you of things you have forgotten. You need to have a complete disclosure prepared before you talk with your spouse because disclosing pieces of information over an extended period—the "dribble method" of disclosure—is very hurtful to your spouse and severely damages any trust that has been rebuilt. During the three to four weeks while you are preparing your disclosure, your spouse should be working with a personal counselor to prepare for the session and building a network of safe people to support his or her own recovery process.

Be wise in choosing who facilitates the disclosure process. The optimum situation is a disclosure session facilitated together by your counselor and your spouse's counselor. The two counselors can work together to keep the process safe and supported for each of you. If neither you nor your spouse is seeing a counselor, the second-best option is to have the session mediated by a couple who has walked through sexual addiction and has a substantial amount (three years or more) of recovery behind them. Again, in this situation, it will be necessary to prepare before the time of disclosure takes place.

There are two primary goals of disclosure. The first is for you to be completely honest about your behaviors while acknowledging the lies and deception you have used to keep your actions secret. The second is for your spouse to be made aware of the forms of your betrayal and the full extent of the debt being asked to forgive.

Generally, in a formal time of disclosure, the counselor will ask you to share about all of the sexual behaviors you have been involved in that directly impact your marriage/relationship. This would include fantasy and masturbation, use of pornography, chatting, sexting, sending/receiving nude or sexual pictures, use of dating or hook-up apps, visiting adult bookstores or strip clubs, and any sexual acts with people. You will need to disclose the type of sexual acting out you have done in general but not graphic terms (kissing, touching breast/genitals, giving or receiving unprotected/protected oral, vaginal, or anal intercourse). You need to share the frequency of these behaviors and any non-sexual secrets linked to them (e.g., financial loss or debt incurred because of acting out, loss of job, or others). If you have been involved in a relationship with someone your spouse or loved one knows, you need to disclose that information. Also, if you have committed any of these acts in your home or vehicle, you should disclose this fact to your spouse. You should not disclose graphic details to your spouse, such as the porn sites you visited, the specific locations of sexual encounters, the names of people your wife does not know, what people were wearing, the conversations you had, etc. Some counselors may ask you to share your sexual history and behaviors preceding the marriage to give your spouse context for the way your addiction developed.

After you share, the counselor will give your spouse an opportunity to ask clarifying questions. Your spouse's counselor will help your mate choose questions that clarify understanding without asking for detail that might be harmful to her or his own recovery.

Your spouse will need time to process and grieve the losses associated with your actions. Both of you will need the help of counselors to navigate the painful aftermath of betrayal as you continue to find freedom from your addiction and rebuild trust in the marriage. Many counselors will suggest that your wife prepare and share an emotional impact letter in response to your disclosure. You, then, will write an amends letter based on what she shares with you about her hurts.

One last thought on disclosure is important to share. Your willingness or unwillingness to fully disclose your sinful behaviors to safe people and your spouse shows whether you are truly serious about freedom. You cannot keep secrets and be free. If you fail to disclose everything, if you keep hidden away even one tiny secret, the enemy will use it to sabotage your recovery and destroy your relationships. Don't forget: Secrecy kills; honesty heals.

Published by Covenant Eyes® with permission by authors Troy and Melissa Haas.

Contributor Information:

Counselor **Troy Haas** (M.Div., CADC-II, CSAT, CMAT) serves as the CEO of the HopeQuest Ministry Group (hopequestgroup.org).

Counselor **Melissa Haas** is a Spouse Supporting Therapist (MAMFT, LPC, CSAT, CMAT)

Troy and Melissa have thirty years of ministry experience, including six years as IMB missionaries in Kenya. Troy served fifteen years as director of Restoration Ministries at First Baptist Church of Woodstock.

Troy's personal struggle with addiction and his recovery journey have enabled him to minister to others with authenticity and grace, providing hope that freedom is possible. Troy and his wife Melissa have dedicated their lives to encouraging, enabling, and equipping the body of Christ to live out Galatians 6:1: "Brothers, if someone is caught in a sin, you who are spiritual should restore him gently."

Endnotes

1   Josh McDowell, "The Porn Phenomenon: The Impact of Pornography in the Digital Age," (Barna Research Group, 2016).

2   Porn Stats 2018 Edition, www.covenanteyes.com/ebooks.

3   Samuel L. Perry and George M. Hayward, "Seeing is (Not) Believing: How Viewing Pornography Shapes Religious Lives of Young Americans," National Center for Biotechnology Information, published online 10 Jan 2017, accessed 8 March 2022, https://www.ncbi.nlm.nih.gov/pmc/articles/PMC5439973/.

4   Samuel L. Perry, Addicted to Lust: Pornography in the Lives of Conservative Protestants, (Oxford: Oxford University Press, 2019), 82.

5   Andrew Dugan, Gallup. June 5, 2018, accessed 8 March 2022, https://news.gallup.com/poll/235280/americans-say-pornography-morally-acceptable.aspx.

6   Porn Stats, 16.

7   Kunaharan S, Halpin S, Sitharthan T, Bosshard S, Walla P. Conscious and Non-Conscious Measures of Emotion: Do They Vary with Frequency of Pornography Use? Applied Sciences. 2017; 7(5):493. https://doi.org/10.3390/app7050493.

8   The Porn Phenomenon, 2016 by Josh McDowell Ministry, Barna Group. http://www.barna.com/wp-content/uploads/2018/12/The-Porn-Phenomenon_excerpt.pdf, https://shop.barna.com/products/porn-phenomenon

9   Samuel L. Perry, Addicted to Lust, 5–7.

10 Rebecca Reilly, Diary of a Christian Woman: How I Used 50 Shades of Grey to Spice Up My Marriage, Kindle publishing, 2015.

11 Jeff Schapiro, "Percentage of Christians, Americans Who Have Read 'Fifty Shades of Grey' the Same." The Christian Post. 5 June 2013, accessed 02 Feb 2022, https://www.christianpost.com/news/percentage-of-christians-americans-who-have-read-fifty-shades-of-grey-the-same.html.

12 https://www.lightworkers.com/game-of-thrones-christians/.

13 Business Insider, "How 'Game of Thrones' viewership compares with TV's other most-watched shows," accessed March 3, 2020, https://www.businessinsider.com/game-of-thrones-compared-to-most-popular-tv-shows-of-2018-ratings-2019-4.

14 Director Explains the Perverted Reason for All That Thrones Nudity, accessed March 3, 2020, https://www.syfy.com/syfywire/director_explains_the_per (The Empireonline.com page has been taken down, but reported word for word by dozens of sources. I first heard it on NPR.)

15 "Shame of Thrones: Where Sexual Violence is King," Feb. 24, 2016, accessed March 1, 2021, https://endsexualexploitation.org/articles/14405-2/).

16 Hayden Royster from https://www.lightworkers.com/game-of-thrones-christians/.

17 Proven Men Porn Survey (conducted by Barna Group in 2014), located at https://www.provenmen.org/2014PornSurvey/.

18 Cara C. Macinnis and Gordon Hodson, "Do American States with More Religious or Conservative Populations Search More for Sexual Content on Google?" Spring Link, 03 October 2014, accessed 03 16 2022, https://link.springer.com/article/10.1007/s10508-014-0361-8.

19 Andrew L. Whitehead and Samuel L. Perry, "Unbuckling the Bible Belt: A State-Level Analysis of Religious Factors and Google Searches for Porn," The Journal of Sex Research, 14 Feb 2017, accessed 03 March 15, 2022, https://www.tandfonline.com/doi/abs/10.1080/00224499.2017.1278736.

20 June Hunt, Sexual Addiction, The Way Out of the Web, (Dubuque, Iowa: Kendall Hunt Publishing, 2020), 3.

21 Mark R. Laaser, PhD, Healing the Wounds of Sexual Addiction, (Grand Rapids: Zondervan, revised 2004), 28, 87.

22 Proven Men Porn Survey (conducted by Barna Group in 2014), located at https://www.provenmen.org/pornography-survey-statistics-2014/.

23 Jay Stringer, Unwanted: How Sexual Brokenness Reveals Our Way to Healing, (Carol Stream, IL: Nav Press, illustrated ed. 2018), 76–77.

24 Norman Doidge, MD, The Brain that Changes Itself: Stories of Personal Triumph from the Frontiers of Brain Science, (New York: Penguin Life, reprint 2017), 106–112.

25 Stringer, Unwanted, 81.

26 Norman Doidge, MD, The Brain that Changes Itself, 109–113 and 200–211.

27 Mark Kastleman, The Drug of the New Millennium, The Brain Science Behind Internet Pornography Use, (Provo, UT: PowerThink Publishing, 2007), 77, 84, 92.

28 P.J. Wright, B. Paul, and D. Herbenick, "Preliminary insights from a U.S. probability sample on adolescents' pornography exposure, media psychology, and sexual aggression," J. Health Commun., 26(1), 2012, 39–46. doi:10.1080 /10810730.2021.1887980.

29 BrainFacts.org. "The Workings of the Adolescent Brain." September 16, 2016. YouTube video, 3:14. https://www.youtube.com/watch?v=Y8sO4tqfUEs.

30 Frances Jensen, MD, The Teenage Brain, A Neuroscientist's Survival Guide to Raising Adolescents and Young Adults, (New York: Harper Publishing, Reprint ed. 2016).

31 Proven Men Porn Survey (conducted by Barna Group in 2014), located at https://www.provenmen.org/pornography-survey-statistics-2014/.

32 Proven Men Porn Survey (conducted by Barna Group in 2014).

33 Stringer, Unwanted, 31.

34 Mark R. Laaser, PhD, Healing the Wounds of Sexual Addiction, 78.

35 Patrick J. Carnes, PhD, "The Making of a Sex Addict," 1998, accessed 8 March 2022, https://cdn.ymaws.com/iitap.com/resource/resmgr/arie_files/ m1_article_the-making-of-a-s.pdf.

36 Stringer, Unwanted, Chapter 3.

37 Stringer, Unwanted, 28.

38 Stringer, Unwanted, 29.

39 Holmes, G.R., Offen, L., & Waller, G. "See no evil, hear no evil, speak no evil: Why do relatively few male victims of childhood sexual abuse receive help for abuse-related issues in adulthood?" Clinical Psychology Review, 1997, 17, 69–88.

40 David Finkelhor, PhD, et. al. "The Lifetime Prevalence of Child Sexual Abuse and Sexual Assault Assessed in Late Adolescence," Journal of Adolescent

Health, 24 December 2013, accessed 8 March 2022, http://www.unh.edu/ccrc/pdf/9248.pdf.

41 Dube, S.R., Anda, R.F., Whitfield, C.L., et al. "Long-term Consequences of Childhood Sexual Abuse by Gender of Victim." American Journal of Preventive Medicine, 2005, 28, 430–438.

42 Michael Aaron, "The Pathways of Problematic Sexual Behavior: A Literature Review of Factors Affecting Adult Sexual Behavior in Survivors of Childhood Sexual Abuse, Sexual Addiction & Compulsivity," 19:3, 2012, 199–218.

43 Gregory Jantz, PhD, Healing the Scars of Childhood Abuse: Moving Beyond the Past into a Healthy Future, (Chicago: Revell, 2017).

44 Gregory Jantz, PhD, Healing the Scars of Childhood Abuse, 48–49.

45 Gregory Jantz, PhD, Healing the Scars of Childhood Abuse, 49.

46 Mark R. Laaser, PhD, Healing the Wounds of Sexual Addiction, 75.

47 Mary Ellen Mann, From Pain to Power: Overcoming Sexual Trauma and Reclaiming Your True Identity, (Colorado Springs: Waterbrook, 2015), 19.

48 Psychology Today, "When Is Porn Use a Problem," 19 Feb 2018, accessed 10 March 2022, https://www.psychologytoday.com/us/blog/experimentations/201802/when-is-porn-use-problem.

49 "Here's What You Told Us About What Porn You Watch, and How Often," 26 Aug 2019, accessed 10 March 2022, https://www.abc.net.au/triplej/programs/hack/heres-what-you-told-us-about-what-porn-you-watch/11442772.

50 Set Free Summit 2016, co-hosted by Covenant Eyes and Josh McDowell Ministry, Greensboro, NC.

51 Jessica Harris, Beggar's Daughter: From the Rags of Pornography to the Riches of Grace, (Create Space Independent Publishing, 2016), 83.

52 Stringer, Unwanted, 67.

53 ScienceDaily, "Sex Differences in Memory: Women Better Than Men at Remembering Everyday Events," 21 Feb 2008, accessed June 3, 2020, https://www.sciencedaily.com/releases/2008/02/080220104244.htm).

54 Set Free Summit 2016.

55 Psychology Today, 13 Aug 2012, accessed June 3, 2020, https://www.psychologytoday.com/us/blog/real-healing/201208/overexposed-and-under-prepared-the-effects-early-exposure-sexual-content.

56 Female Porn Users, Why They Watch and How to Help, 2020, Covenant Eyes ebook, page 6, https://www.covenanteyes.com/resources/ashamed-4-reasons-women-look-porn/.

57 Jay Stringer, "Silence: The Sound of Female Sexual Shame," The Covenant Eyes Blog, October 26, 2017. Accessed 1 Oct 2018, https://www.covenanteyes.com/2017/10/26/silence-the-sound-of-female-sexual-shame/.

58 Female Porn Users: Why They Watch and How To Help, 4.

59 Jessica Harris, Beggar's Daughter, 50–51, 53.

60 Crystal Renaud Day, Dirty Girls Come Clean, (Chicago: Moody Publishers, 2011), 136.

61 Marnie C. Ferree, No Stones, Women Redeemed from Sexual Addiction, (IVP Books 2010).

62 Alford S, et al. Science and Success: Sex Education and Other Programs that Work to Prevent Teen Pregnancy, HIV & Sexually Transmitted Infections. (Washington, DC: Advocates for Youth, 2008, 2nd ed.).

63 A Grunseit, et. al. "Sexuality education and young people's sexual behavior: a review of studies." J Adolescent Res. 12 Oct 1997 (4):421–453.

64 Marnie C. Ferree, No Stones, Women Redeemed from Sexual Addiction, 137.

65 David Finkelhor, PhD, et. al. "The Lifetime Prevalence of Child Sexual Abuse and Sexual Assault Assessed in Late Adolescence," Journal of Adolescent Health, 24 December 2013, 329–333, accessed 8 March 2022, http://www.unh.edu/ccrc/pdf/9248.pdf.

66 Stringer, Unwanted, 67.

67 Seven Pillars of Freedom Workbook, 158–163.

68 L.I.F.E. Recovery Guide for Women, 16.

69 Marked Men for Christ: markedmenforchrist.org.

70 Jeffrey, Stuewig, et. al., "Children's Proneness to Shame and Guilt Predict Risky and Illegal Behaviors in Young Adulthood." Child Psychiatry and Human Development, Vol. 46,2 (2015): 217–227. doi:10.1007/s10578-014-0467-1, accessed 22 March 2022, https://www.ncbi.nlm.nih.gov/pmc/articles/PMC4239200/.

71 Claire McCarthy, MD, "Think Hard Before Shaming Children," Harvard Health Publishing, 24 Jan 2020, accessed 22 March 2022, https://www.health.harvard.edu/blog/think-hard-before-shaming-children-2020012418692.

72 Edward T. Welch, Shame Interrupted: How God Lifts the Pain of Worthlessness and Rejection, (Greensboro: New Growth Press, 2012), 30.

73 Grace Church, Greenville, South Carolina, "Shame: Finding Freedom" event, https://gracechurchsc.org/shameconference.

74 Edward T. Welch, Shame Interrupted, 16.

75 This was an online summit hosted by Covenant Eyes and SHE Recovery.

76 2021 Church Leadership Conference, workshop title "Creating Authentic Community," Watermark Community Church, April 2021

77 Norman Doidge, MD, The Brain That Changes Itself.

78 Norman Doidge, MD, The Brain That Changes Itself, 105.

79 Norman Doidge, MD, The Brain That Changes Itself, 108.

80 William M. Struthers, Wired for Intimacy, 85.

81 Dolf Zillmann and Jennings Bryant, "Pornography's Impact on Sexual Satisfaction," Journal of Applied Social Psychology 18 (1988): 438–453.

82 Maas, M.K., Vasilenko, S.A., and Willoughby, B.J. (2018). "A Dyadic Approach to Pornography Use and Relationship Satisfaction Among Heterosexual Couples: The Role of Pornography Acceptance and Anxious Attachment." Journal of sex research, 55(6), 772–782, accessed 29 March 2022, https://doi.org/10.1080/00224499.2018.1440281.

83 James Reeves, Life Change for Every Christian, 2009 Life Change Resources, Fort Worth, Texas.

84 Michael Gryboski, "Rick Warren Likens Pornography to 'Poison'" The Christian Post, 05 September 2016, accessed 30 March 2022, https://www.christianpost.com/news/rick-warren-pornography-is-poison-only-foolish-people-feed-on-trash.html.

85 Ted Shimer, The Freedom Fight: The New Drug and the Truths That Set Us Free, (Houston: High Bridge Books, 2021).

86 Gregory Mast and Hans Halberstadt, To Be A Military Sniper, (Duluth: Zenith Press, 2007).

87 "New Barna study in Partnership with Pepperdine University offers a revealing look at lives of American pastors," Religion News, LLC, 26 January 2017, accessed 30 March 2022, https://religionnews.com/2017/01/26/new-barna-study-in-partnership-with-pepperdine-university-offers-revealing-look-at-lives-of-american-pastors/.

88 Martin M. Smith, et.al., "The Perniciousness of Perfectionism: A Meta-Analytic Review of Perfectionism-Suicide Relationship," Journal of Personality, 86:522–542, July 2018, accessed 30 March 2022, https://www.researchgate.net/publication/318381042_The_perniciousness_of_perfectionism_A_meta-analytic_review_of_the_perfectionism-suicide_relationship.

89 Eric Geiger, "Three Views of Restoring a Fallen Pastor," blog post, 18 July 2016, https://ericgeiger.com/2016/07/3-different-views-of-restoration/.

90 Earl D. Wilson, et. al., Restoring the Fallen: A Team Approach to Caring, Confronting Reconciling, (Westmont, Illinois: InterVarsity Press, 1997), 53.

91 Earl D. Wilson, et. al., Restoring the Fallen, 31–40.

92 Earl D. Wilson, et. al., Restoring the Fallen, 36–37.

93 "Number of Female Senior Pastors in Protestant Churches Doubles in Past Decade," Barn Research, Sept. 14, 2009, accessed 31 March 2022, https://www.barna.com/research/number-of-female-senior-pastors-in-protestant-churches-doubles-in-past-decade/.

94 "Human Sexuality: How Do Men and Women Differ?" American Psychological Society, 2003, accessed 31 March 2022, https://peplau.psych.ucla.edu/wp-content/uploads/sites/141/2017/07/Peplau-2003.pdf.

95 Sheri Keffer, Intimate Deception: Healing the Wounds of Sexual Betrayal, (Grand Rapids: Revell, 2018), 29.

96 Chuck and Cynthia Swindoll, Doing Ministry the Right Way and for the Right Reason, CIFT Pastor's Forum, May 24, 2007, accessed June 26, 2021, https://ciftcounseling.com/wp-content/uploads/2017/07/Chuck-and-Cynthia-Swindoll-May-24-2007-1.mp3.

97 Frank T. Seekins, Hebrew Word Pictures: How Does the Hebrew Alphabet Reveal Prophetic Truths? (Scottsdale, AZ: Hebrew World, 2016), 149.

98 Strong's Concordance: 898. bagad, accessed June 26, 2021, http://biblehub.com/hebrew/898.htm.

99 Omar Minwalla, "The Secret Sexual Basement: The Traumatic Impacts of Deceptive Sexuality on the Intimate Partner and Relationship, accessed June 26, 2021, https://secureservercdn.net/72.167.241.180/226.c7e.myftpupload.com/wp-content/uploads/2021/06/The-Secret-Sexual-Basement_6_21_21.pdf or https://uploads-ssl.webflow.com/61708b185d7d724acc2096da/61a5399eb4455c2a32f84d60_The_Secret_Sexual_Basement_Nov_2021.pdf.

100 Marnie Ferree, Bethesda Workshops: A Place for Healing, accessed June 26, 2021, https://www.bethesdaworkshops.org/for-sex-addicts/#women.

101 Barbara Steffens, Dorit Reichental, and Marnie Breecher, "The Multidimensional Partner Trauma Model" (lecture, APSATS Multidimensional Partner Trauma Model Training, Los Angeles, CA, February 5, 2014). For more information on the Multidimensional Partner Trauma Model (MPTM), visit Association of Partners of Sex Addicts Trauma Specialists (APSATS) website, https://www.apsats.org.

102 Sheri Keffer, Intimate Deception:52–65.

103 Reiche, Edna & Nunes, Sandra & Morimoto, Helena. (2004). Stress, depression, the immune system, and cancer. The lancet oncology. 5. 617–25. 10.1016/S1470-2045(04)01597-9. https://www.researchgate.net/publication/8251080_Stress_depression_the_immune_system_and_cancer.

104 Barbara Steffens, Dorit Reichental, and Marnie Breecher, "Neuro-psychobiological Impact of Trauma & Trauma Triggering" (lecture, APSATS Multidimensional Partner Trauma Model Training, Los Angeles, CA, February 6, 2014). For more information on the impact of medical/personal health issues, see APSATS, "The Multidimensional Partner Trauma Model Training"; Jason and Minwalla, "Sexual Trauma Model"; Minwalla, "Thirteen Dimensions of Sex Addiction-Induced Trauma."

105 Bessel Van Der Kolk, The Body Keeps the Score: Brain, Mind, and Body in the Healing of Trauma (New York: Penguin Books, 2015), 267; Dean Lauterbach, Rajvee Vora, and Madeline Rakow, "The Relationship Between Posttraumatic Stress Disorder and Self-Reported Health Problems," Psychosomatic Medicine 67, no. 6 (2005): 939–47.

106 K Lillberg et al., "Stressful life events and risk of breast cancer in 10,808 women, a cohort study," American Journal of Epidemiology, 157 (2003): 415–23. https://www.researchgate.net/publication/10874318_Stressful_Life_Events_and_Risk_of_Breast_Cancer_in_10808_Women_A_Cohort_Study.

107 "Have it Your Way," Wikipedia, last updated June 24, https://en.wikipedia.org/wiki/List_of_Burger_King_ad_programs

108 A.P. Brown, "The Relationship Among Male Pornography Use, Attachment, and Aggression in Romantic Relationships," Dissertation, BYU ScholarsArchive, (March 1, 2015), 1–74.

109 Barbara A. Steffens and Marsha Means, Your Sexually Addicted Spouse: How Partners Can Cope and Heal (Far Hills, NJ: New Horizon Press, 2009), 3-12; Barbara A. Steffens and Robyn L. Rennie, "The Traumatic Nature of Disclosure for Wives of Sexual Addicts," Sexual Addiction & Compulsivity 13, no. 2–3 (2006): 247–67.

110 Sheri Keffer, Why Porn and the Pulpit Don't Mix, Newport Beach, CA, April 16, 2021, email sent to mailing list of 7000 betrayed partners, raw data.

111 "Dietrich Bonhoeffer Quotes," Goodreads, accessed June 26, 2021, http://www.goodreads.com/quotes/22884-we-are-not-to-simply-bandage-the-wounds-of-victims.

112 The FASTER Scale was created by Michael Dye, who is also the founder of The Genesis Process. https://www.genesisprocess.org/.

113 Robert A. Heinlein, Time Enough for Love: The Lives of Lazarus Long, A Berkley Medallion Book, (New York: G. P. Putnam's Sons, 1974), 31.

114 John Elmore, Freedom Starts Today: Overcoming Struggles and Addictions One Day at a Time, (Ada, Michigan: Baker Books, 2021), 21.

115 Jonathan Dedmon, "Is the Internet Bad for Your Marriage? Online affairs, pornographic sites playing greater role in divorces." Press Release from The Dilenschneider Group, Inc., Nov. 14, 2002, accessed 7 June 2018, http://www.prnewswire.com/news-releases/is-the-internet-bad-for-your-marriage-online-affairs-pornographic-sites-playing-greater-role-in-divorces-76826727.html.

116 Pam Peeke and Mariska van Aalst, The Hunger Fix: The Three-Stage Detox and Recovery Plan for Overeating and Food Addiction, (Emmaus, Pennsylvania: Rodale Books, 2012), 49.

117 Matt Blanchard & Barry A. Farber, "Lying in Psychotherapy: Why and what clients don't tell their therapist about therapy and their relationship," Counselling Psychology Quarterly, 29:1, 2016, 90–112, DOI: 10.1080/09515070.2015.1085365.

118 John Elmore, Freedom Starts Today, 114.

119 2016 Set Free Summit, co-hosted by Covenant Eyes and Josh McDowell Ministry, Greensboro, NC.

120 Aaron Earls, "The Church Growth Gap: The Big Get Bigger While the Small Get Smaller," Christianity Today, 6 March 2019, accessed 5 April 2022, https://www.christianitytoday.com//news/2019/march/lifeway-research-church-growth-attendance-size.html.

121 Martellozzo, Elena, et. al., "I wasn't sure it was normal to watch it . . ." A quantitative and qualitative examination of the impact of online pornography on the values, attitudes, beliefs, and behaviours of children and young people. London: Middlesex University, 2017, doi:10.6084/ m9.figshare.3382393, accessed 5 April 2022, https://www.researchgate.net/ publication/304490439_I_wasn%27t_sure_it_was_normal_to_watch_it_A_ quantitative_and_qualitative_examination_of_the_impact_of_online_pornog- raphy_on_the_values_attitudes_beliefs_and_behaviours_of_children_and_ young_people.

122 Culture Reframed, accessed 6 April 2022, https://www.culturereframed.org/ the-porn-crisis/.

123 "The Digital Divide: How the Online Behavior of Teens is Getting Past Par- ents," McAfee.com. June 2012.

124 Monica Anderson, "Parents, Teens and Digital Monitoring." Pew Research Center, 7 January 2016, accessed 5 April 2022, https://www.pewresearch.org/ internet/2016/01/07/parents-teens-and-digital-monitoring/#:~:text=For%20 instance%2C%20the%20new%20survey,of%20his%20or%20her%20cell- phone.

125 https://www.goodreads.com/author/quotes/9810.Albert_Einstein.

126 2016 Set Free Summit, co-hosted by Covenant Eyes and Josh McDowell Ministry

127 See the full definitions at watermark.org/about/values.

128 Patrick M.Lencioni, The Advantage: Why Organizational Health Trumps Everything Else In Business, (Hoboken: Jossey-Bass, 2012), 27.

129 Brad Witter, "Marilyn Monroe Didn't Actually Pose for the First Issue of 'Play- boy'," Biography, updated Sept 8, 2020, accessed 6 April 2022, https://www. biography.com/news/marilyn-monroe-playboy-first-issue-didnt-pose.

130 Lonnie Lazar, "Pocket Porn Comes to iPhone," Cult of Mac, June 20, 2008, accessed 6 April 2022, https://www.cultofmac.com/2117/pocket-porn-comes-to-iphone/.

131 Priscilla Frank, "The History of the Pin-Up Girl, From the 1800s to the Pres- ent," Huffington Post, updated Dec 6, 2018, accessed 6 April 2022, https:// www.huffpost.com/entry/pin-up-girl-history_n_6077082.

132 Louis Sahagun, "Pinup Queen Betty Page Dies at 85," Los Angeles Times, Dec 12, 2018, accessed 5 April 2022, https://www.latimes.com/local/obituaries/ la-me-page12-2008dec12-story.html.

133 FindLaw Attorney Writers, "Movie Day at the Supreme Court or "I Know It When I See It": A History of the Definition of Obscenity," last updated 26 April 2016, accessed 6 April 2022, https://corporate.findlaw.com/litigation-disputes/movie-day-at-the-supreme-court-or-i-know-it-when-i-see-it-a.html.

134 ibid

135 ibid

136 Tim Wu, "How Laws Die," Slate News and Politics, Oct 15, 2007, accessed 6 April 22, https://slate.com/news-and-politics/2007/10/how-laws-die.html.

137 Geoffrey R. Stone, "Sexual Expression and Free Speech: How Our Values Have (D)evolved," Human Rights Magazine, Vol. 43, No. 4, American Bar Association, accessed 6 April 2022, https://www.americanbar.org/groups/crsj/publications/human_rights_magazine_home/the-ongoing-challenge-to-define-free-speech/sexual-expression-and-free-speech/.

138 ibid

139 Geoff Nunberg, "Prurient Interests," Commentary Broadcast on "Fresh Air," May 28, 2002, http://people.ischool.berkeley.edu/~nunberg/prurient.html.

140 Dani Pinter, Esq., video from August 11, 2016, https://endsexualexploitation.org/articles/video-distributing-pornography-illegal-obscenity-law-explained/.

141 Alexandra DeSanctis, "Exclusive: U.S. Representatives Call On Barr to Prosecute Obscene Pornography," National Review, Dec 6, 2019, accessed 6 April 2022, https://www.nationalreview.com/corner/exclusive-u-s-representatives-call-on-barr-to-prosecute-obscene-pornography/.

142 William M. Struthers, Wired for Intimacy: How Pornography Hijacks the Male Brain, (New South Wales: ReadHowYouWant Publishing, 2010).

143 Ready: How to Heal and Protect Your Ministry from Pornography, Covenant Eyes, https://learn.covenanteyes.com/ready-ministry-guide, page 13.

144 Stephen Newland, "The Power of Accountability," AFCPE, Q3, 2018, accessed April 4, 2022, https://www.afcpe.org/news-and-publications/the-standard/2018-3/the-power-of-accountability/.

A free ebook edition is available with the purchase of this book.

To claim your free ebook edition:

1. Visit MorganJamesBOGO.com
2. Sign your name CLEARLY in the space
3. Complete the form and submit a photo of the entire copyright page
4. You or your friend can download the ebook to your preferred device

Morgan James BOGO™

A **FREE** ebook edition is available for you or a friend with the purchase of this print book.

CLEARLY SIGN YOUR NAME ABOVE

Instructions to claim your free ebook edition:
1. Visit MorganJamesBOGO.com
2. Sign your name CLEARLY in the space above
3. Complete the form and submit a photo of this entire page
4. You or your friend can download the ebook to your preferred device

Print & Digital Together Forever.

Snap a photo

Free ebook

Read anywhere

CPSIA information can be obtained
at www.ICGtesting.com
Printed in the USA
JSHW021421070423
40074JS00002B/12

9 781636 980256